NEOLIBERALISM'S WAR ON HIGHER EDUCATION

SECOND EDITION

Henry A. Giroux

HAYMARKET BOOKS
CHICAGO, ILLINOIS

This updated paperback edition
published in 2020 by
Haymarket Books
PO Box 180165
Chicago, IL 60618
773-583-7884
www.haymarketbooks.org
info@haymarketbooks.org

ISBN: 978-1-64259-037-1

Distributed to the trade in the US through Consortium Book Sales and Distribution (www.cbsd.com) and internationally through Ingram Publisher Services
International (www.ingramcontent.com).

Cover design by Rachel Cohen. Cover images of protesters from University of California, Berkeley, in coalition with university employee unions, calling for a campus strike rallying against banks and budget cuts to higher education (AP Photo/
Jeff Chiu), and of Earl Hall at Columbia University in New York, photographed
in 2005.

This book was published with the generous support of Lannan Foundation and
the Wallace Global Fund.

Library of Congress Cataloging-in-Publication data is available.

Printed in Canada.

NEOLIBERALISM'S WAR ON HIGHER EDUCATION

TABLE OF CONTENTS

For Rania

To those brave and committed teachers who are struggling to educate young people for a more just and democratic world

Acknowledgments

This book could not have been completed without the help of many people. My late dear friend Roger Simon provided a range of insightful ideas regarding the Quebec student protest. I will miss his friendship and the many conversations we had. Grace Pollock once again provided editorial advice and skills that continually improve the quality of my writing. Lynn Worsham has always been a wonderful colleague, and I want to thank her for publishing an earlier version of "Intellectual Violence in the Age of Gated Intellectuals" in *JAC*. I especially want to thank my administrative assistant, Maya Sabados, for reading and editing every word of this book. Her interventions were invaluable, and her insights, editorial help, and administrative skills have greatly improved the quality of the manuscript. Some of the ideas in this book have been published in a series of shorter articles in *Truthout, CounterPunch,* and *Truthdig.* Chapter six draws heavily on "Neoliberalism and the Weaponizing of Language and Education," in *Race & Class* 16, no. 1 (2019): 26–45.

INTRODUCTION

The Language
of Neoliberal Education

MITJA SARDOČ INTERVIEWS HENRY A. GIROUX[1]

MITJA SARDOČ: FOR SEVERAL DECADES NOW, NEOLIBERALISM HAS BEEN AT THE FOREFRONT OF DISCUSSIONS NOT ONLY IN THE ECONOMY AND FINANCE BUT HAS INFILTRATED OUR VOCABULARY IN A NUMBER OF AREAS AS DIVERSE AS GOVERNANCE STUDIES, CRIMINOLOGY, HEALTH CARE, JURISPRUDENCE, EDUCATION, ETC. WHAT HAS TRIGGERED THE USE AND APPLICATION OF THIS "ECONOMISTIC" LANGUAGE ASSOCIATED WITH THE PROMOTION OF EFFECTIVENESS AND EFFICIENCY?

Henry A. Giroux: Neoliberalism has become the dominant ideology of the times and has established itself as a central feature of politics. Not only does it define itself as a political and economic system whose aim is to consolidate power in the hands of a corporate and financial elite, it also wages a war over ideas. In this instance, it has defined itself as a form of common sense and functions as a mode of public pedagogy that produces a template for structuring not just markets but all of social life. In this sense, it has and continues to function not only through public and higher education to produce and distribute market-based values, identities, and modes of agency, but also in wider cultural apparatuses and platforms to privatize, deregulate, economize, and subject all of the commanding institutions and relations of every-

1

day life to the dictates of privatization, efficiency, deregulation, and commodification.

Since the 1970s, as more and more of the commanding institutions of society come under the control of neoliberal ideology, its notions of common sense—an unchecked individualism, harsh competition, an aggressive attack on the welfare state, the evisceration of public goods, and its attack on all models of sociality at odds with market values—have become the reigning hegemony of capitalist societies. What many on the left have failed to realize is that neoliberalism is about more than economic structures, it is also a powerful pedagogical force—especially in the era of social media—that engages in full-spectrum dominance at every level of civil society. Its reach extends not only into education but also to an array of digital platforms as well as the broader sphere of popular culture. Under neoliberal modes of governance, regardless of the institution, every social relation is reduced to an act of commerce. Neoliberalism's promotion of effectiveness and efficiency gives credence to its willingness and success in making education central to politics. It also offers a warning to progressives, as Pierre Bourdieu insisted, that the left cannot afford to underestimate the struggles waged in the name of the symbolic and cultural and have not always been strategic in addressing this issue as a matter central to politics itself.

MS: ACCORDING TO THE ADVOCATES OF NEOLIBERALISM, EDUCATION REPRESENTS ONE OF THE MAIN INDICATORS OF FUTURE ECONOMIC GROWTH AND INDIVIDUAL WELL-BEING. HOW—AND WHY—DID EDUCATION BECOME ONE OF THE CENTRAL ELEMENTS OF THE "NEOLIBERAL REVOLUTION"?

HAG: Advocates of neoliberalism have always recognized that education is a site of contestation over which there are very high stakes regarding how young people are educated, who is to be educated, and what vision of the present and future should be most valued and privileged. Higher education in the sixties went through a revolutionary period in the United States and many other countries as students sought to both redefine education as a democratic public sphere and to open it up to a variety of groups that up to that point had been excluded. Conservatives were extremely frightened over this shift and did everything they could to counter it. Evidence of this is clear in the production of the Powell Memo published in 1971 and later in the Trilateral Commission's book-length report, *The Crisis of Democracy*, published in 1975. From the 1960s on the conservatives, especially the neoliberal right, has waged a war on education in order to rid it of its potential role as a democratic public sphere. At the same time, they sought aggressively to restructure its modes of governance, undercut the power of faculty, privilege knowledge that was instrumental to the market, define students mainly as clients and consumers, and reduce the function of higher education largely to training students for the global workforce. At the core of the neoliberal investment in education is a desire to undermine the university's commitment to the truth, critical thinking, and its obligation to stand for justice and assume responsibility for safeguarding the interests of young people as they enter a world of marked massive inequalities, exclusion, and violence at home and abroad. Higher education may be one of the few institutions left in neoliberal societies that offers a protective space to question, challenge, and think against the grain. Neoliberalism considers such a space to be dangerous, and they have done everything possible to eliminate higher education as a space where students can realize themselves as critical citizens, faculty can participate in the governing structure, and education can define itself as a right rather than as a privilege.

MS: ALMOST BY DEFINITION, REFORMS AND OTHER INITIATIVES AIMED TO IMPROVE EDUCATIONAL PRACTICES HAVE BEEN ONE OF THE PIVOTAL MECHANISMS TO INFILTRATE THE NEOLIBERAL AGENDA OF EFFECTIVENESS AND EFFICIENCY. WHAT ASPECT OF NEOLIBERALISM AND ITS EDUCATIONAL AGENDA DO YOU FIND MOST PROBLEMATIC? WHY?

HAG: Increasingly aligned with market forces, higher education is mostly primed for teaching business principles and corporate values, while university administrators are prized as CEOs or bureaucrats in a neoliberal-based audit culture. Many colleges and universities have been McDonald's-ized as knowledge is increasingly viewed as a commodity resulting in curricula that resemble fast-food menus. In addition, faculty are subjected increasingly to a model of labor relations designed to make them powerless when it comes to any control over their say in how the university should be run. In the age of precarity and flexibility, the majority of faculty have been reduced to part-time positions and subjected to low wages. They have lost control over the conditions of their labor, suffered reduced benefits, and become frightened about addressing social issues critically in their classrooms for fear of losing their jobs. Short term positions carry the risk of contingent faculty being terminated for being critical of the university, higher education, and a host of other issues. Moreover, the dominance of non-tenured faculty in higher education, especially in the United States where they number about 73 percent of the faculty, creates a multiclass system of faculty that resonates and helps to legitimate class stratification in a range of public institutions and society.[2] The latter may be the central issue curbing free speech and academic freedom in the academy. Moreover, many of these faculty are barely able to make ends meet because of their impoverished salaries, and some are on food stamps. If faculty are treated like service workers, students fare no better, and are now relegated to the status of customers and clients. Moreover, they are not only inundated with the competitive, privatized, and market-driven values of neoliberalism, they are also punished by those values in the form of exorbitant tuition rates, astronomical debts owed to banks and other financial institutions, and in too many cases a lack of meaningful employment. The neoliberal war on higher education is evident not only in its attempts to defund public colleges and universities, model the university after the culture of business, raise tuition for students, privatize education, commodify knowledge, and expand the ranks of the administration with corporate-friendly bureaucrats, it is also obvious in the way the mission of higher education has been redefined to embrace market values rather than values crucial to a democratic society.[3] Commercial and private interest now drive the purpose and mission of higher education. The notion that higher education is a public good and a crucial democratic public sphere that should serve the interests of society at large has either been forgotten or is held in disdain.

Neoliberalism undermines the ability of educators and others to create the conditions that give students the opportunity to acquire the knowledge and the civic courage necessary to make desolation and cynicism unconvincing and hope practical. As an ideology, neoliberalism is at odds with any viable notion of democracy which it sees as the enemy of the market. Yet, democracy cannot work if citizens are not autonomous, self-judging, curious, reflective, and independent—qualities that are indispensable for students if they are going to make vital judgments and choices about participating in and shaping decisions that affect everyday life, institutional reform, and governmental policy.

MS: WHY ARE LARGE-SCALE ASSESSMENTS AND QUANTITATIVE DATA, IN GENERAL, CENTRAL PARTS OF THE "NEOLIBERAL TOOLKIT" IN EDUCATIONAL RESEARCH?

HAG: These are the tools of accountants and have nothing to do with larger visions or questions about what matters as part of a university education. The overreliance on metrics and measurement has become a tool used to remove questions of responsibility, morality, and justice from the language and policies of education. I believe the neoliberal toolkit, as you put it, is part of the discourse of civic illiteracy that now runs rampant in higher educational research, a kind of mind-numbing investment in a metric-based culture that kills the imagination and wages an assault on what it means to be critical, thoughtful, daring, and willing to take risks. Metrics in the service of an audit culture has become the new face of a culture of positivism, a kind of empirical-based panopticon that turns ideas into numbers and the creative impulse into ashes. Large scale assessments and quantitative data are the driving mechanisms in which everything is absorbed into the culture of business. The distinction between information and knowledge has become irrelevant in this model and anything that cannot be captured by numbers is treated with disdain. In this new audit panopticon, the only knowledge that matters is that which can be measured. What is missed here, of course, is that measurable utility is a curse as a universal principle because it ignores any form of knowledge based on the assumption that individuals need to know more than how things work or what their practical utility might be. This is a language that cannot answer the question of what the responsibility of the university and educators might be in a time of tyranny, in the face of the unspeakable, and the current widespread attack on immigrants, Muslims, and others considered disposable. This is a language that is both afraid and unwilling to imagine what alternative worlds inspired by the search for equality and justice might be possible in an age beset by the increasing dark forces of authoritarianism.

MS: WHILE THE ANALYSIS OF THE NEOLIBERAL AGENDA IN EDUCATION IS WELL DOCUMENTED, THE ANALYSIS OF THE LANGUAGE OF NEOLIBERAL EDUCATION IS AT THE FRINGES OF SCHOLARLY INTER-

EST. IN PARTICULAR, THE EXPANSION OF THE NEOLIBERAL VOCABULARY WITH EGALITARIAN IDEAS SUCH AS FAIRNESS, JUSTICE, EQUALITY OF OPPORTUNITY, WELL-BEING, ETC. HAS RECEIVED (AT BEST) ONLY LIMITED ATTENTION. WHAT FACTORS HAVE CONTRIBUTED TO THIS SHIFT OF EMPHASIS?

HAG: Neoliberalism has upended how language is used in both education and the wider society. It works to appropriate discourses associated with liberal democracy that have become normalized in order to both limit their meanings and use them to mean the opposite of what they have meant traditionally, especially with respect to human rights, justice, informed judgment, critical agency, and democracy itself. It is waging a war over not just the relationship between economic structures but over memory, words, meaning, and politics. Neoliberalism takes words like freedom and limits it to the freedom to consume, spew out hate, and celebrate notions of self-interest and a rabid individualism as the new common sense. Equality of opportunity means engaging in ruthless forms of competition, a war of all against all ethos, and a survival of the fittest mode of behavior. The vocabulary of neoliberalism operates in the service of violence in that it reduces the capacity for human fulfillment in the collective sense, diminishes a broad understanding of freedom as fundamental to expanding the capacity for human agency, and diminishes the ethical imagination by reducing it to the interest of the market and the accumulation of capital. Words, memory, language, and meaning are weaponized under neoliberalism. Certainly, neither the media nor progressives have given enough attention to how neoliberalism colonizes language because neither group has given enough attention to viewing the crisis of neoliberalism as not only an economic crisis but also a crisis of ideas.

Education is not viewed as a force central to politics and as such the intersection of language, power, and politics in the neoliberal paradigm has been largely ignored. Moreover, at a time when civic culture is being eradicated, public spheres are vanishing, and notions of shared citizenship appear obsolete, words that speak to the truth, reveal injustices, and provide informed critical analysis has also begun to disappear. This makes it all the more difficult to engage critically the use of neoliberalism's colonization of language. In the United States, Trump's prodigious tweets signify not only a time in which governments engage in the pathology of endless fabrications, but also how they function to reinforce a pedagogy of infantilism designed to animate his base in a glut of shock while reinforcing a culture of war, fear, divisiveness, and greed in ways that disempower his critics.

MS: YOU HAVE WRITTEN EXTENSIVELY ON NEOLIBERALISM'S EXCLUSIVELY INSTRUMENTAL VIEW OF EDUCATION, ITS REDUCTIONIST UNDERSTANDING OF EFFECTIVENESS, AND ITS DISTORTED IMAGE OF FAIRNESS. IN WHAT WAY SHOULD RADICAL PEDAGOGY FIGHT BACK NEOLIBERALISM AND ITS EDUCATIONAL AGENDA?

HAG: First, higher education needs to reassert its mission as a public good in order to reclaim its egalitarian and democratic impulses. Educators need to initiate and expand a national conversation in which higher education can be defended as a democratic public sphere and the classroom as a site of deliberative inquiry, dialogue, and critical thinking, a site that makes a claim on the radical imagination and a sense of civic courage. At the same time, the discourse on defining higher education as a democratic public sphere can provide the platform for a more expressive commitment in developing a social movement in defense of public goods and against neoliberalism as a threat to democracy. This also means rethinking how education can be funded as a public good and what it might mean to fight for policies that both stop the defunding of education and fight to relocate funds from the death-dealing military and incarceration budgets to those supporting education at all levels of society. The challenge here is for higher education not to abandon its commitment to democracy and to recognize that neoliberalism operates in the service of the forces of economic domination and ideological repression. Second, educators need to acknowledge and make good on the claim that a critically literate citizen is indispensable to a democracy, especially at a time when higher education is being privatized and subject to neoliberal restructuring efforts. This suggests placing ethics, civic literacy, social responsibility, and compassion at the forefront of learning so as to combine knowledge, teaching, and research with the rudiments of what might be called the grammar of an ethical and social imagination. This would imply taking seriously those values, traditions, histories, and pedagogies that would promote a sense of dignity, self-reflection, and compassion at the heart of a real democracy. Third, higher education needs to be viewed as a right, as it is in many countries including Germany, France, Norway, Finland,

and Brazil, rather than a privilege for a limited few, as it is in the United States, Canada, and the United Kingdom. Fourth, in a world driven by data, metrics, and the replacement of knowledge by the overabundance of information, educators need to enable students to engage in multiple literacies extending from print and visual culture to digital culture. They need to become border crossers who can think dialectically, and learn not only how to consume culture but also to produce it. Fifth, faculty must reclaim their right to control over the nature of their labor, shape policies of governance, and be given tenure track lines with the guarantee of secure employment and protection for academic freedom and free speech.

MS: WHY IS IT IMPORTANT TO ANALYZE THE RELATIONSHIP BETWEEN NEOLIBERALISM AND CIVIC LITERACY PARTICULARLY AS AN EDUCATIONAL PROJECT?

HAG: The ascendancy of neoliberalism in American politics has made visible a plague of deep-seated civic illiteracy, a corrupt political system and a contempt for reason that has been decades in the making. It also points to the withering of civic attachments, the undoing of civic culture, the decline of public life, and the erosion of any sense of shared citizenship. As market mentalities and moralities tighten their grip on all aspects of society, democratic institutions and public spheres are being downsized, if not altogether disappearing. As these institutions vanish—from public schools and alternative media to health care centers—there is also a serious erosion of the discourse of community, justice, equality, public values, and the common good. At the same time reason and truth are not simply contested, or the subject of informed arguments as they should be, but wrongly vilified—banished to Trump's poisonous world of fake news. For instance, under the Trump administration, language has been pillaged, truth and reason disparaged, and words and phrases emptied of any substance or turned into their opposite, all via the endless production of Trump's Twitter storms and the ongoing clown spectacle of Fox News. This grim reality points to a failure in the power of the civic imagination, political will, and open democracy. It is also part of a politics that strips the social of any democratic ideals and undermines any understanding of education as a public good. What we are witnessing under neoliberalism is not simply a political project to consolidate power in the hands of the corporate and financial elite but also a reworking of the very meaning of literacy and education as crucial to what it means to create an informed citizenry and democratic society. In an age when literacy and thinking become dangerous to the antidemocratic forces governing all the commanding economic and cultural institutions of the United States, truth is viewed as a liability, ignorance becomes a virtue, and informed judgments and critical thinking are demeaned and turned into rubble and ashes. Under the reign of this normalized architecture of alleged common sense, literacy is regarded with disdain, words are reduced to data, and science is confused with pseudoscience. Traces of critical thought appear more and more at the margins of the culture as ignorance becomes the primary organizing principle of American society.

Ignorance now fuses with a reckless use of state power that holds both human life and the planet hostage. Under such circumstances, thinking becomes dangerous and the object of organized disgust for any vestige of the truth. However, there is more at stake here than the production of a toxic form of illiteracy and the shrinking of political horizons. What we are witnessing is a closing of the political coupled with explicit expressions of cruelty and "widely sanctioned ruthlessness."[4] Moreover, the very conditions that enable people to make informed decisions are under siege as schools are defunded, media becomes more corporatized, oppositional journalists are killed, and reality TV becomes the model for mass entertainment.

Under such circumstances, there is a full-scale attack on thoughtful reasoning, empathy, collective resistance, and the compassionate imagination. In some ways, the dictatorship of ignorance resembles what the writer John Berger calls "ethicide": and Joshua Sperling defines as "the blunting of the senses; the hollowing out of language; the erasure of connection with the past, the dead, place, the land, the soil; possibly, too, the erasure even of certain emotions, whether pity, compassion, consoling, mourning, or hoping."[5] Under the forty-year reign of neoliberalism, language has been militarized and handed over to advertisers, game show idiocy, and a political and culturally embarrassing anti-intellectualism sanctioned by the White House. Couple this with a celebrity culture that produces an ecosystem of babble, shock, and tawdry entertainment. Add on the cruel and clownish anti–public intellectuals such as Jordan Peterson who defend inequality, infantile forms of masculinity, and define ignorance and a warrior mentality as part of the natural order, all the while dethroning any viable sense of agency and the political.

The culture of manufactured illiteracy is also reproduced through a media apparatus that trades in illusions and the spectacle of violence. Under these circumstances, illiteracy becomes the norm and education becomes central to a version of neoliberal zombie politics that functions largely to remove democratic values, social relations, and compassion from the ideology, policies, and commanding institutions that now control American society. In the age of manufactured illiteracy, there is more at work than simply an absence of learning, ideas, or knowledge. Nor can the reign of manufactured illiteracy be solely attributed to the rise of the new social media, a culture of immediacy, and a society that thrives on instant gratification. On the contrary, manufactured illiteracy is a political and educational project central to a right-wing corporatist ideology and set of policies that work aggressively to depoliticize people and make them complicitous with the neoliberal and racist political and economic forces that impose misery and suffering upon their lives. There is more at work here than what Ariel Dorfman calls a "felonious stupidity," there are also the workings of a deeply malicious form of twenty-first-century neoliberal fascism and a culture of cruelty in which language is forced into the service of violence while waging a relentless attack on the ethical imagination and the notion of the common good. In the current historical moment illiteracy and ignorance offer the pretense of a community, and in doing so has undermined the importance of civic literacy both in higher education and the larger society.

MS: IS THERE ANY SHORTCOMING IN THE ANALYSIS OF SUCH A COMPLEX (AND CONTROVERSIAL) SOCIAL PHENOMENON AS NEOLIBERALISM AND ITS EDUCATIONAL AGENDA? PUT DIFFERENTLY IS THERE ANY ASPECT OF THE NEOLIBERAL EDUCATIONAL AGENDA THAT ITS CRITICS HAVE FAILED TO ADDRESS?

HAG: Any analysis of an ideology such as neoliberalism will always be incomplete. And the literature on neoliberalism in its different forms and diverse contexts is quite abundant. What is often underplayed in my mind are three things. First, too little is said about how neoliberalism functions not simply as an economic model for finance capital but as a public pedagogy that operates through a diverse number of sites and platforms. Second, not enough has been written about its war on a democratic notion of sociality and the concept of the social. Third, at a time in which echoes of a past fascism are on the rise, not enough is being said about the relationship between neoliberalism and fascism, or what I call neoliberal fascism, especially the relationship between the widespread suffering and misery caused by neoliberalism and the rise of white supremacy. I define neoliberal fascism as both a project and a movement, which functions as an enabling force that weakens, if not destroys, the commanding institutions of a democracy while undermining its most valuable principles. Consequently, it provides a fertile ground for the unleashing of the ideological architecture, poisonous values, and racist social relations sanctioned and produced under fascism. Neoliberalism and fascism conjoin and advance in a comfortable and mutually compatible project and movement that connects the worst excesses of capitalism with fascist ideals—the veneration of war, a hatred of reason and truth; a populist celebration of ultra-nationalism and racial purity; the suppression of freedom and dissent; a culture which promotes lies, spectacles, a demonization of the other, a discourse of decline, brutal violence, and ultimately state violence in heterogeneous forms. As a project, it destroys all the commanding institutions of democracy and consolidates power in the hands of a financial elite. As a movement, it produces and legitimates massive economic inequality and suffering, privatizes public goods, dismantles essential government agencies, and individualizes all social problems. In addition, it transforms the political state into the corporate state and uses the tools of surveillance, militarization, and law and order to discredit the critical press and media in order to undermine civil liberties while ridiculing and censoring critics. What critics need to address is that neoliberalism is the face of a new fascism and as such it speaks to the need to repudiate the notion that capitalism and democracy are the same thing, renew faith in the promises of a democratic socialism, create new political formations around an alliance of diverse social movements, and take seriously the need to make education a primary element of politics.

CHAPTER ONE

Neoliberalism's War on Democracy

It is certain, in any case, that ignorance, allied with power,
is the most ferocious enemy justice can have.

—James Baldwin

Four decades of neoliberal policies have resulted in an economic Darwinism that promotes privatization, commodification, free trade, and deregulation. It privileges personal responsibility over larger social forces, reinforces the gap between the rich and poor by redistributing wealth to the most powerful and wealthy individuals and groups, and it fosters a mode of public pedagogy that privileges the entrepreneurial subject while encouraging a value system that promotes self-interest, if not an unchecked selfishness.[1] Since the 1970s, neoliberalism or free-market fundamentalism has become not only a much-vaunted ideology that now shapes all aspects of life in the United States but also a predatory global phenomenon "that drives the practices and principles of the International Monetary Fund, the World Bank, and World Trade Organization, transnational institutions which largely determine the economic policies of developing countries and the rules of international trade."[2]

With its theater of cruelty and mode of public pedagogy, neoliberalism as a form of economic Darwinism attempts to undermine all forms of solidarity capable of challenging market-driven values and social relations, promoting the virtues of an unbridled individualism almost pathological in its disdain for community, social responsibility, public values, and the public good. As the welfare state is dismantled and spending is cut to the point where government becomes unrecognizable—*except* to promote policies that benefit the rich, corporations, and the defense industry—the already weakened federal and state governments are increasingly replaced by what João Biehl has called proliferating "zones of social abandonment" and "terminal exclusion."[3]

One consequence is that social problems are increasingly criminalized while social protections are either eliminated or fatally weakened. Not only are public servants described as the new "welfare queens" and degenerate freeloaders but young people are also increasingly subjected to harsh disciplinary measures both in and out of schools, often as a result of a violation of the most trivial rules.[4] Another characteristic of this crushing form of economic Darwinism is that it thrives on a kind of social amnesia that erases critical thought, historical analysis, and any understanding of broader systemic relations. In this regard, it does the opposite of critical memory work by eliminating those public spheres where people learn to translate private troubles into public issues. That is, it breaks "the link between public agendas and private worries, the very hub of the democratic process."[5] Once set in motion, economic Darwinism unleashes a mode of thinking in which social problems are reduced to individual flaws and political considerations collapse into the injurious and self-indicting discourse of character. Many Americans are preoccupied less with political and moral outrage over a country whose economic and political system is in the hands of a tiny, exorbitantly rich elite than they are with the challenges of being isolated and surviving at the bottom of a savage neoliberal order. This makes it all the simpler for neoliberalism to convince people to remain attached to a set of ideologies, values, modes of governance, and policies that generate massive suffering and hardships. Neoliberalism's "best trick" is to persuade individuals, as a matter of common sense, that they should "imagine [themselves] as . . . solitary agent[s] who can and must live the good life promised by capitalist culture."[6]

As George Lakoff and Glenn Smith argue, the anti-public philosophy of economic Darwinism makes a parody of democracy by defining freedom as "the liberty to seek one's own interests and well-being, without being responsible for the interests or well-being of anyone else. It's a morality of personal, but not social, responsibility. The only freedom you should have is what you can provide for yourself, not what the Public provides for you to start out."[7] Put simply, we alone become responsible for the problems we confront when we can no longer conceive how larger forces control or constrain our choices and the lives we are destined to lead.

Yet the harsh values and practices of this new social order *are* visible—in the increasing incarceration of young people, the modeling of public schools after prisons, state violence waged against peaceful student protesters, and state policies that bail out investment bankers but leave the middle and working classes in a state of poverty, despair, and insecurity. Such values are also evident in the Republican Party's social Darwinist budget plans that reward the rich and cut aid for those who need it the most. For instance, the 2012 Romney/Ryan budget plan "proposed to cut the taxes of households earning over $1 million by an average of $295,874 a year,"[8] at a cruel cost to those most disadvantaged populations who rely on social programs. In order to pay for tax reductions to benefit the rich, the Romney/Ryan budget would have cut funds for food stamps, Pell grants, health care benefits, unemployment insurance, veterans' benefits, and other crucial social programs.[9] As Paul Krugman has argued, the Ryan budget

> isn't just looking for ways to save money [it's] also trying to make life harder for the poor—for their own good. In March [2012], explaining his cuts in aid for the unfortunate, [Ryan] declared, "We don't want to turn the safety net into a hammock that lulls able-bodied people into lives of dependency and complacency, that drains them of their will and their incentive to make the most of their lives."[10]

Krugman rightly replies, "I doubt that Americans forced to rely on unemployment benefits and food stamps in a depressed economy feel that they're living in a comfortable hammock."[11] An extremist version of neoliberalism, Ryanomics is especially vicious toward US children, 16.1 million of whom currently live in poverty.[12] Marian Wright Edelman captures the harshness and savagery of the Ryan budget passed by the House of Representatives before being voted down in the Senate. She writes:

Ryanomics is an all out assault on our poorest children while asking not a dime of sacrifice from the richest 2 percent of Americans or from wealthy corporations. Ryanomics slashes hundreds of billions of dollars from child and family nutrition, health, child care, education, and child protection services, *in order* to extend and add to the massive Bush tax cuts for millionaires and billionaires at a taxpayer cost of $5 trillion over 10 years. On top of making the Bush tax cuts permanent, the top income bracket would get an additional 10 percent tax cut. Millionaires and billionaires would on average keep at least an additional quarter of a million dollars each year and possibly as much as $400,000 a year according to the Citizens for Tax Justice.[13]

As profits soar for corporations and the upper 1 percent, both political parties are imposing austerity measures that punish the poor and cut vital services for those who need them the most.[14] Rather than raising taxes and closing tax loopholes for the wealthy and corporations, the Republican Party would rather impose painful spending cuts that will impact the poor and vital social services. For example, the 2013 budget cuts produced by sequestration slash $20 million from the Maternal, Infant, and Early Child Home Visiting Program, $199 million from public housing, $6 million from emergency food and shelter, $19 million from housing for the elderly, $116 million from higher education, and $96 million from homeless assistance grants—and these are only a small portion of the devastating cuts enacted.[15] Seventy thousand children will be kicked off of Head Start, ten thousand teachers will be fired, and "the long-term unemployed will see their benefits cut by about 10 percent."[16] Under the right-wing insistence on a politics of austerity, Americans are witnessing not only widespread cuts in vital infrastructures, education, and social protections but also the emergence of policies produced in the spirit of revenge aimed at the poor, the elderly, and others marginalized by race and class. As Robert Reich, Charles Ferguson, and a host of recent commentators have noted, this extreme concentration of power in every commanding institution of society promotes predatory practices and rewards sociopathic behavior. Such a system creates an authoritarian class of corporate and hedge-fund swindlers that reaps its own profits by

placing big bets with other people's money. The winners in this system are top Wall Street executives and traders, private-equity managers and hedge-fund moguls, and the losers are most of the rest of us. The system is largely responsible for the greatest concentration of the nation's income and wealth at the very top since the Gilded Age of the nineteenth century, with the richest 400 Americans owning as much as the bottom 150 million put together. And these multimillionaires and billionaires are now actively buying . . . election[s]—and with [them], American democracy.[17]

Unfortunately, the US public has largely remained silent, if not also complicit in the rise of a neoliberal version of authoritarianism. While workers in Wisconsin, striking teachers in Chicago, and young people across the globe have challenged this politics and machinery of corruption, war, brutality, and social and civil death, they represent a small and marginalized part of the larger movement that will be necessary to initiate massive collective resistance to the aggressive violence being waged against all those public spheres that further the promise of democracy in the United States, the United Kingdom, France, and a host of other countries. The actions of teachers, workers, student protesters, and others have been crucial in drawing public attention to the constellation of forces that are pushing the United States and other neoliberal-driven countries into what Hannah Arendt called "dark times"or what might be described as an increasingly authoritarian public realm that constitutes a clear and present danger to democracy. The questions now being asked must be seen as the first step toward exposing the dire social and political costs of concentrating wealth, income, and power into the hands of the upper 1 percent. What role higher education will play in both educating and mobilizing students is a crucial issue that will determine whether a new revolutionary ideal can take hold in order to address the ideals of democracy and its future.

NEOLIBERAL IDEOLOGY AND THE RHETORIC OF FREEDOM

In addition to amassing ever-expanding amounts of material wealth, the rich now control the means of schooling and other cultural apparatuses in the United States. They have disinvested in critical education while reproducing notions of "common sense" that incessantly replicate the basic values, ideas, and relations necessary to sustain the institutions of economic Darwinism. Both major political parties, along with plutocrat "reformers," support educational reforms that increase conceptual and cultural illiteracy. Critical learning has been replaced with mastering test-taking, memorizing facts, and learning how *not* to question knowledge or authority. Pedagogies that unsettle common sense, make power accountable, and connect classroom knowledge to larger civic issues have become dangerous at all levels of schooling. This method of rote pedagogy, heavily enforced by mainstream educational reformists, is, as Zygmunt Bauman notes, "the most effective prescription for grinding communication to a halt and for [robbing] it of the presumption and expectation of meaningfulness and sense."[18] These radical reformers are also attempting to restructure how higher education is organized. In doing so, they are putting in place modes of governance that mimic corporate structures by increasing the power of administrators at the expense of faculty, reducing faculty to a mostly temporary and low-wage workforce, and reducing students to customers—ripe for being trained for low-skilled jobs and at-risk for incurring large student loans.

This pedagogy of market-driven illiteracy has eviscerated the notion of freedom, turning it largely into the desire to consume and invest exclusively in relationships that serve only one's individual interests. Losing one's individuality is now tantamount to losing one's ability to consume. Citizens are treated by the political and economic elite as restless children and are "invited daily to convert the practice of citizenship into the art of shopping."[19] Shallow consumerism coupled with an indifference to the needs and suffering of others has produced a politics of disengagement and a culture of moral irresponsibility. At the same time, the economically Darwinian ethos that places individual interest at the center of everyday life undercuts, if not removes, moral considerations about what we know and how we act from larger social costs and moral considerations. In media discourse, language has been stripped of the terms, phrases, and ideas that embrace a concern for the other. With meaning utterly privatized, words are reduced to signifiers that mimic spectacles of violence, designed to provide entertainment rather than thoughtful analysis. Sentiments circulating in the dominant culture parade either idiocy or a survival-of-the-fittest ethic, while anti-public rhetoric strips society of the knowledge and values necessary for the development of a democratically engaged and socially responsible public.

In such circumstances, freedom has truly morphed into its opposite. Neoliberal ideology has construed as pathological any notion that in a healthy society people depend on one another in multiple, complex, direct, and indirect ways. As Lewis Lapham observes, "Citizens are no longer held in thoughtful regard . . . just as thinking and acting are removed from acts of public conscience."[20] Economic Darwinism has produced a legitimating ideology in which the conditions for critical inquiry, moral responsibility, and social and economic justice disappear. The result is that neoliberal ideology increasingly resembles a call to war that turns the principles of democracy against democracy itself. Americans now live in an atomized and pulverized society, "spattered with the debris of broken interhuman bonds,"[21] in which "democracy becomes a perishable commodity"[22] and all things public are viewed with disdain.

NEOLIBERAL GOVERNANCE

At the level of governance, neoliberalism has increasingly turned mainstream politics into a tawdry form of money-laundering in which the spaces and registers that circulate power are controlled by those who have amassed large amounts of capital. Elections, like mainstream politicians, are now bought and sold to the highest bidder. In the Senate and House of Representatives, 47 percent are millionaires—the "estimated median net worth of a current US senator stood at an average of $2.56 million while the median net worth of members of Congress is $913,000."[23] Elected representatives no longer even purport to do the bidding of the people who elect them. Rather, they are now largely influenced by the demands of lobbyists, who have enormous clout in promoting the interests of the elite, financial services sector, and megacorporations. In 2012, there were just over fourteen thousand registered lobbyists in Washington, DC, which amounts to approximately twenty-three lobbyists for every member of Congress. Although the number of lobbyists has steadily increased by about 20 percent since 1998, the Center for Responsive Politics found that "total spending on lobbying the federal government has almost tripled since 1998, to $3.3 billion."[24] As Bill Moyers and Bernard Weisberger succinctly put it, "A radical minority of the superrich has gained ascendency over politics, buying the policies, laws, tax breaks, subsidies, and rules that consolidate a permanent state of vast inequality by which they can further help themselves to America's wealth and resources."[25] How else to explain that the 2013 bill designed to regulate the banking and financial sectors was drafted for legislators by Citigroup lobbyists?[26] There is more at stake here than legalized corruption, there is the arrogant dismantling of democracy and the production of policies that extend rather than mitigate human suffering, violence, misery, and everyday hardships. Democratic governance has been replaced by the sovereignty of the market, paving the way for modes of governance intent on transforming democratic citizens into entrepreneurial agents. The language of the market and business culture have now almost entirely supplanted any celebration of the public good or the calls to enhance civil society characteristic of past generations. Moreover, authoritarian governance now creeps into every institution and aspect of public life. Instead of celebrating Martin Luther King for his stands against poverty, militarization, and racism, US society holds him up as an icon denuded of any message of solidarity and social struggle. This erasure and depoliticization of history and politics is matched by the celebration of a business culture in which the US public transforms Bill Gates into a national hero. At the same time, civil rights heroine Rosa Parks cedes her position to the Kardashian sisters, as the prominence of civic culture is canceled out by herd-like public enthusiasm for celebrity culture, reality TV, and the hyper-violence of extreme sports. The older heroes sacrificed in order to alleviate the suffering of others, while the new heroes drawn from corporate and celebrity culture live off the suffering of others.

Clearly, US society is awash in a neoliberal culture of idiocy and illiteracy. It produces many subjects who are indifferent to others and are thus incapable of seeing that when the logic of extreme individualism is extended into the far reaches of the national security state, it serves to legitimate the breakdown of the social bonds necessary for a democratic society and reinforces a culture of cruelty that upholds solitary confinement as a mode of punishment for thousands of incarcerated young people and adults.[27] Is it any wonder that with the breakdown of critical education and the cultural apparatuses that support it, the American public now overwhelmingly supports state torture and capital punishment while decrying the necessity of a national health care system? Fortunately, there are signs of rebellion among workers, young people, students, and teachers, indicating that the US public has not been entirely colonized by the bankers, hedge fund managers, and other apostles of neoliberalism. For example, in Connecticut, opponents of public-school privatization replaced three right-wing, pro-charter school board members. In Chicago, reform efforts prevented the city from outsourcing the lease of Midway Airport and breast cancer screening for uninsured women. And, in Iowa, as a result of pressure from progressives, the governor rejected corporate bids to purchase Iowa's statewide fiber-optics network.

Neoliberal governance has produced an economy and a political system almost entirely controlled by the rich and powerful—what a Citigroup report called a "plutonomy," an economy powered by the wealthy.[28] I have referred to these plutocrats as "the new zombies": they are parasites that suck the resources out of the planet and the rest of us in order to strengthen their grasp on political and economic power and fuel their exorbitant lifestyles.[29] Power is now global, gated, and driven by a savage disregard for human welfare, while politics resides largely in older institutions of modernity such as nation states. The new plutocrats have no allegiance to national communities, justice, or human rights, just potential markets and profits. The work of citizenship has been set back decades by this new group of winner-take-all global predators.[30] Policies are now enacted that provide massive tax cuts to the rich and generous subsidies to banks and corporations—alongside massive disinvestments in job creation programs, the building of critical infrastructures, and the development of crucial social programs ranging from health care to school meal programs for disadvantaged children.

Neoliberalism's massive disinvestment in schools, social programs, and an aging infrastructure is not about a lack of money. The real problem stems from government priorities that inform both how the money is collected and how it is spent.[31] More than 60 percent of the federal budget goes to military spending, while only 6 percent is allocated toward education. The United States spends more than $92 billion on corporate subsidies and only $59 billion on social welfare programs.[32] John Cavanagh has estimated that if there were a tiny tax imposed on Wall Street stock and derivatives transactions, the government could raise $150 billion annually.[33] In addition, if the tax code were adjusted in a fair manner to tax the wealthy, another $79 billion could be raised. Finally, Cavanagh notes that $100 billion in tax income is lost annually through tax haven abuse; proper regulation would make it costly for corporations to declare "their profits in overseas tax havens like the Cayman Islands."[34]

At the same time, the financialization of the economy and culture has resulted in the poisonous growth of monopoly power, predatory lending, abusive credit card practices, and misuses of CEO pay. The false but central neoliberal tenet that markets can solve all of society's problems grants unchecked power to money and has given rise to "a politics in which policies that favor the rich ... have allowed the financial sector to amass vast economic and political power."[35] As Joseph Stiglitz points out, there is more at work in this form of governance than a pandering to the wealthy and powerful: there is also the specter of an authoritarian society "where people live in gated communities," large segments of the population are impoverished or locked up in prison, and Americans live in a state of constant fear as they face growing "economic insecurity, healthcare insecurity, [and] a sense of physical insecurity."[36] In other words, the authoritarian nature of neoliberal political governance and economic power is also visible in the rise of a national security state in which civil liberties are being drastically abridged and violated.

As the war on terror becomes a normalized state of existence, the most basic rights available to American citizens are being shredded. The spirit of revenge, militarization, and fear now permeates the discourse of national security. For instance, under Presidents Bush and Obama, the idea of habeas corpus, with its guarantee that prisoners have minimal rights, has given way to policies of indefinite detention, abductions, targeted assassinations, drone killings, and an expanding state surveillance apparatus. The Obama administration has designated forty-six inmates for indefinite detention at Guantánamo because, according to the government, they can be neither tried nor safely released. Moreover, another "167 men now confined at Guantanamo . . . have been cleared for release yet remain at the facility."[37]

With the passing of the National Defense Authorization Act in 2012, the rule of legal illegalities has been extended to threaten the lives and rights of US citizens. The law authorizes military detention of individuals who are suspected of belonging not only to terrorist groups such as al-Qaida but also to "associated forces." As Glenn Greenwald illuminates, this "grants the president the power to indefinitely detain in military custody not only accused terrorists, but also their supporters, all without charges or trial."[38] The vagueness of the law allows the possibility of subjecting to indefinite detention US citizens who are considered to be in violation of the law. Of course, that might include journalists, writers, intellectuals, and anyone else who might be accused because of their dealings with alleged terrorists. Fortunately, US district judge Katherine Forrest of New York agreed with Chris Hedges, Noam Chomsky, and other writers who have challenged the legality of the law. Judge Forrest recently acknowledged the unconstitutionality of the law and ruled in favor of a preliminary barring of the enforcement of the National Defense Authorization Act.[39] Unfortunately, on July 17, 2013, an appeals court in New York ruled in favor of the Obama administration, allowing the government to detain indefinitely without due process persons designated as enemy combatants.

The antidemocratic practices at work in the Obama administration also include the US government's use of state secrecy to provide a cover for practices that range from the illegal use of torture and the abduction of innocent foreign nationals to the National Security Agency's use of a massive surveillance campaign to monitor the phone calls, e-mails, and Internet activity of all Americans. A shadow mass surveillance state has emerged that eschews transparency and commits unlawful acts under the rubric of national security. Given the power of the government to engage in a range of illegalities and to make them disappear through an appeal to state secrecy, it should come as no surprise that warrantless wiretapping, justified in the name of national security, is on the rise at both the federal and state levels. For instance, the New York City Police Department "implemented surveillance programs that violate the civil liberties of that city's Muslim-American citizens [by infiltrating] mosques and universities [and] collecting information on individuals suspected of no crimes."[40] The US public barely acknowledged this shocking abuse of power. Such antidemocratic policies and practices have become the new norm in US society and reveal a frightening and dangerous move toward a twenty-first-century version of authoritarianism.

NEOLIBERALISM AS THE NEW LINGUA FRANCA OF CRUELTY

The harsh realities of a society defined by the imperatives of punishment, cruelty, militarism, secrecy, and exclusion can also be seen in a growing rhetoric of insult, humiliation, and slander. Teachers are referred to as "welfare queens" by right-wing pundits; conservative radio host Rush Limbaugh claimed that Michael J. Fox was "faking" the symptoms of Parkinson's disease when he appeared in a political ad for Democrat Claire McCaskill; and the public is routinely treated to racist comments, slurs, and insults about Barack Obama by a host of shock jocks, politicians, and even a federal judge.[41] Poverty is seen not as a social problem but as a personal failing, and poor people have become the objects of abuse, fear, and loathing. The poor, as right-wing ideologues never fail to remind us, are lazy—and, for that matter, how could they truly be poor if they own TVs and cell phones? Cruel, racist insults and the discourse of humiliation are now packaged in a mindless rhetoric as unapologetic as it is ruthless—this has become the new lingua franca of public exchange.

Republican presidential candidate Mitt Romney echoed the harshness of the new lingua franca of cruelty when asked during the 2012 campaign about the government's responsibility to the 50 million Americans who don't have health insurance. Incredibly, Romney replied that they already have access to health care because they can go to hospital emergency rooms.[42] In response, a New York Times editorial stated that emergency room care "is the most expensive and least effective way of providing care" and that such a remark "reeks of contempt for those left behind by the current insurance system, suggesting that they must suffer with illness until the point where they need an ambulance."[43] Indifferent to the health care needs of the poor and middle class, Romney also conveniently ignores the fact that, as indicated in a Harvard University study, "more than 62% of all personal bankruptcies are caused by the cost of overwhelming medical expenses."[44] The new lingua franca of cruelty and its politics of disposability are on full display here. To paraphrase Hannah Arendt, we live in a time when revenge has become the cure-all for most of our social and economic ills.

NEOLIBERALISM AND THE RETREAT FROM ETHICAL CONSIDERATIONS

Not only does neoliberal rationality believe in the ability of markets to solve all problems, it also removes economics and markets from ethical considerations. Economic growth, rather than social needs, drives politics. Long-term investments are replaced by short-term gains and profits, while compassion is viewed as a weakness and democratic public values are derided. As Stanley Aronowitz points out, public values and collective action have given way to the "absurd notion the market should rule every human activity," including the "absurd neoliberal idea that users should pay for every public good from parks and beaches to highways [and] higher education."[45] The hard work of critical analysis, moral judgments, and social responsibility have given way to the desire for accumulating profits at almost any cost, short of unmistakably breaking the law and risking a jail term (which seems unlikely for Wall Street criminals). Gordon Gekko's "Greed is good" speech in the film *Wall Street* has been revived as a rallying cry for the entire financial services industry, rather than seen as a critique of excess. With society overtaken by the morality of self-interest, profit-seeking weaves its way into every possible space, relationship, and institution. For example, the search for high-end profits has descended upon the educational sector with a vengeance, as private bankers, hedge fund elites, and an assortment of billionaires are investing in for-profit and charter schools while advocating policies that disinvest in public education. At the same time the biotech, pharmaceutical, and defense industries and a range of other corporations are investing in universities to rake in profits while influencing everything from how such institutions are governed and define their mission to what they teach and how they treat faculty members and students. Increasingly, universities are losing their power not only to produce critical and civically engaged students but also to offer the type of education that enables them to refute the neoliberal utopian notion that paradise amounts to a world of voracity and avarice without restrictions, governed by a financial elite who exercise authority without accountability or challenge. Literacy, public service, human rights, and morality in this neoliberal notion of education become damaged concepts, stripped of any sense of reason, responsibility, or obligation to a just society.

In this way, neoliberalism proceeds, in zombie-like fashion, to impose its values, social relations, and forms of social death upon all aspects of civic life. This is marked by not only a sustained lack of interest in the public good, a love of inequitious power relations, and a hatred of democracy. There is also the use of brutality, state violence, and humiliation to normalize a neoliberal social order that celebrates massive inequalities in income, wealth, and access to vital services. This is a social Darwinism without apology, a ruthless form of casino capitalism whose advocates have suggested, without irony, that what they do is divinely inspired.[46] Politics has become an extension of war, just as state-sponsored violence increasingly finds legitimation in popular culture and a broader culture of cruelty that promotes an expanding landscape of selfishness, insecurity, and precarity that undermines any sense of shared responsibility for the well-being of others. Too many young people today learn quickly that their fate is solely a matter of individual responsibility, legitimated through market-driven laws that embrace self-promotion, hypercompetitiveness, and surviving in a society that increasingly reduces social relations to social combat. Young people today are expected to inhabit a set of relations in which the only obligation is to live for oneself and to reduce the obligations of citizenship to the demands of a consumer culture.

Gilded Age vengeance has also returned in the form of scorn for those who are either failed consumers or do not live up to the image of the United States as a white Christian nation. Reality TV's overarching theme, echoing Hobbes's "war of all against all," brings home the lesson that punishment is the norm and reward the exception. Unfortunately, it no longer mimics reality, it is the new reality. There is more at work here than a flight from social responsibility. Also lost is the importance of those social bonds, modes of collective reasoning, and public spheres and cultural apparatuses crucial to the construction of the social state and the formation of a sustainable democratic society. Nowhere is the dismantling of the social state and the transformation of the state into a punishing machine more evident than in the recent attacks on youth, labor rights, and higher education being waged by Republican governors in a number of key states such as Michigan, Wisconsin, Florida, and Ohio.

What is often missed in discussions of these attacks is that the war on the social state and the war on education represent part of the same agenda of destruction and violence. The first war is being waged for the complete control by the rich and powerful of all modes of wealth and income while the second war is conducted on the ideological front and represents a battle over the very capacity of young people and others to imagine a different and more critical mode of subjectivity and alternative mode of politics. If the first war is on the diverse and myriad terrain of political economy the second is being waged though what C. Wright Mills once called the major cultural apparatuses, including public and higher education. This is a struggle to shape indentities, desires, and modes of subjectivity in accordance with market values, needs, and relations. Both of these wars register as part of a larger effort to destroy any vestige of a democratic imaginary, and to relegate the value of the ethical responsibility and the social question to the wasteland of political thought. Paul Krugman is on target in arguing that in spite of massive suffering caused by the economic recession—a recession that produced "once-unthinkable levels of economic distress"—there is "growing evidence that our governing elite just doesn't care."[47] Of course, Krugman is not suggesting that if the corporate and financial elite cared the predatory nature of capitalism would be transformed. Rather, he is suggesting that economic Darwinism leaves no room for compassion or ethical considerations, which makes its use of power much worse than more liberal models of a market-based society.

POLITICS OF DISPOSABILITY AND THE ATTACK ON HIGHER EDUCATION

The not-so-hidden order of politics underlying the second Gilded Age and its heartless version of economic Darwinism is that some populations, especially those marginalized by class, race, ethnicity, or immigration status, are viewed as excess populations to be removed from the body politic, relegated to sites of terminal containment or exclusion. Marked as disposable, such populations become targets of state surveillance, violence, torture, abduction, and injury. Removed from all vestiges of the social contract, they have become the unmentionables of neoliberalism. For them, surviving—not getting ahead—marks the space in which politics and power converge. The politics of disposability delineates these populations as unworthy of investment or of sharing in the rights, benefits, and protections of a substantive democracy.[48] Pushed into debt, detention centers, and sometimes prison, the alleged human waste of free-market capitalism now inhabits zones of terminal exclusion—zones marked by forms of social and civil death.[49] Particularly disturbing is the lack of opposition among the US public to this view of particular social groups as disposable—this, perhaps more than anything else, signals the presence of a rising authoritarianism in the United States. Left unchecked, economic Darwinism will not only destroy the social fabric and undermine democracy; it will also ensure the marginalization and eventual elimination of those intellectuals willing to fight for public values, rights, spaces, and institutions not wedded to the logic of privatization, commodification, deregulation, militarization, hypermasculinity, and a ruthless "competitive struggle in which only the fittest could survive."[50] This new culture of cruelty and disposability has become the hallmark of neoliberal sovereignty, and it will wreak destruction in ways not yet imaginable—even given the horrific outcomes of the economic and financial crisis brought on by economic Darwinism. All evidence suggests a new reality is unfolding, one characterized by a deeply rooted crisis of education, agency, and social responsibility.

The current assault threatening higher education and the humanities in particular cannot be understood outside of the crisis of economics, politics, and power. Evidence of this new historical conjuncture is clearly seen in the growing number of groups considered disposable, the collapse of public values, the war on youth, and the assault by the ultra-rich and megacorporations on democracy itself. This state of emergency must take as its starting point what Tony Judt has called "the social question," with its emphasis on addressing acute social problems, providing social protections for the disadvantaged, developing public spheres aimed at promoting the collective good, and protecting educational spheres that enable and deepen the knowledge, skills, and modes of agency necessary for a substantive democracy to flourish.[51] What is new about the current threat to higher education and the humanities in particular is the increasing pace of the corporatization and militarization of the university, the squelching of academic freedom, the rise of an ever increasing contingent of part-time faculty, the rise of a bloated manegerial class, and the view that students are basically consumers and faculty providers of a saleable commodity such as a credential or a set of workplace skills. More striking still is the slow death of the university as a center of critique, vital source of civic education, and crucial public good.

Or, to put it more specifically, the consequence of such dramatic transformations is the near-death of the university as a democratic public sphere. Many faculties are now demoralized as they increasingly lose rights and power. Moreover, a weak faculty translates into one governed by fear rather than by shared responsibilities, one that is susceptible to labor-bashing tactics such as increased workloads, the casualization of labor, and the growing suppression of dissent. Demoralization often translates less into moral outrage than into cynicism, accommodation, and a retreat into a sterile form of professionalism. Faculty now find themselves staring into an abyss, unwilling to address the current attacks on the university or befuddled over how the language of specialization and professionalization has cut them off from not only connecting their work to larger civic issues and social problems but also developing any meaningful relationships to a larger democratic polity.

As faculties no longer feel compelled to address important political issues and social problems, they are less inclined to communicate with a larger public, uphold public values, or engage in a type of scholarship accessible to a broader audience.[52] Beholden to corporate interests, career building, and the insular discourses that accompany specialized scholarship, too many academics have become overly comfortable with the corporatization of the university and the new regimes of neoliberal governance. Chasing after grants, promotions, and conventional research outlets, many academics have retreated from larger public debates and refused to address urgent social problems. Assuming the role of the disinterested academic or the clever faculty star on the make, endlessly chasing theory for its own sake, these so-called academic entrepreneurs simply reinforce the public's perception that they have become largely irrelevant. Incapable, if not unwilling, to defend the university as a crucial site for learning how to think critically and act with civic courage, many academics have disappeared into a disciplinary apparatus that views the university not as a place to think but as a place to prepare students to be competitive in the global marketplace.

This is particularly disturbing given the unapologetic turn that higher education has taken in its willingness to mimic corporate culture and ingratiate itself to the national security state.[53] Universities face a growing set of challenges arising from budget cuts, diminishing quality of instruction, the downsizing of faculty, the militarization of research, and the revamping of the curriculum to fit the interests of the market, all of which not only contradicts the culture and democratic value of higher education but also makes a mockery of the very meaning and mission of the university as a place both to think and to provide the formative culture and agents that make a democracy possible. Universities and colleges have been largely abandoned as democratic public spheres dedicated to providing a public service, expanding upon humankind's great intellectual and cultural achievements, and educating future generations to be able to confront the challenges of a global democracy.

Higher education increasingly stands alone, even in its attenuated state, as a public arena where ideas can be debated, critical knowledge produced, and learning linked to important social issues. Those mainstream cultural apparatuses that once offered alternative points of view, challenged authority, and subordinated public values to market interests have largely been hijacked by the consolidation of corporate power. As Ashley Lutz,

Bob McChesney, and many others have noted, approximately 90 percent of the media is currently controlled by six corporations.[54] This is a particularly important statistic in a society in which the free circulation of ideas is being replaced by ideologies, values, and modes of thought managed by the dominant media. One consequence is that dissent is increasingly met with state repression, as indicated by the violence inflicted on the Occupy Wall Street protesters, and critical ideas are increasingly viewed or dismissed as banal, if not reactionary. For many ultra-conservatives, reason itself is viewed as dangerous, along with any notion of science that challenges right-wing fundamentalist world views regarding climate change, evolution, and a host of other social issues.[55] As Frank Rich has observed, the war against literacy and informed judgment is made abundantly clear in the populist rage sweeping the country in the form of the Tea Party, a massive collective anger that "is aimed at the educated, not the wealthy."[56] This mode of civic illiteracy is rooted in racism and has prompted a revival of overtly racist language, symbols, and jokes. Confederate flags are a common feature of Tea Party rallies, as are a variety of racially loaded posters, barbs, and derogatory, racist shouting aimed at President Obama.

Democracy can only be sustained through modes of civic literacy that enable individuals to connect private troubles to larger public issues as part of a broader discourse of critical inquiry, dialogue, and engagement. Civic literacy, in this context, provides a citizenry with the skills for critical understanding while enabling them to actually intervene in society. The right-wing war on education must be understood as a form of organized irresponsibility; that is, it represents a high-intensity assault on those cultures of questioning, forms of literacy, and public spheres in which reason and critique merge with social responsibility as a central feature of critical agency and democratization. As the political philosopher Cornelius Castoriadis insists, for democracy to be vital "it needs to create citizens who are critical thinkers capable of putting existing institutions into question so that democracy again becomes . . . a new type of regime in the full sense of the term."[57]

The right-wing war on critical literacy is part of an ongoing attempt to destroy higher education as a democratic public sphere that enables intellectuals to stand firm, take risks, imagine the otherwise, and push against the grain. It is important to insist that as educators we ask, again and again, how higher education can survive in a society in which civic culture and modes of critical literacy collapse as it becomes more and more difficult to distinguish opinion and emotive outbursts from a sustained argument and logical reasoning. Equally important is the need for educators and young people to take on the challenge of defending the university. Toni Morrison gets it right:

> If the university does not take seriously and rigorously its role as a guardian of wider civic freedoms, as interrogator of more and more complex ethical problems, as servant and preserver of deeper democratic practices, then some other regime or ménage of regimes will do it for us, in spite of us, and without us.[58]

Defending the humanities, as Terry Eagleton has recently argued, means more than offering an academic enclave for students to learn history, philosophy, art, and literature. It also means stressing how indispensable these fields of study are for all students if they are to be able to make any claim whatsoever to being critical and engaged individual and social agents. But the humanities do more. They also provide the knowledge, skills, social relations, and modes of pedagogy that constitute a formative culture in which the historical lessons of democratization can be learned, the demands of social responsibility can be thoughtfully engaged, the imagination can be expanded, and critical thought can be affirmed. As an adjunct of the academic-military-industrial complex, however, higher education has nothing to say about teaching students how to think for themselves in a democracy, how to think critically and engage with others, and how to address through the prism of democratic values the relationship between themselves and the larger world. We need a permanent revolution around the meaning and purpose of higher education, one in which academics are more than willing to move beyond the language of critique and a discourse of both moral and political outrage, however necessary to a sustained individual and collective defense of the university as a vital public sphere central to democracy itself.

We must reject the idea that the university should be modeled after "a sterile Darwinian shark tank in which the only thing that matters is the bottom line."[59] We must also reconsider how the university in a post-9/11 era is being militarized and increasingly reduced to an adjunct of the growing national security state. The public has apparently given up on the idea of either funding higher education or valuing it as a public good indispensable to the life of any viable democracy. This is all the more reason for academics to be at the forefront of a coalition of activists, public servants, and others in both rejecting the growing corporate management of higher education and developing a new discourse in which the university, and particularly the humanities, can be defended as a vital social and public institution in a democratic society.

BEYOND NEOLIBERAL MISEDUCATION

As universities turn toward corporate management models, they increasingly use and exploit cheap faculty labor. Many colleges and universities are drawing more and more upon adjunct and nontenured faculty, many of whom occupy the status of indentured servants who are overworked, lack benefits, receive little or no administrative support, and are paid salaries that qualify them for food stamps.[60] Students increasingly fare no better in sharing the status of a subaltern class beholden to neoliberal policies and values. For instance, many are buried under huge debt, celebrated by the collection industry because it is cashing in on their misfortune. Jerry Aston, a member of that industry, wrote in a column after witnessing a protest rally by students criticizing their mounting debt that he "couldn't believe the accumulated wealth they represent—for our industry."[61] And, of course, this type of economic injustice is taking place in an economy in which rich plutocrats such as the infamous union-busting Koch brothers each saw "their investments grow by $6 billion in one year, which is three million dollars per hour based on a 40-hour 'work' week."[62] Workers, students, youth, and the poor are all considered expendable in this neoliberal global economy. Yet the one institution, education, that offers the opportunities for students to challenge these antidemocratic tendencies is under attack in ways that are unparalleled, at least in terms of the scope and intensity of the assault by the corporate elite and other economic fundamentalists.

Casino capitalism does more than infuse market values into every aspect of higher education; it also wages a full-fledged assault on the very notion of public goods, democratic public spheres, and the role of education in creating an informed citizenry. When Rick Santorum argued that intellectuals were not wanted in the Republican Party, he was articulating what has become common sense in a society wedded to narrow instrumentalist values and various modes of fundamentalism. Critical thinking and a literate public have become dangerous to those who want to celebrate orthodoxy over dialogue, emotion over reason, and ideological certainty over thoughtfulness.[63] Hannah Arendt's warning that "it was not stupidity but a curious, quite authentic inability to think"[64] at the heart of authoritarian regimes is now embraced as a fundamental tenet of Republican Party politics.

Right-wing appeals to austerity provide the rationale for slash-and-burn policies intended to deprive governmental social and educational programs of the funds needed to enable them to work, if not survive. Along with health care, public transportation, Medicare, food stamp programs for low-income children, and a host of other social protections, higher education is being defunded as part of a larger scheme to dismantle and privatize all public services, goods, and spheres. But there is more at work here than the march toward privatization and the never-ending search for profits at any cost; there is also the issue of wasteful spending on a bloated war machine, the refusal to tax fairly the rich and corporations, and the draining of public funds in order to support the US military presence in Iraq, Afghanistan, and elsewhere. The deficit argument and the austerity policies advocated in its name are a form of class warfare designed largely for the state to be able to redirect revenue in support of the commanding institutions of the corporate-military-industrial complex and away from funding higher education and other crucial public services. The extent of the budget reduction assault is such that in 2012 "states reduced their education budgets by $12.7 billion."[65] Of course, the burden of such reductions falls upon poor minority and other low-income students, who will not be able to afford the tuition increases that will compensate for the loss of state funding.

What has become clear in light of such assaults is that many universities and colleges have become unapologetic accomplices to corporate values and power, and in doing so increasingly regard social problems as either irrelevant or invisible.[66] The transformation of higher education both in the United States and abroad is evident in a number of registers. These include decreased support for programs of study that are not business oriented, reduced support for research that does not increase profits, the replacement of shared forms of governance with business management models, the ongoing exploitation of faculty labor, and the use of student purchasing power as the vital measure of a student's identity, worth, and access to higher education.[67]

As I point out throughout this book, one consequence of this on-going disinvestment in higher education is the expansion of a punishing state that increasingly criminalizes a range of social behaviors, wages war on the poor instead of poverty, militarizes local police forces, harasses poor minority youth, and spends more on prisons than on higher education.[68] The punishing state produces fear and sustains itself on moral panics. Dissent gives way to widespread insecurity, uncertainty, and an obsession with personal safety. Political, moral, and social indifference is the result, in part, of a public that is increasingly constituted within an educational landscape that reduces thinking to a burden and celebrates civic illiteracy as a prerequisite for negotiating a society in which moral disengagement and political corruption go hand in hand.[69] The assault on the university is symptomatic of the deep educational, economic, and political crisis facing the United States. It is but one lens through which to recognize that the future of democracy depends on the educational and ethical standards of the society we inhabit.[70]

This lapse of the US public into a political and moral coma is induced, in part, by an ever-expanding, mass-mediated celebrity culture that trades in hype and sensation. It is also accentuated by a governmental apparatus that sanctions modes of training that undermine any viable notion of critical schooling and public pedagogy. While there is much being written about how unfair the Left is to the Obama administration, what is often forgotten by these liberal critics is that Obama has aligned himself with educational practices and policies as instrumentalist and anti-intellectual as they are politically reactionary, and therein lies one viable reason for not supporting his initiatives and administration.[71] What liberals refuse to entertain is that the Left is correct in attacking Obama for his cowardly retreat from a number of progressive issues and his dastardly undermining of civil liberties. In fact, they do not go far enough in their criticisms. Often even progressives miss that Obama's views on education are utterly reactionary and provide no space for the nurturance of a radically democratic imagination. Hence, while liberals point to some of Obama's progressive policies—often in a New Age discourse that betrays their own supine moralism—they fail to acknowledge that Obama's educational policies do nothing to contest, and are in fact aligned with, his weak-willed compromises and authoritarian policies. In other words, Obama's educational commitments undermine the creation of a formative culture capable of questioning authoritarian ideas, modes of governance, and reactionary policies. The question is not whether Obama's policies are slightly less repugnant than those of his right-wing detractors. On the contrary, it is about how the Left should engage politics in a more robust and democratic way by imagining what it would mean to work collectively and with "slow impatience" for a new political order outside of the current moderate and extreme right-wing politics and the debased, uncritical educational apparatus that supports it.[72]

THE ROLE OF CRITICAL EDUCATION

One way of challenging the new authoritarianism is to reclaim the relationship between critical education and social change. The question of what kind of subjects and modes of individual and social agency are necessary for a democracy to survive appears more crucial now than ever before, and this is a question that places matters of education, pedagogy, and culture at the center of any understanding of politics. We live at a time when too few Americans appear to have an interest in democracy beyond the every-four-years ritual performance of voting, and even this act fails to attract a robust majority of citizens. The term "democracy" has been emptied of any viable meaning, hijacked by political scoundrels, corporate elites, and the advertising industry. The promise that democracy exhibits as an ongoing struggle for rights, justice, and a future of hope has been degraded into a misplaced desire to shop and to fulfill the pleasure quotient in spectacles of violence, while the language of democracy is misappropriated and deployed as a rationale for racist actions against immigrants, Muslims, and the poor. Of course, while more and more nails are being put into the coffin of democracy, there are flashes of resistance, such as those among workers in Wisconsin, the Occupy Wall Street movement, and the more recent strike by Chicago teachers. Public employees, fast food workers, Walmart employees, disaffected youth, and others are struggling to expose the massive injustices and death-dealing machinations of the 1 percent and the pernicious effects of casino capitalism. But this struggle is just beginning and only time will tell how far it goes.

The time has come not only to redefine the promise of democracy but also to challenge those who have poisoned its meaning. We have already witnessed such a challenge by protest movements both at home and abroad in which the struggle over education has become one of the most powerful fulcrums for redressing the detrimental effects of neoliberalism. What these struggles, particularly by young people, have in common is the attempt to merge the powers of persuasion and critical, civic literacy with the power of social movements to activate and mobilize real change. They are recovering a notion of the social and reclaiming a kind of humanity that should inspire and inform our collective willingness to imagine what a real democracy might look like. Cornelius Castoriadis rightly argues that "people need to be educated for democracy by not only expanding the capacities that enable them to assume public responsibility but also through active participation in the very process of governing."[73]

As the crucial lens through which to create the formative culture in which politics and power can be made visible and held accountable, pedagogy plays a central role. But as Archon Fung notes, criticism is not the only public responsibility of intellectuals, artists, journalists, educators, and others who engage in critical pedagogical practices. "Intellectuals can also join citizens—and sometimes governments—to construct a world that is more just and democratic. One such constructive role is aiding popular movements and organizations in their efforts to advance justice and democracy."[74] In this instance, understanding must be linked to the practice of social responsibility and the willingness to fashion a politics that addresses real problems and enacts concrete solutions. As Heather Gautney points out,

> We need to start thinking seriously about what kind of political system we really want. And we need to start pressing for things that our politicians did NOT discuss at the conventions. Real solutions—like universal education, debt forgiveness, wealth redistribution, and participatory political structures—that would empower us to decide together what's best. Not who's best.[75]

Critical thinking divorced from action is often as sterile as action divorced from critical theory. Given the urgency of the historical moment, we need a politics and a public pedagogy that make knowledge meaningful in order to make it critical and transformative. Or, as Stuart Hall argues, we need to produce modes of analysis and knowledge in which "people can invest something of themselves . . . something that they recognize is of them or speaks to their condition."[76] A notion of higher education as a democratic public sphere is crucial to this project, especially at a time in which the apostles of neoliberalism and other forms of political and religious fundamentalism are ushering in a new age of conformity, cruelty, and disposability. But as public intellectuals, academics can do more.

First, they can write for multiple audiences, expanding public spheres, especially online, to address a range of social issues including, importantly, the relationship between the attack on the social state and the defunding of higher education. In any democratic society, education should be viewed as a right, not an entitlement, and this suggests a reordering of state and federal priorities to make that happen. For instance, the military budget could be cut by two-thirds and those funds invested instead in public and higher education. There is nothing utopian about this demand, given the excess of military power in the United States, but addressing this task requires a sustained critique of the militarization of American society and a clear analysis of the damage it has caused both at home and abroad. Brown University's Watson Institute for International Studies, with the efforts of a number of writers such as Andrew Bacevich, has been doing this for years and offers a treasure trove of information that could be easily accessed and used by public intellectuals in and outside of the academy. A related issue, as Angela Davis, Michelle Alexander, and others have argued, is the need for public intellectuals to become part of a broader social movement aimed at dismantling the prison-industrial complex and the punishing state, which drains billions of dollars in funds to put people in jail when such funds could be used to fund public and higher education or other social supports that may help prevent criminalized behaviors in the first place. The punishing state is a dire threat not only to public and higher education but also, more broadly, to democracy itself. It is the pillar of the authoritarian state, undermining civil liberties, criminalizing a range of social behaviors related to concrete social problems, and intensifying the legacy of Jim Crow against poor people of color. The US public does not need more prisons; it needs more schools.

Second, academics, artists, journalists, and other cultural workers need to connect the rise of subaltern, part-time labor in the university as well as the larger society with the massive inequality in wealth and income that now corrupts every aspect of American politics and society. Precarity has become a weapon both to exploit adjuncts, part-time workers, and temporary laborers and to suppress dissent by keeping them in a state of fear over losing their jobs. Insecure forms of labor increasingly produce "a feeling of passivity born of despair."[77] Multinational corporations have abandoned the social contract and any vestige of supporting the social state. They plunder labor and perpetuate the mechanizations of social death whenever they have the chance to accumulate capital. This issue is not simply about restoring a balance between labor and capital, it is about recognizing a new form of serfdom that kills the spirit as much as it depoliticizes the mind. The new authoritarians do not ride around in tanks; they have private jets, they fund right-wing think tanks, and they lobby for reactionary policies that privatize everything in sight while filling their bank accounts with massive profits. They are the embodiment of a culture of greed, cruelty, and disposability.

Third, academics can fight for the rights of students to get a free education, a formidable and critical education not dominated by corporate values, to have a say in its shaping, and to experience what it means to expand and deepen the practice of freedom and democracy. Young people have been left out of the discourse of democracy. They are the new disposable individuals, a population lacking jobs, a decent education, and any hope of a future better than the one their parents inherited. They are a reminder of how finance capital has abandoned any viable vision of the future, including one that would support future generations. This is a mode of politics and capital that eats its own children and throws their fate to the vagaries of the market. If a society is in part judged by how it views and treats its children, US society by all accounts has truly failed in a colossal way and, in doing so, provides a glimpse of the heartlessness at the core of the new authoritarianism.

Last, public intellectuals should also address and resist the ongoing shift in power relations between faculty and the managerial class. Too many faculty are now removed from the governing structures of higher education and as a result have been abandoned to the misery of impoverished wages, excessive class loads, no health care, and few, if any, social benefits. This is shameful and is not merely an issue of the education system but a deeply political matter, one that must address how neoliberal ideology and policy have imposed on higher education an antidemocratic governing structure that mimics the broader authoritarian forces now threatening the United States.[78]

I want to conclude by quoting from James Baldwin, a courageous writer who refused to let the hope of democracy die in his lifetime, and who offered that mix of politics, passion, and courage that deserves not just admiration but emulation. His sense of rage was grounded in a working-class sensibility, eloquence, and heart that illuminate a higher standard for what it means to be a public and an engaged intellectual. His words capture something that is missing from the US cultural and political landscape, something affirmative that needs to be seized upon, rethought, and occupied by intellectuals, academics, artists, and other concerned citizens—as part of both the fight against the new authoritarianism and its cynical, dangerous, and cruel practices, and the struggle to reclaim a belief in justice and mutuality that seems to be dying in all of us. In *The Fire Next Time*, Baldwin writes:

> One must say Yes to life, and embrace it wherever it is found—and it is found in terrible places. . . . For nothing is fixed, forever and forever, it is not fixed; the earth is always shifting, the light is always changing, the sea does not cease to grind down rock. Generations do not cease to be born, and we are responsible to them because we are the only witnesses they have. The sea rises, the light fails, lovers cling to each other, and children cling to us. The moment we cease to hold each other, the moment we break faith with one another, the sea engulfs us and the light goes out.

CHAPTER TWO

Dystopian Education in a Neoliberal Society

I n the United States and abroad, public and higher education is under assault by a host of religious, economic, ideological, and political fundamentalists. As regards public schools, the most serious attack is being waged by religious conservatives and advocates of neoliberalism whose reform efforts focus narrowly on high-stakes testing, skill-based teaching, traditional curriculum, and memorization drills.[1] Ideologically, the pedagogical emphasis is the antithesis of a critical approach to teaching and learning, emphasizing a pedagogy of conformity and a curriculum marked by a vulgar "vocationalist instrumentality."[2] At the level of policy, the assault is driven by an aggressive attempt to disinvest in public schools, replace them with charter schools, and remove state and federal governments completely from public education in order to allow education to be organized and administered by a variety of privatizing, market-driven forces and for-profit corporations.[3] In this instance, public schools are defined through practices of repression, removed from any larger notion of the public good, reduced to "simply another corporate asset bundled in credit default swaps," valuable solely for their rate of exchange and trade value on the open market.[4] Clearly, public education should not be harnessed to the script of cost-benefit analyses, the national security state, or the needs of corporations, which often leads to the loss of egalitarian and democratic values, ideals, and responsibilities.

At the same time, a full-fledged assault is also being waged on higher education in North America, the United Kingdom, and various European countries. While the nature of the assault varies across countries, there is a common set of assumptions and practices driving the transformations of higher education into an adjunct of corporate power and values. The effects of the assault are not hard to discern. Universities are being defunded, tuition fees are skyrocketing, faculty salaries are shrinking as workloads are increasing, and faculty are being reduced to a subaltern class of migrant laborers. Corporate management schemes are being put in place, "underpinned by market-like principles, based on metrics, control, and display of performance."[5] The latter is reinforcing an audit culture that mimics the organizational structures of a market economy. In addition, class sizes are ballooning, curriculum is stripped of liberal values, research is largely assessed for its ability to produce profits, administrative staffs are being cut back, governance has been handed over to paragons of corporate culture, and valuable services are being either outsourced or curtailed.

The neoliberal paradigm driving these attacks on public and higher education abhors democracy and views public and higher education as a toxic civic sphere that poses a threat to corporate values, power, and ideology. As democratic public spheres, colleges and universities are allegedly dedicated to teaching students to think critically, take imaginative risks, learn how to be moral witnesses, and procure the skills that enable one to connect to others in ways that strengthen the democratic polity, and this is precisely why they are under attack by the concentrated forces of neoliberalism.[6] Self-confident citizens are regarded as abhorrent by conservatives and evangelical fundamentalists who, traumatized by the campus turmoil of the sixties, largely view dissent, if not critical thought itself, as a dire threat to corporate power and religious authority.[7] Similarly, critical thought, knowledge, dialogue, and dissent are increasingly perceived with suspicion by the new corporate university that now defines faculty as entrepreneurs, students as customers, and education as a mode of training.[8]

Welcome to the dystopian world of corporate education, in which learning how to think, appropriate public values, and become an engaged critical citizen is viewed as a failure rather than a success. Instead of producing "a generation of leaders worthy of the challenges,"[9] the dystopian mission of public and higher education is to produce robots, technocrats, and trained workers. There is more than a backlash at work in these assaults on public and higher education; there is a sustained effort to dismantle education from the discourse of democracy, public values, critical thought, social responsibility, and civic courage. Put more bluntly, the dystopian shadow that has fallen on public and higher education reveals the coming darkness of a counterrevolution that is putting into place a mode of corporate sovereignty constituting a new, updated form of authoritarianism. During the Cold War, US officials never let us forget that authoritarian countries put their intellectuals into prison. While such practices do not prevail in the United States or other capitalist democracies, the fate of critical intellectuals today is no better, since they are either fired or denied tenure for being too critical, or relegated to an intolerable state of dire poverty and existential impoverishment in part-time appointments that pay low wages.[10]

Education within the last three decades has been removed from its utopian possibilities of educating young people to be reflective, critical, and socially engaged agents. The post-WWII Keynesian period up to the civil rights movement and the campus uprisings in the 1960s witnessed an ongoing expansion of public and higher education as democratic public spheres. Democratic ideals were never far from the realms of public and higher education, though they often lacked full support of both the public and the university administration. While not all educators willingly addressed matters of equity, inclusion, racism, and the role of education as a public good, such issues never disappeared from public view. Under neoliberal regimes, however diverse, the notion of public and higher education, as well as the larger notion of education as the primary register of the greater culture, are viewed as too dangerous by the apostles of free-market capitalism. Critical thought and the imaginings of a better world present a direct threat to a neoliberal paradigm in which the future replicates the present in an endless circle, with capital and the identities that legitimate it merging with each other into what might be called the dead zone of casino capitalism. This dystopian impulse thrives on producing myriad forms of violence embracing the symbolic and the structural as part of a broader attempt to define education in purely instrumental and anti-intellectual terms. It is this replacement of educated hope with an aggressive dystopian project in particular that characterizes the current assault on higher education in various parts of the globe extending from the United States and the United Kingdom to Greece and Spain.

In light of this dystopian attempt to remove education from any notion of critique, dialogue, and empowerment, it would be an understatement to suggest that there is something very wrong with US public and higher education. For a start, this counterrevolution is giving rise to punitive evaluation schemes, harsh disciplinary measures, and the ongoing deskilling of many teachers that together are reducing many excellent educators to the debased status of technicians and security personnel. Additionally, as more and more wealth is distributed to the richest Americans and corporations, states are drained of resources and are shifting the burden of their deficits onto public schools and other vital public services. With 40 percent of wealth going to the top 1 percent, public services are drying up from lack of revenue, and more and more young people find themselves locked out of the dream of getting a decent education or a job, robbed of any hope for the future.[11]

While the nation's schools and infrastructure suffer from a lack of resources, right-wing politicians are enacting policies that lower the taxes of the rich and megacorporations. For the elite, taxes are seen as constituting a form of class warfare waged by the state against the rich, who view the collection of taxes as a form of state coercion. What is ironic in this argument is the startling fact that not only are the rich not taxed fairly but they also receive billions in corporate subsidies. But there is more at stake here than untaxed wealth and revenue; there is also the fact that wealth corrupts and buys power. And this poisonous mix of wealth, politics, and power translates into an array of antidemocratic practices that have created an unhealthy society in every major index ranging from infant mortality rates to a dysfunctional political system.[12]

Hidden in this hollow outrage by the wealthy is the belief that the real enemy is any form of government that needs to raise revenue in order to build and maintain infrastructures, provide basic services for those who need them, and develop investments such as a transportation system and schools that are not tied to the logic of the market. One consequence of this vile form of actual class warfare is a battle over crucial resources, a battle that has dire political and educational consequences especially for the poor and middle classes, if not democracy itself. This battle in the United States is particularly fierce over the issue of taxes. As David Theo Goldberg points out, neoliberal ideology makes clear—as part of its project of hollowing out public institutions—that "paying taxes has devolved from a central social responsibility to a game of creative work-arounds. Today, taxes are not so much the common contribution to cover the costs of social benefits and infrastructure relative to one's means, as they are a burden to be avoided."[13]

Money no longer simply controls elections; it also controls policies that shape public education, if not practically all other social, cultural, and economic institutions.[14] One indicator of such corruption is that hedge fund managers now sit on school boards across the country, doing everything in their power to eliminate public schools and punish unionized teachers who do not support charter schools. In New Jersey hundreds of teachers have been sacked because of alleged budget deficits. Not only is Governor Christie using the deficit argument to fire teachers, he also uses it to break unions and balance the budget on the backs of students and teachers. How else to explain Christie's refusal to endorse reinstituting the "millionaires' taxes," or his craven support for lowering taxes on the top twenty-five hedge fund officers in New Jersey, who in 2009 raked in $25 billion, enough to fund 658,000 entry-level teachers?[15]

In this conservative right-wing reform culture, the role of public and higher education, if we are to believe the Heritage Foundation and billionaires such as Bill Gates, is to produce students who laud conformity, believe job training is more important than education, and view public values as irrelevant. While Gates, former DC education chancellor Michelle Rhee, and secretary of education Arne Duncan would argue they are the true education reformers, the fact of the matter is that education in their view is tied to job training, quantitative measurements, and the development of curricula to prepare students for particular occupations. Teaching to the test, undercutting the power of teachers, and removing subjects such as art, literature, music, and critical thinking from the school curriculum are at the core of their conservative vision for reform. Moreover, their relentless attempts to turn public schools into charter schools are in direct opposition to their claims that their policies serve the public good and empower young people, especially poor minorities. Students in this corporate-driven world view are no longer educated for democratic citizenship. On the contrary, they are being trained to fulfill the need for human capital.[16] At the same time, this emphasis on defining schools through an audit culture and various accountability regimes conveniently allows the financial elite to ignore those forces that affect schools such as poverty, unemployment, poor health care, inequality, and other important social and economic forces. Removing matters of equity from issues of excellence and learning also makes it easier for right-wing foundations and conservative foundations to blame teachers and unions for the failure of schools, making it all the easier to turn public schools, universities, and colleges over to for-profit forces.

What is lost in this approach to schooling is what Noam Chomsky describes as "creating creative and independent thought and inquiry, challenging perceived beliefs, exploring new horizons and forgetting external constraints."[17] At the same time, public schools and colleges are under assault not because they are failing (though some are) but because they are one of the few public spheres left where people can learn the knowledge and skills necessary to allow them to think critically and hold power and authority accountable. It is worth repeating that not only are the lines between the corporate world and public and higher education blurring, but all modes of education (except for the elite) are being reduced to what Peter Seybold calls a "corporate service station," in which the democratic ideals at the heart of public and higher education are up for sale.[18] At the heart of this crisis of education are larger questions about the formative culture necessary for a democracy to survive, the nature of civic education and teaching in dark times, the role of educators as civic intellectuals, and what it means to understand the purpose and meaning of education as a site of individual and collective empowerment.

This current right-wing emphasis on low-level skills distracts the US public from examining the broader economic, political, and cultural forces that bear down on schools. Matters concerning the influence on schools of corporations, textbook publishers, commercial industries, and the national security state are rendered invisible, as if schools and the practices they promote exist in a bubble. At work here is a dystopian pedagogy that displaces, infantilizes, and depoliticizes both students and large segments of the US public. Under the current regime of neoliberalism, schools have been transformed into a private right rather than a public good. Students are being educated to become consumers rather than thoughtful, critical citizens. Increasingly, as public schools are put in the hands of for-profit corporations, hedge fund elites, and other market-driven sources, their value is derived from their ability to turn a profit and produce compliant students eager to join the workforce.[19]

What is truly scandalous about the current dismantling of and disinvestment in public schooling is that those who advocate such changes are called the new education reformers. They are not reformers at all. They are reactionaries and financial mercenaries, and resemble dystopian zombies in spewing toxic educational gore. In their wake, teaching is turned into the practice of conformity, and curricula are driven by an anti-intellectual obsession with student test scores. In addition, students are educated to be active consumers and compliant subjects, increasingly unable to think critically about themselves and their relationship to the larger world. This virus of repression, conformity, and instrumentalism is turning public and higher education into a repressive site of containment, devoid of poetry, critical learning, or soaring acts of curiosity and imagination. As Diane Ravitch sums it up, what is driving the current public school reform movement is a profoundly anti-intellectual project that promotes "more testing, more privately managed schools, more deregulation, more firing of teachers, [and] more school closings."[20]

At the level of higher education, the script is similar with a project designed to defund higher education, impose corporate models of governance, purge the university of critical thinkers, turn faculty into a low-wage army of part-time workers, and allow corporate money and power to increasingly decide course content and determine what faculty get hired. As public values are replaced by corporate values, students become clients, faculty are deskilled and depoliticized, tuition rises, and more and more working-class and poor minority students are excluded from the benefits of higher education. There are no powerful and profound intellectual dramas in this view of schooling, just the noisy and demonstative rush to make schools another source of profit for finance capital with its growing legion of bankers, billionaires, and hedge fund scoundrels.

Public schooling and higher education are also increasingly harnessed to the needs of corporations and the warfare state. One consequence is that many public schools, especially those occupied by poor minority youth, have become the equivalent of factories for dumbing down the curricula and turning teachers into what amounts to machine parts. At the same time, such schools have become increasingly militarized and provide a direct route for many youth into the prison-industrial complex via the "school-to-prison pipeline."[21] What is buried under the educational-reform rhetoric of hedge fund and casino capitalism is the ideal of offering public school students a civic education that provides the capacities, knowledge, and skills that enable students to speak, write, and act from a position of agency and empowerment. At the college level, students are dazzled with a blitz of spaces that now look like malls, while in between classes they are endlessly entertained by a mammoth sports culture that is often as debasing as it is dangerous in its hypermasculinity, racism, and overt sexism.[22]

Privatization, commodification, militarization, and deregulation are the new guiding categories through which schools, teachers, pedagogy, and students are defined. The current assaults on public and higher education are not new, but they are more vile and more powerful than in the past. Crucial to any viable resistance is the need to understand the historical context in which education has been transformed into an adjunct of corporate power as well as the ways in which the current right-wing reform operates within a broader play of forces that bear down in antidemocratic ways on the purpose of schooling and the practice of teaching itself. Making power visible is important but only a first step in understanding how it works and how it might be challenged. But recognizing such a challenge is not the same thing as overcoming it. Part of this task necessitates that educators anchor their own work in classrooms, however diverse, in projects that engage the promise of an unrealized democracy against its existing, often repressive forms. And this is only a first step.

Public and higher education, along with the pedagogical role of the larger culture, should be viewed as crucial to any viable notion of democracy, while the pedagogical practices they employ should be consistent with the ideal of the good society. This means teaching more than the knowledge of traditional canons. In fact, teachers and students need to recognize that as a moral and political practice pedagogy is about the struggle over identity just as much as it is a struggle over what counts as knowledge. At a time when censorship is running amok in public schools and dissent is viewed as a distraction or unpatriotic, the debate over whether we should view schools as political institutions seems not only moot but irrelevant. Pedagogy is a mode of critical intervention, one that endows teachers with a responsibility to prepare students not merely for jobs but for being in the world in ways that allow them to influence the larger political, ideological, and economic forces that bear down on their lives. Schooling is an eminently political and moral practice because it is directive of and also actively legitimates what counts as knowledge, sanctions particular values, and constructs particular forms of agency.

One of the most notable features of contemporary conservative reform efforts is the way in which they increasingly position teachers as a liability and in doing so align with modes of education that are as demeaning as they are deskilling. These reforms are not innocent and actually promote failure in the classroom. And when that is successful, they open the door for more public schools to be closed, provide another chance at busting the union, and allow such schools to be taken over by private and corporate interests. Under the influence of market-based pedagogies, public school teachers are subjected to what can only be described as repressive disciplinary measures in the school and an increasing chorus of verbal humiliation from politicians outside of the classroom. Academics do not fare much better and are often criticized for being too radical, for not working long hours, and for receiving cushy paychecks—a position at odds with the fact that more than 70 percent of academic labor is now either part-time or on a non-tenure track. Many contingent faculty earn so little income that they are part of the growing new class of workers who qualify for food stamps. With no health insurance and lacking other crucial benefits, they are truly on their own.

Teachers and academics are not only on the defensive in the neoliberal war on schools, they are also increasingly pressured to assume a more instrumentalist and mercenary role. Such approaches leave them with no time to be creative, use their imagination, work with other teachers, or develop classroom practices that are not wedded to teaching to the test and other demeaning empirical measures. Of course, the practice of disinvesting in public schools and higher education has a long history, but it has strengthened since the election of Ronald Reagan in 1980 and intensified in the new millennium. How else to explain that many states invest more in building prisons than educating students, especially those who are poor, disabled, and immersed in poverty? What are we to make of the fact that there are more Black men in prison than in higher education in states such as Louisiana and California?[23] The right-wing makeover of public education has resulted in some states, Texas for example, banning the teaching of critical thinking in their classrooms, while in Arizona legislation has been passed that eliminates all curricular material from the classroom that includes the histories of Mexican Americans. The latter case is particularly loathsome. Masquerading as legislation designed to teach students how—no irony intended—to value each other and eliminate the hatred of other ethnic groups and races, Bill HB2281 bans ethnic studies. According to the bill, it is illegal for a school district to have any courses or classes that will "promote the overthrow of the U.S. government, promote resentment of a particular race or class of people, are designed primarily for students of a particular ethnic group or advocate ethnic solidarity instead of the treatment of pupils as individuals."[24] Schools that do not comply with this racist law will lose 10 percent of their monthly share of state aid.

It gets worse. In addition to eliminating the teaching of the history and culture of those ethnic groups considered a threat or disposable, the Arizona Department of Education "began telling school districts that teachers whose spoken English it deems to be heavily accented or ungrammatical must be removed from classes for students still learning English."[25] The targets here include not only ethnic studies but also those educators who inhabit ethnic identities. This is an unadulterated expression of educational discrimination and apartheid, and it is as disgraceful as it is racist. It is worth noting that these states also want to tie the salaries of faculty in higher education to performance measures based on a neoliberal model of evaluation. In this case, these racist reforms share an unholy alliance with neoliberal reforms that make teachers voiceless, if not powerless, to reject them by preoccupying them with modes of pedagogy as repressive as they are anti-intellectual and depoliticized.

Fighting for democracy as an educational project means encouraging a culture of questioning in classrooms, one that explores both the strengths and weaknesses of the current era. This notion of questioning is not simply about airing conflicting points of view, nor is it about substituting dogma for genuine dialogue and critical analysis. Most importantly, it is about a culture of questioning that raises ideas to the status of public values and a broader encounter with the larger social order. At issue here are pedagogical practices that are not only about the search for the truth but also about taking responsibility for intervening in the world by connecting knowledge and power, learning and values to interrelated modes of commitment and social engagement. I think Zygmunt Bauman is right in arguing that "if there is no room for the idea of *a wrong* society, there is hardly much chance for the idea of a good society to be born, let alone make waves."[26] The relevant question in this instance is what kind of future do our teachings presuppose? What forms of literacy and agency do we make available to our students through our pedagogical practices? How do we understand and incorporate in classroom pedagogies the ongoing search for equity and excellence, truth and justice, knowledge and commitment? I believe that this broader project of addressing democratization as a pedagogical practice should be central to any worthwhile attempt to engage in classroom teaching. And this is a political project. As educators, we have to begin with a vision of schooling as a democratic public sphere, and then we have to figure out what the ideological, political, and social impediments are to such a goal and organize collectively to derail them. In other word, educators need to start with a project, not a method. They need to view themselves through the lens of civic responsibility and address what it means to educate students in the best of those traditions and knowledge forms we have inherited from the past and also in terms of what it means to prepare them to be in the world as critically engaged agents.

Educators need to be more forceful and committed to linking their overall investment in democracy to modes of critique and collective action that address the presupposition that democratic societies are never too just or just enough. Moreover, such a commitment suggests that a viable democratic society must constantly nurture the possibilities for self-critique, collective agency, and forms of citizenship in which teachers and students play a fundamental role. Rather than being forced to participate in a pedagogy designed to raise test scores and undermine forms of critical thinking, students must be involved pedagogically in critically discussing, administrating, and shaping the material relations of power and ideological forces that structure their everyday lives. Central to such an educational project is the continual struggle by teachers to connect their pedagogical practices to the building of an inclusive and just democracy, which should be open to many forms, offers no political guarantees, and provides an important normative dimension to politics as an ongoing process that never ends. Such a project is based on the realization that a democracy open to exchange, question, and self-criticism never reaches the limits of justice; it is never just enough and never finished. It is precisely the open-ended and normative nature of such a project that provides a common ground for educators to share their resources with a diverse range of intellectual pursuits while refusing to believe that such struggles in schools ever come to an end.

In order to connect teaching with the larger world so as to make pedagogy meaningful, critical, and transformative, educators will have to focus their work on important social issues that connect what is learned in the classroom to the larger society and the lives of their students. Such issues might include the ongoing destruction of the ecological biosphere, the current war against youth, the hegemony of neoliberal globalization, the widespread attack by corporate culture on public schools, the relentless attack on the welfare system, the increasing rates of incarceration of people of color, the dangerous growth of the prison-industrial complex, the increasing gap between the rich and the poor, the rise of a generation of students who are laboring under the burden of debt, and the increasing spread of war globally.

Once again, educators need to do more than create the conditions for critical learning for their students; they also need to responsibly assume the role of civic educators willing to share their ideas with other educators and the wider public. This suggests writing and speaking to a variety of audiences through a host of public means of expression including the lecture circuit, Internet, radio interviews, alternative magazines, and the church pulpit, to name only a few. Such writing needs to become public by crossing over into spheres and avenues of expression that speak to more general audiences in a language that is clear but not theoretically simplistic. Capitalizing on their role as intellectuals, educators can address the challenge of combining scholarship and commitment through the use of a vocabulary that is neither dull nor obtuse, while seeking to reach a broad audience. More importantly, as teachers organize to assert the importance of their role and that of public schooling in a democracy, they can forge new alliances and connections to develop social movements that include and also expand beyond working with unions.

Educators also need to be more specific about what it means to be self-critical as well as attentive to learning how to work collectively with other educators through a vast array of networks across a number of public spheres. This might mean sharing resources with educators in a variety of fields and sites, extending from other teachers to community workers and artists outside of the school. This also suggests that educators become more active in addressing the ethical and political challenges of globalization. Public schools, teachers, and higher education faculties need to unite across the various states and make a case for public and higher education. At the very least, they could make clear to a befuddled American public that the deficit theory regarding school cutbacks is a fraud.

There is plenty of money to provide quality education to every student in the United States—and this certainly holds true for the United Kingdom and Canada as well. As Salvatore Babones points out, "The problem isn't a lack of money. The problem is where the money is going."[27] The issue is not about the absence of funds as much as it is about where funds are being invested and how more revenue can be raised to support public education in the United States. The United States spends around $960 billion on its wars and defense-related projects.[28] In fact, the cost of war over a ten-year period "will run at least $3.7 trillion and could reach as high as $4.4 trillion, according to the research project "Costs of War" by Brown University's Watson Institute for International Studies."[29] Military spending seems to know no bounds. The United States could spend as much as a trillion dollars for a fleet of F-35 fighter planes with stealth technology. Each plane costs $90 million, and the military is "spending more on this plane than Australia's entire GDP ($924 billion)."[30] Many military experts urged the Pentagon to ditch the project because of cost overruns and a series of technological problems that more recently have resulted in the Pentagon grounding all F-35s. In just this one example, billions are being wasted on faulty military planes when the money could be used to fund food programs for needy children, scholarships for low-income youth, and shelter for the homeless. As Babones argues, the crucial recognition here is that

> research consistently shows that education spending creates more jobs per dollar than any other kind of government spending. A University of Massachusetts study ranked military spending worst of five

major fiscal levers for job creation. The UMass study ranked education spending the best. A dollar spent on education creates more than twice as many jobs than a dollar spent on defense. Education spending also outperforms health care, clean energy and tax cuts as a mechanism for job creation.[31]

Surely, this budget could be trimmed appropriately to divert much-needed funds to education, given that a nation's highest priority should be investing in its children rather than in the production of organized violence. As capital, finance, trade, and culture become extraterritorial and increasingly removed from traditional political constraints, it becomes all the more pressing to put global networks and political organizations into play to contend with the reach and power of neoliberal globalization. Engaging in intellectual practices that offer the possibility of alliances and new forms of solidarity among public school teachers and cultural workers such as artists, writers, journalists, academics, and others who engage in forms of public pedagogy grounded in a democratic project represents a small, but important, step in addressing the massive and unprecedented reach of global capitalism.

Educators also need to register and make visible their own subjective involvement in what they teach, how they shape classroom social relations, and how they defend their positions within institutions that often legitimate educational processes based on narrow ideological interests and political exclusions. This suggests making one's authority and classroom work the subject of critical analysis with students but taken up in terms that move beyond the rhetoric of method, psychology, or private interests. Pedagogy in this instance can be addressed as a moral and political discourse in which students are able to connect learning to social change, scholarship to commitment, and classroom knowledge to public life. Such a pedagogical task suggests that educators speak truth to power, exercise civic courage, and take risk in their role as public intellectuals. Theodor Adorno is insightful here in arguing that "the undiminished presence of suffering, fear and menace necessitates that thought that cannot be realized should not be discarded."[32] This suggests, in part, that academics must overcome an intense obsession with the demands of their own circumscribed professional pursuits, rejecting the privatized notion of scholarship and agency that dominates academic life. Too many academics are willing to depoliticize their work by insulating theory, teaching, and research from the discourse, structures, and experiences of everyday life. This is not merely a matter of intellectuals selling out but of standing still, refusing to push against the grain to address the crimes and rubbish of the new Gilded Age. Of course, there are many academics, teachers, and right-wing pundits who argue that the classroom should be free of politics and hence a space where matters of power, values, and social justice should not be addressed. The usual object of scorn in this case is the charge that teachers who believe in civic education indoctrinate students. In this ideologically pure world, authority in the classroom is reduced to a transparent pedagogy in which nothing controversial can be stated and teachers are forbidden to utter one word related to any of the major problems facing the larger society. Of course, this position is as much a flight from responsibility as it is an instance of a dreadful pedagogy.

One useful approach to embracing the classroom as a political site but at the same time eschewing any form of indoctrination is for educators to think through the distinction between a *politicizing pedagogy*, which insists wrongly that students think as we do, and a *political pedagogy*, which teaches students by example and through dialogue about the importance of power, social responsibility, and of taking a stand (without standing still) while rigorously engaging the full range of ideas about an issue.

Political pedagogy offers the promise of nurturing students to think critically about their understanding of classroom knowledge and its relationship to the issue of social responsibility. Yet it would also invoke the challenge of educating students not only to engage the world critically but also to be responsible enough to fight for those political and economic conditions that make democratic participation in both schools and the larger society viable. Such a pedagogy affirms the experience of the social and the obligations it evokes regarding questions of responsibility and transformation. In part, it does this by opening up for students important questions about power, knowledge, and what it might mean for them to critically engage the conditions under which life is presented to them. In addition, the pedagogy of freedom would provide students with the knowledge and skills to analyze and work to overcome those social relations of oppression that make living unbearable for those who are poor, hungry, unemployed, deprived of adequate social services, and viewed under the aegis of neoliberalism as largely disposable. What is important about this type of critical pedagogy is the issue of responsibility as both a normative issue and a strategic act. Responsibility not only highlights the performative nature of pedagogy by raising questions about the relationship that teachers have to students but also the relationship that students have to themselves and others.

Central here is the importance for educators to encourage students to reflect on what it means for them to connect knowledge and criticism to becoming agents of social change, buttressed by a profound desire to overcome injustice and a spirited commitment to social agency. Political education teaches students to take risks, challenge those with power, and encourage them to be reflexive about how power is used in the classroom. Political education proposes that the role of the teacher as public intellectual is not to consolidate authority but to question and interrogate it, and that teachers and students should temper any reverence for authority with a sense of critical awareness and an acute willingness to hold it accountable for its consequences. Moreover, political education foregrounds education not within the imperatives of specialization and professionalization but within a project designed to expand the possibilities of democracy by linking education to modes of political agency that promote critical citizenship and address the ethical imperative to alleviate human suffering.

On the other hand, politicizing education silences in the name of orthodoxy and imposes itself on students while undermining dialogue, deliberation, and critical engagement. Politicizing education is often grounded in a combination of self-righteousness and ideological purity that silences students as it enacts "correct" positions. Authority in this perspective rarely opens itself to self-criticism or for that matter to any criticism, especially from students. Politicizing education cannot decipher the distinction between critical teaching and pedagogical terrorism because its advocates have no sense of the difference between encouraging human agency and social responsibility and molding students according to the imperatives of an unquestioned ideological position and sutured pedagogical script. Politicizing education is more religious than secular and more about training than educating; it harbors a great dislike for complicating issues, promoting critical dialogue, and generating a culture of questioning.

If teachers are truly concerned about how education operates as a crucial site of power in the modern world, they will have to take more seriously how pedagogy functions on local and global levels to secure and challenge the ways in which power is deployed, affirmed, and resisted within and outside traditional discourses and cultural spheres. In this instance, pedagogy becomes an important theoretical tool for understanding the institutional conditions that place constraints on the production of knowledge, learning, and academic labor itself. Pedagogy also provides a discourse for engaging and challenging the production of social hierarchies, identities, and ideologies as they traverse local and national borders. In addition, pedagogy as a form of production and critique offers a discourse of possibility, a way of providing students with the opportunity to link meaning to commitment and understanding to social transformation—and to do so in the interest of the greatest possible justice. Unlike traditional vanguardist or elitist notions of the intellectual, critical pedagogy and education should embrace the notion of rooting the vocation of intellectuals in pedagogical and political work tempered by humility, a moral focus on suffering, and the need to produce alternative visions and policies that go beyond a language of sheer critique.

I now want to shift my frame a bit in order to focus on the implications of the concerns I have addressed thus far and how they might be connected to developing an academic agenda for teachers as public intellectuals, particularly at a time when neoliberal agendas increasingly guide social policy.

Once again, in opposition to the privatization, commodification, commercialization, and militarization of everything public, educators need to define public education as a resource vital to the democratic and civic life of the nation. At the heart of such a task is the challenge for teachers, academics, cultural workers, and labor organizers to join together in opposition to the transformation of public education into a commercial sector—to resist what Bill Readings has called a consumer-oriented corporation more concerned about accounting than accountability.[33] As Bauman reminds us, schools are one of the few public spaces left where students can learn the "skills for citizen participation and effective political action. And where there is no [such] institution, there is no 'citizenship' either."[34] Public education may be one of the few sites available in which students can learn about the limits of commercial values, address what it means to learn the skills of social citizenship, and learn how to deepen and expand the possibilities of collective agency and democratic life.

Defending education at all levels of learning as a vital public sphere and public good rather than merely a private good is necessary to develop and nourish the proper balance between democratic public spheres and commercial power, between identities founded on democratic principles and identities steeped in forms of competitive, self-interested individualism that celebrate selfishness, profit-making, and greed. This view suggests that public education be defended through intellectual work that self-consciously recalls the tension between the democratic imperatives and possibilities of public institutions and their everyday realization within a society dominated by market principles. If public and higher education are to remain sites of critical thinking, collective work, and thoughtful dialogue, educators need to expand and resolutely defend how they view the meaning and purpose of their work with young people. As I have stressed repeatedly, academics, teachers, students, parents, community activists, and other socially concerned groups must provide the first line of defense in protecting public education as a resource vital to the moral life of the nation, open to people and communities whose resources, knowledge, and skills have often been viewed as marginal. This demands not only a revolutionary educational idea and concrete analysis of the neoliberal and other reactionary forces at work in dismantling public education but also the desire to build a powerful social movement as a precondition to real change and free quality education for everyone.

Such a project suggests that educators develop a more inclusive vocabulary for aligning politics and the task of leadership. In part, this means providing students with the language, knowledge, and social relations to engage in the "art of translating individual problems into public issues, and common interests into individual rights and duties."[35] Leadership demands a politics and pedagogy that refuses to separate individual problems and experience from public issues and social considerations. Within such a perspective, leadership displaces cynicism with hope, challenges the neoliberal notion that there are no alternatives with visions of a better society, and develops a pedagogy of commitment that puts into place modes of critical literacy in which competency and interpretation provide the basis for actually intervening in the world.

Leadership invokes the demand to make the pedagogical more political by linking critical thought to collective action, human agency to social responsibility, and knowledge and power to a profound impatience with a status quo founded upon deep inequalities and injustices.

One of the crucial challenges faced by educators is rejecting the neoliberal collapse of the public into the private, the rendering of all social problems as biographical in nature. The neoliberal obsession with the private not only furthers a market-based politics that reduces all relationships to the exchange of money and the accumulation of capital, it also depoliticizes politics itself and reduces public activity to the realm of utterly privatized practices and utopias, underscored by the reduction of citizenship to the act of purchasing goods. Within this discourse all forms of solidarity, social agency, and collective resistance disappear into the murky waters of a politics in which the demands of privatized pleasures and ready-made individual choices are organized on the basis of market mentalities and moralities that cancel out all modes of social responsibility, commitment, and action. This is a reactionary public pedagogy that finds its vision in the creation of atomized individuals who live in a moral vacuum and regress to sheer economic Darwinism or infantilism. One of the major challenges now facing educators, especially in light of the current neoliberal attack on public workers, is to reclaim the language of the social, agency, solidarity, democracy, and public life as the basis for rethinking how to name, theorize, and strategize a new kind of education as well as more emancipatory notions of individual and social agency, as well as collective struggle.

This challenge suggests, in part, positing new forms of social citizenship and civic education that have a purchase on people's everyday lives and struggles. Teachers and faculty bear an enormous responsibility in opposing neoliberalism—the most dangerous ideology of our time—by bringing democratic political culture back to life. Part of this effort demands creating new locations of struggle, vocabularies, and values that allow people in a wide variety of public spheres to become more than they are now, to question what it is they have become within existing institutional and social formations, and "to give some thought to their experiences so that they can transform their relations of subordination and oppression."[36] One element of this struggle could take the form of resisting attacks on existing public spheres, such as schools, while creating new spaces in clubs, neighborhoods, bookstores, trade unions, alternative media sites, and other places where dialogue and critical exchanges become possible. At the same time, challenging neoliberalism means fighting against the state's ongoing reconfiguration into the role of an enlarged police precinct, designed to repress dissent, regulate immigrant populations, incarcerate youth who are considered disposable, and safeguard the interests of global investors. It also means shifting spending priorities in favor of young people and a sustainable democracy.

Revenue for investing in young people, social services, health care, crucial infrastructures, and the welfare state has not disappeared. It has simply been moved into other spending categories or used to benefit a small percentage of the population. As mentioned above, military spending is bloated and supports a society organized for the mass production of violence. Such spending needs to be cut to the bone and could be done without endangering the larger society. In addition, as John Cavanagh has suggested, educators and others need to fight for policies that provide a small tax on stocks and derivatives, eliminate the use of overseas tax havens by the rich, and create tax policies in which the wealthy are taxed fairly.[37] Cavanagh estimates that the enactment of these three policies could produce as much as $330 billion in revenue annually, enough to vastly improve the quality of education for all children throughout the United States.[38]

As governments globally give up their role of providing social safety nets, maintaining public services, and regulating corporate greed, capital escapes beyond the reach of democratic control, leaving marginalized individuals and groups at the mercy of their own meager resources to survive. In such circumstances, it becomes difficult to create alternative public spheres that enable people to become effective agents of change. Under neoliberalism's reign of terror, public issues collapse into privatized discourses and a culture of personal confessions, greed, and celebrity worship emerges to set the stage for depoliticizing public life and turning citizenship and governance into a form of consumerism. Celebrity has become the principal expression of value in a society in which only commodified objects have any value. The rich and the powerful dislike public education as much as they despise any real notion of democracy and they will do all in their power to defend their narrow ideological and economic interests.

The growing attack on public and higher education in American society, as well as in the United Kingdom and many other neoliberal countries, may say less about the reputed apathy of the populace than about the bankruptcy of old political languages and orthodoxies and the need for new vocabularies and visions for clarifying our intellectual, ethical, and political projects, especially as they work to reabsorb questions of agency, ethics, and meaning back into politics and public life. In the absence of such a language and the social formations and public spheres that make democracy and justice operative, politics becomes narcissistic and caters to the mood of widespread pessimism and the cathartic allure of the spectacle. In addition, public service and government intervention are sneered at as either bureaucratic or a constraint upon individual freedom. Any attempt to give new life to a substantive democratic politics must address the issue of how people learn to be political agents as well as what kind of educational work is necessary within what kind of public spaces to enable people to use their full intellectual resources to provide a profound critique of existing institutions and to undertake a struggle to make the operation of freedom and autonomy achievable for as many people as possible in a wide variety of spheres.

As engaged educators, we are required to understand more fully why the tools we used in the past feel inadequate in the present, often failing to respond to problems now facing the United States and other parts of the globe. More specifically, educators face the challenge posed by the failure of existing critical discourses to bridge the gap between how society represents itself and how and why individuals fail to understand and critically engage such representations in order to intervene in the oppressive social relationships they often legitimate.

Against neoliberalism, educators, students, and other concerned citizens face the task of providing a language of resistance and possibility, a language that embraces a militant utopianism while constantly being attentive to those forces that seek to turn such hope into a new slogan or punish and dismiss those who dare to look beyond the horizon of the given. Hope is the affective and intellectual precondition for individual and social struggle, the mark of courage on the part of intellectuals in and out of the academy who use the resources of theory to address pressing social problems. But hope is also a referent for civic courage that translates as a political practice and begins when one's life can no longer be taken for granted, making concrete the possibility for transforming politics into an ethical space and a public act that confronts the flow of everyday experience and the weight of social suffering with the force of individual and collective resistance and the unending project of democratic social transformation.

There is a lot of talk among educators and the general public about the death of democratic schooling and the institutional support it provides for critical dialogue, nurturing the imagination, and creating a space of inclusiveness and critical teaching. Given that educators and others now live in a democracy emptied of any principled meaning, the ability of human beings to imagine a more equitable and just world becomes more difficult. I would hope educators, of all groups, would be the most vocal and militant in challenging this assumption by making clear that at the heart of any notion of a substantive democracy is the assumption that learning should be used to expand the public good, create a culture of questioning, and promote democratic social change. Individual and social agency become meaningful as part of the willingness to think in oppositional, if not utopian, terms "in order to help us find our way to a more human future."[39] Under such circumstances, knowledge can be used for amplifying human freedom and promoting social justice, not for simply creating profits. The diverse terrains of critical education and critical pedagogy offer some insights for addressing these issues, and we would do well to learn as much as possible from them in order to expand the meaning of the political and revitalize the pedagogical possibilities of cultural politics and democratic struggles. The late Pierre Bourdieu has argued that intellectuals need to create new ways for doing politics by investing in political struggles through a permanent critique of the abuses of authority and power, especially under the reign of neoliberalism. Bourdieu wanted educators to use their skills and knowledge to break out of the microcosm of academia and the classroom, combine scholarship with commitment, and "enter into sustained and vigorous exchange with the outside world (especially with unions, grassroots organizations, and issue-oriented activist groups) instead of being content with waging the 'political' battles, at once intimate and ultimately, and always a bit unreal, of the scholastic universe."[40]

At a time when our civil liberties are being destroyed and public institutions and goods all over the world are under assault by the forces of a rapacious global capitalism, there is a concrete urgency on the horizon that demands not only the most engaged forms of political opposition on the part of teachers but also new modes of resistance and collective struggle buttressed by rigorous intellectual work, social responsibility, and political courage. The time has come for educators to distinguish caution from cowardice and recognize the need for addressing the dire crisis public education is now facing. As Jacques Derrida reminds us, democracy "demands the most concrete urgency . . . because as a concept it makes visible the promise of democracy, that which is to come."[41] We have seen glimpses of such a promise among those brave students and workers who have demonstrated in Montreal, Paris, London, Athens, Toronto, Mexico City, and many other cities across the globe.

As engaged intellectuals, teachers can learn from such struggles by turning the colleges and public schools into vibrant critical sites of learning and unconditional spheres of pedagogical and political resistance. The power of the existing dominant order does not merely reside in the economic or in material relations of power, but also in the realm of ideas and culture. This is why educators must take sides, speak out, and engage in the hard pedagogical work of debunking corporate culture's assault on teaching and learning, orient their teaching for social change, and connect learning to public life. At the very least, educators can connect knowledge to the operations of power in their classroom, providing a safe space for students to address a variety of important issues ranging from the violation of human rights to crimes against humanity. Assuming the role of public intellectual suggests being a provocateur in the classroom; it means asking hard questions, listening carefully to what students have to say, and pushing teaching against the grain. But it also means stepping out of the classroom and working with others to create public spaces where it becomes possible not only to "shift the way people think about the moment but potentially to energize them to do something differently in that moment," to link one's critical imagination with the possibility of activism in the public sphere.[42] This is, of course, a small step, but if we do not want to repeat the present as the future or, even worse, become complicit in the workings of dominant power, it is time for educators to collectively mobilize their energies by breaking down the illusion of unanimity that dominant power propagates while working diligently, tirelessly, and collectively to reclaim the promises of a truly global, democratic future. There is no room for a dystopian pedagogy in a democratic society because it destroys the foundation for a formative culture necessary to provide the modes of shared sociality and social agents who possess the knowledge, skills, and values that support an ongoing collective struggle for democratization. In light of the current neoliberal assault on all democratic public spheres, along with the urgency of the problems faced by those marginalized because of their class, race, age, or sexual orientation, I think it is all the more crucial to imagine a politics that both challenges and rejects the dystopian "dreamworlds" of consumption, privatization, deregulation, and the neverending search for accumulating profits. At the heart of such a struggle is the need for a new radical imagination—in this case, one that is willing to develop new social movements, a fresh language for politics, an intense struggle to preserve the democratic educational possibilities of higher education, and alternative public spheres. All of which are crucial to sustain a democratic formative culture to challenge the neoliberal authoritarianism that generates massive social inequality, deepens market savagery, promotes massive privatization, and unleashes a global war against any viable notion of social citizenship and critical education.

CHAPTER THREE

At the Limits of Neoliberal Higher Education

Global Youth Resistance and the American/British Divide

We need a wholesale revision of how a democracy both listens to and treats young people.

—Andy Mycock

The global reach and destructiveness of neoliberal values and disciplinary controls are not only evident in the widespread hardships and human suffering caused by the economic recession of 2008, they are also visible in the ongoing and ruthless assault on the social state, workers, unions, higher education, students, and any vestige of the social at odds with neoliberal values. Under the regime of market fundamentalism, institutions that were meant to limit human suffering and misfortune and protect the public from the excesses of the market have been either weakened or abolished, as have been many of those public spheres where private troubles can be understood as social problems and addressed as such.[1] Government institutions and policies to protect workers' rights and regulate corporations have been weakened just as the institutional basis of the welfare state has been undermined along with "the ideas of social provision that supported it."[2] Many programs inaugurated during FDR's New Deal and Lyndon Johnson's Great Society eras have either been eliminated or are now under attack by conservative politicians, especially Texas senator Ted Cruz and other adherents of the Tea Party. One startling example of growing inequality is the reinstatement of ability grouping in public schools, which is a blatant return to the old forms of tracking students by class and race.[3] Such tracking already exists in higher education by virtue of the correlation between a student's opportunity to get a quality education and the ability to pay soaring tuition rates at the best public and private schools. Under neoliberalism, privatization has run rampant, engulfing institutions as different in their goals and functions as public schools and core public services, on the one hand, and prisons, on the other. This shift from the social contract to savage forms of corporate sovereignty is part of a broader process of "reducing state support of social goods [and] means that states—the institutions best placed to defend the gains workers and other popular forces have made in previous struggles—are instead abandoning them."[4] In this brave new world, there is rapidly growing inequality in income and wealth, the financial sector now occupies an unprecedented position in the economy, and one consequence is a "scale of worldwide misery not seen since the 1930s."[5]

Faced with massive deficits, the US federal government, along with that of many states, is refusing to raise taxes either on the rich or on wealthy corporations while at the same time enacting massive cuts in everything from Medicaid programs, food banks, and worker retirement funds to higher education and health care programs for children. As one example, Florida governor Rick Scott has

> proposed slashing corporate income and property taxes, laying off 6,700 state employees, cutting education funding by $4.8 billion, and cutting Medicaid by almost $4 billion. Scott's ultimate plan is to phase the Sunshine state's corporate income tax out entirely. He [wants] to gut Florida's unemployment insurance system, leaving unemployed workers "with much less economic protection than unemployed workers in any other state in the country."[6]

As social problems are privatized and public spaces are commodified, there has been an increased emphasis on individual solutions to socially produced problems, while at the same time market relations and the commanding institutions of capital are divorced from matters of politics, ethics, and responsibility. Free market ideology, with its emphasis on the privatization of public wealth, the elimination of social protections, and its deregulation of economic activity, now shapes practically every commanding political and economic institution in the United States. In these circumstances, notions of the public good, community, and the obligations of citizenship are replaced by the overburdened demands of individual responsibility and an utterly privatized ideal of freedom.

In the current market-driven society, with its ongoing uncertainties and collectively induced anxieties, core public values that safeguard the common good have been abandoned under a regime that promotes a survival-of-the-fittest economic doctrine. As Jeffrey Sachs points out, "Income inequality is at historic highs, but the rich claim they have no responsibility to the rest of society. They refuse to come to the aid of the destitute, and defend tax cuts at every opportunity. Almost everybody complains, almost everybody aggressively defends their own narrow, short-term interests, and almost everybody abandons any pretense of looking ahead or addressing the needs of others."[7] Shared sacrifice and shared responsibilities now give way to shared fears and a disdain for investing in the common good or, for that matter, the security of future generations of young people. Conservatives and liberals alike seem to view public values as either a hindrance to the profit-seeking goals of the allegedly free market or as an enervating drain on society. Espousing a notion of the common good is now treated as a sign of weakness, if not a dangerous pathology.[8]

Public spheres that once offered at least the glimmer of progressive ideas, enlightened social policies, noncommodified values, and critical exchange have been increasingly commercialized—or replaced by private spaces and corporate settings whose ultimate fidelity is to expanding profit margins. For example, higher education is increasingly defined as an adjunct of corporate power and culture. Public spaces such as libraries are detached from the language of public discourse and viewed increasingly as a waste of taxpayers' money. No longer vibrant political spheres and ethical sites, public spaces are reduced to dead spaces in which it becomes almost impossible to construct those modes of knowledge, communication, agency, and meaningful interventions necessary for an aspiring democracy. What has become clear is that the neoliberal attack on the social state, workers, and unions is now being matched by a full-fledged assault on higher education. Such attacks are not happening just in the United States but in the many other parts of the globe where neoliberalism is waging a savage battle to eliminate all of those public spheres that might offer a glimmer of opposition to and protection from market-driven policies, institutions, ideology, and values. Higher education is being targeted by conservative politicians and governments because it embodies, at least ideally, a sphere in which students learn that democracy, as Jacques Rancière suggests, entails rupture, relentless critique, and dialogue about official power, its institutions, and its never-ending attempts to silence dissent.[9]

THE NEOLIBERAL ATTACK ON HIGHER EDUCATION

As Ellen Schrecker observes, "Today the entire enterprise of higher education, not just its dissident professors, is under attack, both internally and externally."[10] In England and the United States, universities and businesses are forming stronger ties, the humanities are being underfunded, student tuition is rising at astronomical rates, knowledge is being commodified, and research is valued through the lens of an audit culture. In England, the Browne Report—an ostensibly independent review of British higher education, released in 2009—has established modes of governance, financing, and evaluation that for all intents and purposes make higher education an adjunct of corporate values and interests.[11] Delivering improved employability has reshaped the connection between knowledge and power while rendering faculty and students as professional entrepreneurs and budding customers. The notion of the university as a center of critique and a vital democratic public sphere that cultivates the knowledge, skills, and values necessary for the production of a democratic polity is giving way to a view of the university as a marketing machine essential to the production of neoliberal subjects.[12] This is completely at odds with the notion that higher education, in particular, is wedded to the presupposition that literacy in its various economic, political, cultural, and social forms is essential to the development of a formative culture that provides the foundation for producing critically engaged and informed citizens.

Clearly, any institution that makes a claim to literacy, critical dialogue, informed debate, and reason is now a threat to a political culture in which ignorance, stupidity, lies, misinformation, and appeals to common sense have become the dominant, if not most valued, currency of exchange. And this seems to apply as well to the dominant media. How else to explain the widespread public support for politicians in the United States such as Herman Cain, who is as much a buffoon as he is an exemplar of illiteracy and ignorance in the service of the political spectacle? In fact, one can argue reasonably that the entire slate of 2012 presidential Republican Party candidates, extending from Cain to Rick Santorum to Rick Perry and Michele Bachmann, embodied not simply a rejection of science, evidence, informed argument, and other elements associated with the Enlightenment but a deep-seated disdain and hatred for any vestige of a critical mind. During the 2012 campaign, almost every position taken by the Republican primary candidates harked back to a pre-Enlightenment period when faith and cruelty ruled the day and ignorance was the modus operandi for legitimating political and ethical impotence. Mitt Romney, the eventual Republican Party front-runner, not only supported such views but also appeared to have little regard for the truth, as he constantly changed his positions on a number of issues to simply fit the demands of his various audiences. Even the post-election attempt by the Republican Party to find new faces of leadership, such as Florida senator Marco Rubio, perpetuated the legacy of ignorance and denial that plagues the party. For example, Rubio, in his response to Obama's State of the Union address, "dismissed the idea that the U.S. government could do anything to combat climate change," crassly implying that climate change was not man-made and was not a vital political and environmental issue.[13] Rubio has also made comments about hearing what he called "reasonable debate" from both sides about whether climate change is man-made. In this regressive, neoliberal worldview, ignorance and scientific evidence are weighed equally, as if one balances the other. This type of ideological fundamentalism buttressed by a willful ignorance is especially disingenuous in light of a large number of scientific studies that affirm the existence of man-made global warming. "In fact, a study, published in 2010 in the *Proceedings of the National Academy of Sciences*, surveyed 1,372 climate researchers and found that 97 to 98 percent of them agree that climate change is anthropogenic."[14]

Beneath the harsh rule of a neoliberal sovereignty, education, if not critical thought itself, is removed from its civic ties and rendered instrumental, more closely tied to the production of ignorance and conformity than informed knowledge and critical exchange. Under such circumstances, it is not surprising that higher education, or for that matter any other critical public sphere in the United States and increasingly in England, occupies a high-profile target for dismantlement and reform by neoliberal and right-wing politicians and other extremists. While there is ample commentary on the dumbing down of the culture as a result of the corporate control of the dominant media, what is often missed in this argument is how education has come under a similar attack, and not simply because there is an attempt to privatize or commercialize such institutions.

Under casino capitalism, higher education matters only to the extent that it promotes national prosperity and drives economic growth, innovation, and transformation. But there is more at stake here in turning the university into an adjunct of the corporation: there is also an attempt to remove it because it is one of the few remaining institutions in which dissent, critical dialogue, and social problems can be critically engaged. Young people in the United States now recognize that the university has become part of a Ponzi scheme designed to impose on students an unconscionable amount of debt while subjecting them to the harsh demands and power of commanding financial institutions for years after they graduate. Under this economic model of subservience, there is no future for young people, there is no time to talk about advancing social justice, addressing social problems, promoting critical thinking, cultivating social responsibility, or engaging noncommodified values that might challenge the neoliberal world view.

One of the most flagrant examples of how the university as a place to think is being dismantled can be seen in the Browne Report. Chaired by Lord Browne of Madingley, the former chief executive of BP, the Browne Report recommended a series of deeply conservative changes to British higher education, including raising the cap on fees that universities could charge students. The report's guiding assumptions suggest that "student choice," a consumer model of pedagogy, an instrumentalist culture of auditing practices, and market-driven values are at the core of the new neoliberal university. Like most neoliberal models of education, higher education matters only to the extent that it promotes national prosperity and drives economic growth, innovation, and transformation.[15] Tuition will be tripled in some cases. Numerous schools will be closed. Higher education will be effectively remade according to the dictates of a corporate culture.

On March 26, 2011, students in London joined with labor union activists, public service employees, and others in a massive demonstration protesting the savage cuts in jobs, services, and higher education proposed by the Conservative-Liberal Democratic coalition government formed in May 2010. Yet the government appears indifferent to the devastating consequences its policies will produce. Simon Head has suggested that the Browne policies represent a severe threat to academic freedom. In actuality, the neoliberal policies outlined in the report represent a fundamental threat to the future of democracy as well as the university—one of the few remaining institutions left in which dissent, critical dialogue, and social problems can be critically engaged.[16] What is often lost in critiques of the neoliberal university is the connection to broader society. Democracy necessitates a culture of questioning and a set of institutions in which complicated ideas can be engaged, authority challenged, power held accountable, and public intellectuals produced.

In the United States, the neoliberal model takes a somewhat different form since states control the budgets for higher education. Under the call for austerity, states have begun the process of massively defunding public universities while simultaneously providing massive tax breaks for corporations and the rich. At the same time, higher education in its search for funding has "adopted the organizational trappings of medium-sized or large corporations."[17] University presidents are now viewed as CEOs, faculty as entrepreneurs, and students as consumers. In some universities, college deans are shifting their focus beyond the campus in order to take on "the fund-raising, strategic planning, and partner-seeking duties that were once the bailiwick of the university president."[18] Academic leadership is now defined in part through the ability to partner with corporate donors. In fact, deans are increasingly viewed as the heads of complex businesses, and their job performance is rated according to their fundraising capacity.

College presidents now willingly and openly align themselves with corporate interests. The *Chronicle of Higher Education* has reported that "presidents from 19 of the top 40 research universities with the largest operating budgets sat on at least one company board."[19] As business culture permeates higher education, all manner of school practices—from food service and specific modes of instruction to the hiring of temporary faculty—is now outsourced to private contractors. In the process of adopting market values and cutting costs, classes have ballooned in size, matched only by a top-heavy layer of managerial elites, who now outnumber faculty at American universities. For faculty and students alike, there is an increased emphasis on rote learning and standardized testing. Tuition fees have skyrocketed, making it impossible for thousands of working-class youth to gain access to higher education. Moreover, the value of higher education is now tied exclusively to the need for credentials. Disciplines and subjects that do not fall within the purview of mathematical utility and economic rationality are seen as dispensable.

Among the most serious consequences facing faculty in the United States under the reign of neoliberal austerity and disciplinary measures is the increased casualization of academic labor. As universities adopt models of corporate governance, they are aggressively eliminating tenure positions, increasing part-time and full-time positions without the guarantee of tenure, and attacking faculty unions. In a number of states such as Ohio and Utah, legislatures have passed bills outlawing tenure, while in Wisconsin the governor has abrogated the bargaining rights of state university faculty.[20] At a time when higher education is becoming increasingly vocationalized, the ranks of tenure-track faculty are being drastically depleted in the United States, furthering the loss of faculty as stakeholders. Currently, only 27 percent of faculty are either on a tenure track or in a full-time tenure position.[21] As faculty are demoted to contingency forms of labor, they lose their power to influence the conditions of their work; they see their work load increase; they are paid poorly, deprived of office space and supplies, and refused travel money; and, most significantly, they are subject to policies that allow them to be fired at another's will.[22] The latter is particularly egregious because, when coupled with an ongoing series of attacks by right-wing ideologues against left-oriented and progressive academics, many nontenured faculty begin to censor themselves in their classes. At a time when critical faculty might be fired for their political beliefs, have their names posted on right-wing web sites, be forced to turn over their e-mail correspondence to right-wing groups,[23] or face harassment by the conservative press, it is crucial that protections be put in place that safeguard their positions and enable them to exercise the right of academic freedom.[24]

Neoliberal and right-wing political attacks on higher education and the rise of student protests movements in England and the United States, in particular, must be viewed within a broader political landscape that goes far beyond a critique of massive increases in student tuition. A broader analysis is needed to provide insights into how neoliberal policies and modes of resistance manifest themselves in different historical contexts while also offering possibilities for building alliances among different student groups across a range of countries. What both the United Kingdom and the United States share is a full-fledged attack by corporate and market-driven forces to destroy higher education as a democratic public sphere, despite the ongoing "desirability of an educated population to sustain a vibrant democracy and culture that provides a key component of the good life."[25]

STUDENTS AGAINST NEOLIBERAL AUTHORITARIANISM

In the face of the mass uprisings in England, Europe, Canada, and the Middle East, many commentators have raised questions about why comparable forms of widespread resistance did not take place earlier among US youth. Before the California student movement of 2009–2010 and the Occupy Wall Street protests, everyone from left critics to mainstream radio commentators voiced surprise and disappointment that US youth appeared unengaged by the collective action of their counterparts in other countries. In a wave of global protests that indicted the lack of vision, courage, and responsibility on the part of their elders and political leaders, young people in London, Paris, Montreal, Tunis, Quebec, and Athens were taking history into their own hands, fighting not merely for a space to survive but also for a society in which matters of justice, dignity, and freedom are objects of collective struggle. These demonstrations have created a new stage on which young people once again are defining what John Pilger calls the "theater of the possible."[26] Signaling a generational and political crisis that is global in scope, young people sent a message to the world that they refuse to live any longer under repressive authoritarian regimes sustained by morally bankrupt market-driven policies and repressive governments. Throughout Europe, students protested the attack on the social state, the savagery of neoliberal policies, and the devaluation of higher education as a public good. In doing so, they defied a social order in which they could not work at a decent job, have access to a quality education, or support a family—a social order that offered them a meager life stripped of self-determination and dignity. In London, students have been at the forefront of a massive progressive movement protesting against a Cameron-Clegg government that has imposed, under the ideological rubric of austerity-driven slash-and-burn policies, drastic cuts to public spending. These draconian policies are designed to shift the burden and responsibility of the recession from the rich to the most vulnerable elements of society, such as the elderly, workers, lower-income people, and students.

While young people in the United States did not take to the streets as quickly as their European counterparts, they have embraced the spirit of collective protests with the Occupy Wall Street movement. In the United States young people are not simply protesting tuition increases, the defunding of academia, and the enormous debt many of them are laboring under, they are also situating such concerns within a broader attack on the fundamental institutions and ideology of casino capitalism in its particularly virulent neoliberal form. Claiming that they are left out of the discourse of democracy, student protesters have not only made clear that inequality is out of control but that power largely resides in the hands of the top 1 percent, who control almost every aspect of society, from the government and the media to the schools and numerous cultural apparatuses. The Occupy Wall Street movement, taking a lesson from the Quebec student movement, is leading the move away from a focus on isolated issues in an attempt to develop a broader critique as the basis for an energized social movement less interested in liberal reforms than in a wholesale restructuring of US society under more radical and democratic values, social relations, and institutions of power. Ironically, very few progressives saw this movement coming and had for all intents and purposes written off the possibility of a new youth movement protesting against the savage policies of neoliberalism.

Some commentators, including Courtney Martin, a senior correspondent for the *American Prospect*, suggested that the problem is one of privilege. In a 2010 article for the magazine titled "Why Class Matters in Campus Activism," Martin argues that US students are often privileged and view politics as something that happens elsewhere, far removed from local activism.[27]

> Many of us from middle- and upper-income backgrounds have been socialized to believe that it is our duty to make a difference, but undertake such efforts abroad—where the "real" poor people are. We found nonprofits aimed at schooling children all over the globe while rarely acknowledging that our friend from the high school football team can't afford the same kind of opportunities we can. Or we create Third World bicycle programs while ignoring that our lab partner has to travel two hours by bus, as he is unable to get a driver's license as an undocumented immigrant. We were born lucky, so we head to the bars—oblivious to the rising tuition prices and crushing bureaucracy inside the financial aid office.[28]

This theme is taken up in greater detail in Martin's latest book, *Do It Anyway: A New Generation of Activists*. Sadly, however, the analysis Martin provides in that book suffers, like her piece in the *American Prospect*, from the same sort of privilege it critiques. It suggests not only that privileged middle-class kids are somehow the appropriate vanguard of change for this generation but also that they suffer from both a narcissistic refusal to look inward and a narrow, ego-driven sense of politics that is paternalistic and missionary in focus. This critique is too simplistic, overlooks complexity, and ignores social issues in a manner as objectionable as the attitudes it purports to find so misguided.

The other side of the overprivileged youth argument is suggested by longtime activist Tom Hayden, who argues that many students are so saddled with financial debt and focused on what it takes to get a job that they have little time for political activism.[29] According to Hayden, student activism in the United States, especially since the 1980s, has been narrowly issues-based, ranging from a focus on student unionization and gender equity to environmental topics and greater minority enrollment, thus circumscribing in advance youth participation in larger political spheres.[30] While Martin and Hayden both offer enticing narratives to explain the belated onslaught of student resistance, Simon Talley, a writer for *Campus Progress*, may be closer to the truth in claiming that students in the United States have had less of an investment in higher education than European students because for the last thirty years they have been told that higher education neither serves a public good nor is a valuable democratic public sphere.[31]

These commentators, however much they sometimes got it right, still underestimated the historical and current impacts of the conservative political climate on American campuses and the culture of youth protest. This conservatism took firm hold with the election of Ronald Reagan and the emergence of both neoconservative and neoliberal disciplinary apparatuses since the 1980s. Youth have in fact been very active in the last few decades, but in many instances to deeply conservative ends. As Susan Searls Giroux has argued, a series of well-funded, right-wing campus organizations have made much use of old and new media to produce bestselling screeds as well as interactive websites for students to report injustices in the interests of protesting the alleged left-totalitarianism of the academy. In her book *Between Race and Reason: Violence, Intellectual Responsibility and the University to Come,* Susan Searls Giroux writes:

> Conservative think tanks provide $20 million annually to the campus Right, according to the People for the American Way, to fund campus organizations such as Students for Academic Freedom, whose credo is "You can't get a good education if they're only telling you half the story" and boasts over 150 campus chapters. Providing an online complaint form for disgruntled students to fill out, the organization's website monitors insults, slurs and claims of more serious infractions that students claim to have suffered. Similarly, the Intercollegiate Studies Institute, founded by William F. Buckley, funds over 80 right-wing student publications through its Collegiate Network, which has produced such media darlings as Dinesh D'Souza and Ann Coulter. There is also the Leadership Institute, which trains, supports and does public relations for 213 conservative student groups who are provided with suggestions for inviting conservative speakers to campus, help starting conservative newspapers, or training to win campus elections. Or the Young Americans for Freedom, which sponsors various campus activities such as "affirmative action bake sales" where students are charged variously according to their race or ethnicity, or announcements of "whites only" scholarships.[32]

Resistance among young people has not always been on the side of freedom and justice. Many liberal students for the past few decades, for their part, have engaged in forms of activism that also tend to mimic neoliberal rationalities. The increasing emphasis on consumerism, immediate gratification, and the narcissistic ethic of privatization took its toll in a range of student protests developed over issues such as "a defense of the right to consume alcohol."[33] As Mark Edelman Boren points out in his informative book on student resistance, alcohol-related issues caused student uprisings on a number of American campuses. He recounts one telling example: "At Ohio University, several thousand students rioted in April 1998 for a second annual violent protest over the loss of an hour of drinking when clocks were officially set back at the beginning of daylight savings time; forced out of area bars, upset students hurled rocks and bottles at police, who knew to show up in full riot gear after the previous year's riot. The troops finally resorted to shooting wooden 'knee-knocker' bullets at the rioters to suppress them."[34]

WIDENING THE LENS

All of these explanations have some merit in accounting for the lack of resistance among American students until the Occupy Wall Street movement, but I'd like to shift the focus of the analysis. Student resistance in the United States should be viewed within a broader political landscape, especially for what it might tell us about the direction the current Wall Street protests might take; yet, with few exceptions, this landscape still remains unexamined. First, we have to remember that students in England, in particular, were faced with a series of crises that were more immediate, bold, and radical in their assault on young people and the institutions that bear down heavily on their lives than those in the United States. In the face of the economic recession, educational budgets were and continue to be cut in an extreme, take-no-prisoners fashion; the social state is being radically dismantled; tuition costs have spiked exponentially; and unemployment rates for young people are far higher than in the United States (with the exception of youth in poor minority communities). Students in England have experienced a massive and bold assault on their lives, educational opportunities, and their future. Moreover, these students live in a society where it becomes more difficult to collapse public life into largely private considerations. Students in these countries have access to a wider range of critical public spheres, politics in many of these countries has not collapsed entirely into the spectacle of celebrity/commodity culture, left-oriented political parties still exist, and labor unions have more political and ideological clout than they do in the United States. Alternative newspapers, progressive media, and a profound sense of the political constitute elements of a vibrant, discerning formative culture within a wide range of public spheres that have helped nurture and sustain the possibility to think critically, engage in political dissent, organize collectively, and inhabit public spaces in which alternative and critical theories can be developed.

In the United States, by contrast, the assault on colleges and universities has been less uniform. Because of the diverse nature of how higher education is financed and governed, the cuts to funding and services have been differentially spread out among community colleges, public universities, and elite colleges, thus US students are lacking a unified, oppressive narrative against which to position resistance. Moreover, the campus "culture wars" narrative fueled by the Right has served to galvanize many youth around a reactionary cultural project while distancing them from the very nature of the economic and political assault being waged against their future. All this raises another set of questions. The more important questions, ones that do not reproduce the all-too-commonplace demonization of young people as merely apathetic, are twofold. First, the issue should not be why there have been no student protests until recently, but why previous protests have been largely ignored. Evidence of such nascent protests, in fact, has been quite widespread. The student protests against the draconian right-wing policies attempting to destroy the union rights and collective bargaining power of teachers, promoted by Republican governor Scott Walker in Wisconsin, is one example indicating that students were in fact engaged and concerned. There were also smaller student protests taking place at various colleges, including Berkeley, CUNY, and other campuses throughout the United States. Until recently, student activists constituted a minority of US students, with very few enrolled in professional programs. Most student activists have come from the arts, social sciences, and humanities (the conscience of the college). Second, there is the crucial issue regarding what sort of disabling conditions young people have inherited in American society. What political and cultural shifts have worked together to undermine their ability to be critical agents capable of waging a massive protest movement against the growing injustices they face on a daily basis? After all, the assault on higher education in the United States, while not as severe as in Europe, still provides ample reason for students to be in the streets protesting.

Close to forty-three states have pledged major cuts to higher education in order to compensate for insufficient state funding. This means an unprecedented hike in tuition rates is being implemented, enrollments are being slashed, salaries are being reduced, and need-based scholarships are being eliminated in some states. Pell grants, which enable poor students to attend college, are also being cut. Robert Reich has chronicled some of the specific impacts on university budgets, which include cutting state funding for higher education by $151 million in Georgia, reducing student financial aid by $135 million in Michigan, raising tuition by 15 percent in Florida's eleven public universities, and increasing tuition by 40 percent in just two years in the University of California system.[35] As striking as these increases are, tuition has been steadily rising over the past several decades, becoming a disturbingly normative feature of postsecondary education in the United States.

A further reason that US students took so long to begin to mobilize may be because by the time the average US student now graduates, he or she has not only a degree but also an average debt of about $23,000.[36] As Jeffrey Williams points out in a 2008 article for *Dissent*, "Student Debt and the Spirit of Indenture," this debt amounts to a growing form of indentured servitude for many students. Being burdened by excessive debt upon graduation only to encounter growing rates of unemployment—"unemployment for recent college graduates rose from 5.8 percent to 8.7 percent in 2009"[37]—surely undercuts the opportunity to think about, organize, and engage in social activism. In other words, crippling debt plus few job prospects in a society in which individuals are relentlessly held as being solely responsible for the problems they experience leaves little room for rethinking the importance of larger social issues or the necessity for organized collective action against systemic injustice. In addition, as higher education increasingly becomes a fundamental requirement for employment, many universities have been able to justify the reconfiguration of their mission exclusively in corporate terms. They have replaced education with training while defining students as consumers, faculty as a cheap form of subaltern labor, and entire academic departments as revenue-generating units.[38] No longer seen as a public good or a site of social struggle, higher education is increasingly viewed as a credential mill for success in the global economy.

Meanwhile, not only have academic jobs been disappearing, but given the shift to an instrumentalist education that is decidedly technicist in nature, the culture of critical thinking has been slowly disappearing on US campuses as well. As universities and colleges emphasize market-based skills, students are learning neither how to think critically nor how to connect their private troubles with larger public issues. The humanities continue to be downsized, eliminating some of the most important opportunities many students will ever have to develop a commitment to public values, social responsibilities, and the broader demands of critical citizenship. Moreover, critical thinking has been devalued as a result of the growing corporatization of higher education. Under the influence of corporate values, thought in its most operative sense loses its modus operandi as a critical mediation on "civilization, existence, and forms of evaluation."[39]

It has become increasingly difficult for students to recognize how their formal education and social development in the broadest sense have been systematically devalued, and how this not only undercuts their ability to be engaged critics but contributes to the further erosion of what is left of US democracy. How else to explain the reticence of students within the last decade toward protesting against tuition hikes? The forms of instrumental training they receive undermine any critical capacity to connect the fees they pay to the fact that the United States puts more money into the funding of wars, armed forces, and military weaponry than the next twenty-five countries combined—money that could otherwise fund higher education.[40] The inability to be critical of such injustices and to relate them to a broader understanding of politics suggests a failure to think outside of the prescriptive sensibilities of a neoliberal ideology that isolates knowledge and normalizes its own power relations. In fact, one recent study by Richard Arum and Josipa Roksa found that "45 percent of students show no significant improvement in the key measures of critical thinking, complex reasoning and writing by the end of their sophomore years."[41]

The corporatization of schooling and the commodification of knowledge over the last few decades have done more than make universities into adjuncts of corporate power. They have produced a culture of critical illiteracy and further undermined the conditions necessary to enable students to become truly engaged, political agents. The value of knowledge is now linked to a crude instrumentalism, and the only mode of education that seems to matter is that which enthusiastically endorses learning marketable skills, embracing a survival-of-the-fittest ethic, and defining the good life solely through accumulation and disposal of the latest consumer goods. Academic knowledge has been stripped of its value as a social good. To be relevant, and therefore adequately funded, knowledge has to justify itself in market terms or simply perish.

Enforced privatization, the closing down of critical public spheres, and the endless commodification of all aspects of social life have created a generation of students who are increasingly being reared in a society in which politics is viewed as irrelevant, while the struggle for democracy is being erased from social memory. This is not to suggest that Americans have abandoned the notion that ideas have power or that ideologies can move people. Progressives pose an earnest challenge to right-wing ideologies and policies, but they seem less inclined to acknowledge the diverse ways in which the pedagogical force of the wider culture functions in the production, distribution, and regulation of both power and meaning. By contrast, the conservative willingness to use the educational force of the culture explains in part both the rapid rise of the Tea Party movement and the fact that it seemed to have no counterpart among progressives in the United States, especially young people. This is now changing, given the arrogant, right-wing attacks being waged on unions, public sector workers, and public school educators in Wisconsin, Florida, Ohio, New Jersey, and other states where Tea Party candidates have come to power.[42] Progressives, largely unwilling to engage in a serious manner the educational force of the larger culture as part of their political strategy, have failed to theorize how conservatives successfully seize upon this element of politics in ways that far outstrip its use by the left and other progressive forces. Missing from their critical analyses is any understanding of how public pedagogy has become a central element of politics itself.

Public pedagogy in this sense refers to the array of different sites and technologies of image-based media and screen culture that are reconfiguring the very nature of politics, cultural production, knowledge, and social relations. Market-driven modes of public pedagogy now dominate major cultural apparatuses such as mainstream electronic and print media and other elements of screen culture, whose one-sided activities, permeated by corporate values, proceed more often than not unchallenged. Left to their own devices by progressive movements, which for decades have largely refused to take public pedagogy seriously as part of their political strategy, the new and old media with their depoliticized pedagogies of consumption may finally be encountering some resistance from the rising student protests around the globe.

HIGHER EDUCATION AND THE ERASURE OF CRITICAL FORMATIVE CULTURES

In a social order dominated by the relentless privatization and commodification of everyday life and the elimination of critical public spheres, young people find themselves in a society in which the formative cultures necessary for a democracy to exist have been more or less eliminated, or reduced to spectacles of consumerism made palatable through a daily diet of talk shows, reality TV, and celebrity culture. What is particularly troubling in US society is the absence of the vital formative cultures necessary to construct questioning persons who are capable of seeing through the consumer come-ons, who can dissent and act collectively in an increasingly imperiled democracy. Sheldon Wolin is instructive in his insistence that the creation of a democratic formative culture is fundamental to enabling both political agency and a critical understanding of what it means to sustain a viable democracy. According to Wolin,

> Democracy is about the conditions that make it possible for ordinary people to better their lives by becoming political beings and by making power responsive to their hopes and needs. What is at stake in democratic politics is whether ordinary men and women can recognize that their concerns are best protected and cultivated under a regime whose actions are governed by principles of commonality, equality, and fairness, a regime in which taking part in politics becomes a way of staking out and sharing in a common life and its forms of self-fulfillment. Democracy is not about bowling together but about managing together those powers that immediately and significantly affect the lives and circumstances of others and one's self.[43]

Instead of public spheres that promote dialogue, debate, and arguments with supporting evidence, US society offers young people a conservatizing, consumer-driven culture through entertainment spheres that infantilize almost everything they touch, while legitimating opinions that utterly disregard evidence, reason, truth, and civility. The "Like" button has replaced the critical knowledge and the modes of education needed for long-term commitments and the search for the good society. Intimate and committed social attachments are short-lived, and the pleasure of instant gratification cancels out the interplay of freedom, reason, and responsibility. As a long-term social investment, young people are now viewed in market terms as a liability, if not a pathology. No longer a symbol of hope and the future, they are viewed as a drain on the economy, and if they do not assume the role of functioning consumers, they are considered disposable.

Within the last thirty years, the United States under the reign of market fundamentalism has been transformed into a society that is more about forgetting than learning, more about consuming than producing, more about asserting private interests than democratic rights. In a society obsessed with customer satisfaction and the rapid disposability of both consumer goods and long-term attachments, US youth are not encouraged to participate in politics. Nor are they offered the help, guidance, and modes of education that cultivate the capacities for critical thinking and engaged citizenship. As Zygmunt Bauman points out, in a consumerist society, "the tyranny of the moment makes it difficult to live in the present, never mind understand society within a range of larger totalities."[44] Under such circumstances, according to Theodor Adorno, thinking loses its ability to point beyond itself and is reduced to mimicking existing certainties and modes of common sense. Thought cannot sustain itself and becomes short-lived, fickle, and ephemeral. If young people do not display a strong commitment to democratic politics and collective struggle, then, it is because they have lived through thirty years of what I have elsewhere called "a debilitating and humiliating disinvestment in their future," especially if they are marginalized by class, ethnicity, and race.[45]

What sets this generation of young people apart from past generations is that today's youth have been immersed since birth in a relentless, spreading neoliberal pedagogical apparatus with its celebration of an unbridled individualism and its near pathological disdain for community, public values, and the public good. They have been inundated by a market-driven value system that encourages a culture of competitiveness and produces a theater of cruelty that has resulted in what Bauman calls "a weakening of democratic pressures, a growing inability to act politically, [and] a massive exit from politics and from responsible citizenship."[46] Yet, they refuse to allow this deadening apparatus of force, manufactured ignorance, and ideological domination to shape their lives. Reclaiming both the possibilities inherent in the political use of digital technologies and social media, US students are now protesting in increasing numbers the ongoing intense attack on higher education and the welfare state, refusing a social order shaped by what Axel Honneth describes as "an abyss of failed sociality," one in which "the perceived suffering [of youth] has still not found resonance in the public space of articulation."[47]

Young people, students, and other members of the 99 percent are no longer simply enduring the great injustices they see around them, they are now building new public spaces, confronting a brutalizing police apparatus with their bodies, and refusing to put up with the right-wing notion that they are part of what is often called a "failed generation." Young people, especially, have flipped the script and are making clear that the failures of casino capitalism lie elsewhere, pointing to the psychological and social consequences of growing up under a neoliberal regime that goes to great lengths to enshrine ignorance, privatize hope, derail public values, and reinforce economic inequality and its attendant social injustices. What the Occupy Wall Street protesters, like their counterparts in London, Montreal, Athens, Cairo, and elsewhere, have made clear is that not only is casino capitalism the site of political corruption and economic fraud, but it also reproduces a "failed sociality" that hijacks critical thinking and agency along with any viable attempt of democracy to deliver on its promises.

In the face of a politically organized ignorance on the part of right-wing anti-public intellectuals, think tanks, media organizations, and politicians, the Occupy Wall Street protesters have refused to provide recipes and blueprints about a longed-for utopian future. Instead, they have resurrected the most profound elements of a radical politics, one that recognizes that critical education, dialogue, and new modes of solidarity and communication serve as conditions for their own autonomy and for the sustainability of democratization as an ongoing social movement. This is evident in their embrace of participatory democracy, a consensus model of leadership, the call for direct action, the development of co-op food banks, free health care clinics, and the development of a diverse model of multimedia communication, production, and circulation. What terrifies the corporate rich, bankers, media pundits, and other bloviators about this movement is not that it has captured the attention of the broader public but that it constantly hammers home the message that a substantive democracy requires citizens capable of self-reflection and social criticism, and that such citizens, through their collective struggles, are the products of a critical formative culture in which people are provided with the knowledge and skills to participate effectively in developing a radically democratic society. And this fear on the part of ruling classes and the corporate elite has gone global.

When we see fifteen-year-olds battling against established oppressive orders in the streets of Montreal, Paris, Cairo, and Athens in the hope of forging a more just society, we are being offered a glimpse of what it means for youth to enter "modernist narratives as trouble."[48] This expression of "trouble" exceeds the dominant society's eagerness to view youth as a pathology, as monsters, or as a drain on the market-driven order. Instead, trouble in this sense speaks to something more suggestive of what John and Jean Comaroff call the "productive unsettling of dominant epistemic regimes under the heat of desire, frustration, or anger."[49] The expectations that frame market-driven societies are losing their grip on young people, who can no longer be completely seduced or controlled by the tawdry promises and failed returns of corporate-dominated and authoritarian regimes.

What is truly remarkable about this movement is its emphasis on connecting learning to social change and its willingness to do so through new and collective modes of education. Equally encouraging is that this movement views its very existence and collective identity as part of a larger struggle for the economic, political, and social conditions that give meaning and substance to what it means to make democracy possible. In the United States, the Occupy Wall Street protests have made clear that the social visions embedded in casino capitalism and deeply authoritarian regimes have lost both their utopian thrust and their ability to persuade and intimidate through manufactured consent, threats, coercion, and state violence. Rejecting the terrors of the present along with the modernist dreams of progress at any cost, young people have become, at least for the moment, harbingers of democracy, fashioned through the desires, dreams, and hopes of a world based on the principles of equality, justice, and freedom. One of the most famous slogans of May 1968 was "Be realistic, demand the impossible." The spirit of that slogan is alive once again. But what is different this time is that it appears to be more than a slogan—it now echoes throughout the United States and abroad as both a discourse of critique and as part of a vocabulary of possibility and long-term collective struggle. The current right-wing politics of illiteracy, exploitation, and cruelty can no longer hide in the cave of ignorance, legitimated by their shameful accomplices in the dominant media. The lights have come on all over the United States and young people, workers, and other progressives are on the move. Thinking is no longer seen as an act of stupidity, acting collectively is no longer viewed as unimaginable, and young people are no longer willing to be viewed as disposable. Of course, how this movement plays out over time remains to be seen.

In the United States, the most important question to be raised about US students is no longer why they do not engage in massive protests or why have they not continued the massive protests that characterized the first year of the Occupy Wall Street protest movement, but *when will they join* their youthful counterparts protesting in London, Montreal, Athens, Istanbul, and elsewhere in building a global democratic order in which they can imagine a future different from the present? The test of these movements will be their ability to develop national associations and international alliances that can be sustained for the long run. But this will only happen when young people and others begin to organize collectively in order to develop the formative cultures, public spheres, and institutions that are crucial to helping them confront neoliberalism and the threats it poses to the environment, public goods, and those dispossessed by race, class, and age. Only then will they join together in individual and collective efforts to reclaim higher education as a public good vital for creating new imaginaries and democratic social visions.

CHAPTER FOUR

Intellectual Violence in the Age of Gated Intellectuals

Critical Pedagogy and a Return to the Political

BRAD EVANS AND HENRY A. GIROUX

The more radical the person is, the more fully he or she enters into reality so that, knowing it better, he or she can transform it. This individual is not afraid to confront, to listen, to see the world unveiled. This person is not afraid to meet the people or to enter into a dialogue with them. This person does not consider himself or herself the proprietor of history or of all people, or the liberator of the oppressed; but he or she does commit himself or herself, within history, to fight at their side.

—Paulo Freire

INTRODUCTION

Proverbial wisdom warns that while sticks and stones shall inflict pain, words will never kill us. Yet nothing is further from the truth: inflammatory rhetoric has *always* been a strategic precursor to the drums of warfare. This was perhaps most obvious in recent years in the discursive violence used by the Bush administration to justify the invasions of Iraq and Afghanistan. Moreover, the periodic militaristic pronouncements employed by Israel and the United States as a precursor for a potential attack on Iran demonstrate that discourse can continually authenticate the meaning of violent encounters and produce organized violence. Intellectual discourse is also a veritable minefield littered with the corpses of radical pioneers who dared to venture into uncharted fields. One does not have to look too far to find the most sophisticated regimes of truth being used to offer the surest moral backbone to the most reasoned forms of human atrocities. Recent memory provides sufficient testimony here: we only have to look to the gradual buildup for each of the so-called wars on terror for evidence of "discursive creep." As we seamlessly moved through the various stages of securitization, civil liberties were shredded, terrorism became a term that justified the most violent actions, and the seemingly impossible became the altogether inevitable state of affairs. Among both academic and public intellectuals the paths to recognition, resources, and credibility have become dependent upon one's willingness to shamefully compromise with the utility of force and its compulsion to embed all things potentially subversive.

The university has not in any way been immune to these strategies of absorption, as the lines between the times of civic peace and militarism have become increasingly blurred to the latter's normalization. Increasingly, research and the production of knowledge within the university have become militarized as the role of the university has in fact given way to various methods of intellectual policing, with the main strategic function becoming the need to think how to wage war better. For such reasons academics occupy a somewhat (in)enviable position when it comes to the study of intellectual violence. We remain empirical objects and principal stakeholders due to the political stakes. Drawing upon personal experiences, many critical scholars in the post-9/11 moment have publically attested to and critiqued deeply embedded institutional forms of intellectual violence that have shaped their everyday working relations. They have also been highly critical of what they perceive as state violence around the world, a mode of violence that provides cover for the role that higher education often plays in legitimating such violence. Consequently, various critical scholars, such as Ward Churchill, Patricia Adler, Norman Finkelstein, Bashir Abu-Manneh, Terri Ginsberg, David Graeber, and, more recently, Samer Shehata, have been refused promotions, or, more severely, denied tenure.[1]

All too frequently positions of academic authority have been awarded to opportunistic careerists who remain completely untroubled by the burdens of complicated thought and the fight for ethical and political responsibility. While it is somewhat easier to come to terms with the usual suspects, who remain openly hostile to any form of post-1968 criticality as it challenges the simple comforts of rehearsed orthodoxy, it is the institutionally sanctioned violence that tends to take more subtle forms, frequently masked by the collegiate language of "consensus," "playing the game," and "majoritarianism," that is of greater concern. Such consensus-building majorities brazenly offer the most fantastic appropriation of democratic terms. What passes for the majority here is not a numeric expression but a particularistic relation of force that provides a sure glimpse into the authoritarian personality so apt to Theodor Adorno's sense of inquiry.[2] Some may invariably call this leadership. The dark and poisonous influence of authoritarianism often wraps itself in the discourse of patriotism, rights, duty, and—most shamefully—the mantle of democracy. Yet if leadership is to reclaim its political and ethical standing and have any collegiate relevance whatsoever, it must be afforded by those who are meant to be inspired by the example and not made to feel coerced into submission.

We are not suggesting a uniform experience. Nor do we refuse to acknowledge the many forms of resistance to this mode of creeping academic authoritarianism. Some schools, faculties, and globally reputable institutions still take great pride in their commitment to the opening of possibilities for thinking the political anew and reclaiming a link between the production of knowledge and social change. Such resistance needs to be celebrated and vigorously defended. And so do the principles of a significant number of scholars who still recognize that the essential function of the university is to continue to hold power to account. The neoliberal assault on global academia is, however, now so pervasive and potentially dangerous in its effects that it is must be viewed as more than a "cause for concern." While the system in the United States has been at the forefront of policies that have tied academic merit to market-driven performance indicators, the ideologically driven transformations under way in the United Kingdom point in an equally worrying direction as the need for policy entrepreneurship increasingly becomes the norm.

The closures of entire philosophy programs signify the most visible shift away from reflective thinking to the embrace of a dumbed-down approach to humanities education with no time for anything beyond the objectively neutralizing and politically compromising deceit of pseudo-scientific paradigms that replace education with training and emphasize teaching to the test. Instrumentalism in the service of corporate needs and financial profit now dominates university modes of governance, teaching, research, and the vocabulary used to describe students and their relationship to each other and the larger world. What is most disturbing about the hyper-militarization of the university and of knowledge is the militarization of pedagogy itself. No longer viewed as a political and ethical practice that provides the conditions for critical thought and engaged modes of democratic action, pedagogy has become repressive. That is, this market-driven pedagogy "mobilizes people's feelings primarily to neutralize their senses, massaging their minds and emotions so that the individual succumbs to the charisma of vitalistic power,"[3] if not the normalization of violence itself. Increasingly within the university, thinking critically and embracing forceful new angles of vision are all too frequently viewed as heresy. One consequence is that those who dare challenge institutional conformity through a commitment to academic freedom and intellectual inquiry often find that insightful ideas emerge only to die quickly.

Discourses, ideas, values, and social relations that push against the grain, redefine the boundaries of the sensible, and reclaim the connection between knowledge and power in the interest of social change too often not only become inconvenient but also rapidly accelerate to being viewed as dangerous. If the dissent is pressed too far, it can lead to being fired, prison time, and possibly death. As Gilles Deleuze once maintained, nobody is ever intellectually put into prison for powerlessness or pessimism. It is the courage to articulate the truth that so perturbs. For thought to be "meaningful," then, it has to become empty, inhabiting a "no-fly" space utterly policed by the apologists for conformity. Any pedagogy that aims at turning out informed citizens makes one immediately suspect. And it is not simply academics but all cultural workers who now suffer under this rising tide of ignorance that has become a hallmark of a repressive neoliberal ideology. This leaves us, in part, wondering how any author or artist in the current climate could ever create anything re-motely comparable to oft-cited historical masterpieces that were not sub-jected to intellectually compromised performance deadlines. But we are also left to question whether the term "university" itself is appropriate for certain institutions that declare open hostility to the very academic discipline and forms of intellectual inquiry that gave original meaning to the idea of public education.

Despite their provocative intentions, our concerns take us beyond those all-too-familiar vitriolic forms of extremism that seek to publicly shut down points of difference through good old-fashioned bullying tech-niques. However abhorrent they appear, it is better that such inflamma-tory thoughts are put into the public arena so that nothing is subject to misinterpretation or counterfactual claims of misrepresentation. Indeed, although it is undoubtedly the case that the center ground for global pol-itics more generally has moved to the extreme right of the spectrum in all its various ontotheological, faith-based expressions, the symbolic violence of the vitriolic leaves enough visible traces to be openly condemned with an even greater degree of intellectual effort. Yet our concern is with the more sophisticated forms of intellectual violence that, although some-times openly condescending in their patronizing churlishness, neverthe-less present a formidable challenge due to the weight of their reasoning. Such violence is a familiar neoliberal deceit. It emanates from a progres-sive constituency that draws upon the virtues of enlightened praxis and its normalizing tendencies to make us desire that which even the most momentary forms of conscious and reflective political thought will deem particularly intolerable. These normalizing tendencies can be seen in the support of progressives for the wars in Iraq and Afghanistan, indifference to the corporatization of higher education, and utter silence about the sta-tus of the United States as "one of the biggest open-air prisons on earth."[4] And such intellectual violence occasions with either personal displays of utmost courteousness or talks to a much wider claim of humanitarianism.

There is a bankrupt civility at work here, disingenuous in its com-plicity with violence and disillusioned about the social costs it promotes and the moral coma it attempts to impose on those considered rudely uncivil, code for those who take intellectual risks and are willing to think critically and hold power accountable. The very notion that the univer-sity might have a role to play in either promoting or resisting authoritarian politics, state and corporate-sponsored violence, and war is often met with a condescending lifting of the head or wave of the hand that bespeaks the violence and deep order of politics lurking beneath this banalized appropriation of civility as code for a flight from moral, political, and pedagogical responsibility. This is the civility of authoritarians who flee from open conflict and mask their intellectual violence with weak handshakes, forced smiles, and mellowed voices. Like the punishment dished out to a recalcitrant child, however, through reason of seductive persuasion or reason of a more brutal force, more "mature" (the authoritarian default) ways of thinking about the world must eventually be shown to be the natural basis for authority and rule.

The concept of violence is not taken lightly here. Violence remains poorly understood if it is accounted for simply in terms of how and what it kills, the scale of its destructiveness, or any other element of its annihilative power. Intellectual violence is no exception as its qualities point to a deadly and destructive conceptual terrain. As with all violence, there are two sides to this relation. There is the annihilative power of nihilistic thought that seeks, through strategies of domination and practices of terminal exclusion, to close down the political as a site for differences. Such violence appeals to the authority of a peaceful settlement, though it does so in a way that imposes a distinct moral image of thought that already maps out what is reasonable to think, speak, and act. Since the means and ends are already set out in advance, the discursive frame is never brought into critical question. And there is an affirmative counter that directly challenges authoritarian violence. Such affirmation refuses to accept the parameters of the rehearsed orthodoxy. It brings into question that which is not ordinarily questioned. Foregrounding the life of the subject as key to understanding political deliberation, it eschews intellectual dogmatism with a commitment to the open possibilities in thought. However, as we shall argue in this chapter, rather than countering intellectual violence with a "purer violence" (discursive or otherwise), there is a need to maintain the language of critical pedagogy. By "criticality," we insist upon a form of thought that does not have war or violence as its object. If there is destruction, this is only apparent when the affirmative is denied. And by criticality we also insist upon a form of thought that does not offer its intellectual soul to the seductions of militarized power. Too often we find that while the critical gestures toward profound insights, it is really the beginning of violence that amounts to a death sentence for critical thought. Our task is to avoid this false promise and demand a politics that is dignified and open to the possibility of nonviolent ways of living.

THE TYRANNY OF REASON

Michel Foucault introduced the concept of the biopolitical to denounce the illusion of institutional peace and the inevitability of freedom despite the existence of free-flowing power relations. As he put to question, "When, how and why did someone come up with the idea that it is a sort of uninterrupted battle that shapes peace, and that the civil order—its basis, its essence, its essential mechanisms—is basically an order of battle?"[5] There are two important aspects to deal with here. First, when Foucault refers to "killing" in a biopolitical sense he does not simply refer to the vicious and criminal act of physically taking a life: "When I say 'killing,' I obviously do not mean simply murder as such, but also every form of indirect murder: the fact of exposing someone to death, increasing the risk of death for some people, or, quite simply, political death, expulsion, rejection and so on."[6] And second, despite any semblance of peace, it is incumbent upon the critical cartographer to bring into question normalized practices so as to reveal their scars of battle:

> [My methodology] is interested in rediscovering the blood that has dried in the codes, and not, therefore, the absolute right that lies beneath the transience of history; it is interested not in referring the relativity of history to the absolute of law, but in discovering beneath the stability of the law or the truth, the indefiniteness of history. It is interested in the battle cries that can be heard beneath the formulas of right.[7]

This represents an important shift in our understanding of violence. No longer simply content with exploring extrajuridical forms of violent abuse, attentions instead turn toward those forms of violence that take place in the name of human progress and the emancipatory subject. This type of violence takes place through a hidden order of politics concealed beneath the circuits of discursive regimes of truth, civility, and representations of a commodified culture that is fully and uncritically absorbed in the modernist notion of progress.

The dominant institutions for social progress today are no longer sovereign in any popular sense of the term. State sovereignty has been compromised by corporate sovereignty just as state power now more closely resembles the workings of a carceral state. At the same time, politics has become local and power is now global, unrestricted by the politics of the nation-state and indifferent to the specificity of its practices and outcomes. Power and violence have been elevated into the global space of flows.[8] The most evident development of this has been the veritable "capitalization of peace" in which the global ravages of poverty, war, and violence are tied to neoliberal policies that, proceeding in the name of human togetherness/progress/unity, conceal an inner logic of biopolitical separation and social containment.[9]

As politics is emptied of its ability to control global power, the bankruptcy of biocapitalism becomes evident in the hollowing out of the social state and the increasing force of the dominant discourses and policies that legitimate its extinction. For example, when the Bush and Obama administrations argued that the banks were too big to fail, we were presented with more than another neoliberal conceit regarding supply-side economics and its practice of distributing wealth and income away from the already impoverished to the already enriched. The more dangerous conceit paved the way for the destruction of even the most minimal conditions for a sustainable democracy. This subterfuge at one level argues that the victims of casino capitalism are guilty of waging class warfare while at the same time the ruling elite destroy all those public spheres capable of providing even minimal conditions for individuals to engage the capacities to think, feel, and act as engaged and critical citizens. And they do it in the midst of a decrepit and weakened state of politics that holds corporate power unaccountable, while endlessly repeating the poisonous mantra of deregulation, privatization, and commodification. The banking elite and the mega-financial services openly serve the rich while engaging in widespread ecological devastation as well as destroying the safety nets that serve the poor and the middle class. But since the banking sector is seen to be integral to the vision of planetary peace, its survivability is morally tied to humanity's potential for self-ruination.

The ruinous logic of militarization now provides global finance with the mad machinery of violence in order to dispense with the power of reason and the demands of global social responsibility. To put it another way, since global finance is openly presented to be central to the neoliberal security *dispositif*, we should be under no illusions where military allegiance lies. George W. Bush certainly didn't send troops into Iraq and Afghanistan for the betterment of the victims of market fundamentalism at home or those Iraqis suffering under the ruthless dictatorship of Saddam Hussein. Neither was the more recent securitization of the London Olympics carried out to protect immigrant populations living on the margins in the capital's run-down areas. There is therefore no hegemonic discourse in any conventional sovereign geo-strategic sense of the term. Instead, what appears is a neoliberal will to rule that is upheld by a formidable school of intellectual thought and takes direct aim at the critically minded as a dangerous community to be vanquished. Reason in this sense is unmoored from its emancipatory trappings, reduced to a legitimating discourse for a notion of progress that embraces a mode of technological rationality that operates in the service of repression and the militarization of thought itself.[10]

The contemporary tyranny of reason is not exclusively tied to state power and now works within modes of sovereignty constructed through the logics of biocapitalism and its growing banking and financial sectors. Reason embraces such tyranny through an ossified logic of the market and its principle of risk. It is most revealing to find that economic agencies are at the forefront of this policy that has made economic questions of prime political significance. During the 1990s organizations such as the World Bank increasingly became interested in political concerns as the focus of their work (along with economics more generally) changed from the managed recoveries of national crises to the active promotion of better lives.[11] Transforming their remit from economic management to security governance, such organizations became moral agents in their own right, advocating economic solutions to the ravages of civil wars, criminality, shadow economies, poverty, endemic cultural violence, and political corruption. This was matched by a particular revival in the ideas of political economists such as Friedrich von Hayek and Milton Friedman, who long equated neoliberalism with marketable freedoms. Neoliberalism in this case becomes a source of political and moral legitimacy, determined not only to institute market-based structural reforms but also to establish the conditions for producing particular types of agency, subjects, and social relations that are said to thrive by embracing a logic of risk that promotes insecurity as a principal design for existence.

The unchecked celebration of a neoliberal subject willing to take market-based risks—either financial or through acts of consumption—does more than provide a rationale for the corrupt trading practices of investment bankers and hedge fund power brokers, it also points to the closer connection between those considered the producers of capital and those who are now the new at-risk, disposable populations. The financial elite now view themselves as corporate missionaries promoting policies, practices, and ideas that are not only designated as universal but take their inspiration from God. How else to interpret Goldman Sachs's chief executive Lloyd Blankfein's comment that he is just a banker "doing God's work."[12] Needless to say, those individuals and populations who are outside the accumulation, possession, and flow of capital are considered the new parasites, excess, and global human waste. That is, those considered failed consumers—"enemy combatants," unpatriotic dissidents, poor minority youth, low-income white kids, immigrants, and others inhabiting the margins of global capital and its intellectual ecosystem of vast inequality and ruthless practices of disposability. Capital is not only wedded to the production of profits, it is also invested in a form of intellectual violence that legitimates its savage market-driven practices and the exercise of ruthless power. When applied to the intellectual terrain, to paraphrase C. Wright Mills, we are seeing the breakdown of democracy, the disappearance of critical thought, and "the collapse of those public spheres which offer a sense of critical agency and social imagination."[13] Since the 1970s, we have seen the forces of market fundamentalism strip education of its public values, critical content, and civic responsibilities as part of its broader goal of creating new subjects wedded to the logic of privatization, efficiency, flexibility, consumerism, and the destruction of the social state.

Tied largely to instrumental purposes and measurable paradigms, many institutions of higher education are now committed almost exclusively to economic growth, instrumental rationality, and the narrow civically deprived task of preparing students strictly for the workforce. The question of what kind of education is needed for students to be informed and active citizens is now rarely asked.[14] Hence, it is no surprise, for example, to read that "Thomas College, a liberal arts college in Maine, advertises itself as Home of the Guaranteed Job!"[15] Within this discourse, faculty are largely understood as a subaltern class of low-skilled entrepreneurs, removed from the powers of governance and subordinated to the policies, values, and practices within a market model of the university that envisages pure instrumentality.[16]

Within both higher education and the educational force of the broader cultural apparatus—with its networks of knowledge production in the old and new media—we are witnessing the emergence and dominance of a form of a powerful and ruthless, if not destructive, market-driven notion of governance, teaching, learning, freedom, agency, and responsibility. Such modes of education do not foster a sense of organized responsibility central to a democracy. They corrupt any commitment to critical pedagogy. As David Harvey insists, "The academy is being subjected to neoliberal disciplinary apparatuses of various kinds [while] also becoming a place where neoliberal ideas are being spread."[17]

Not only does neoliberalism undermine civic education and public values as well as confuse education with training, it also treats knowledge as a product, promoting a neoliberal logic that views schools as malls, students as consumers, and faculty as entrepreneurs. Just as democracy appears to be fading throughout the liberal world, so is the legacy of higher education's faith in and commitment to democracy. As the humanities and liberal arts are downsized, privatized, and commodified, higher education finds itself caught in the paradox of claiming to invest in the future of young people while offering them few intellectual, civic, and ethical supports. One such measure of the degree to which higher education has lost its ethical compass can be viewed in the ways in which it disavows any relationship between equity and excellence, eschews the discourse of democracy, and reduces its commitment to learning to the stripped-down goals of either preparing students for the workforce or teaching them the virtues of measurable utility. While such objectives are not without vocational merit, they have little to say about the role that higher education might play in influencing the fate of future citizens and the state of democracy itself, nor do they say much about what it means for academics to be more than technicians or hermetic scholars.

GATED ACADEMICS

Giorgio Agamben came to prominence during the immediate aftermath of 9/11 as his work on the state of exception seemed to strike a precise chord.[18] Central then to Agamben's work was his concern with the spatial figuration of the camp and how sites such as Guantánamo Bay removed any semblance of political, legal, and ethical rights. Bare life thus became a defining critical motif for many who were concerned with the perceived lawlessness of the US administration and its allies as they deployed excessive force against enemies real or newly provoked. We have never been entirely convinced by Agamben's understanding of the modern *nomos* or stripping away of political agency for the globally oppressed. Neither have we been content to focus our attentions simply on the violence that takes place in distinct sites of social abandonment as if all things within law (especially violence) are devoid of complementary relations.

While we do accept that policies of containment are sometimes a preferred method for dealing with troublesome populations who need to be curtailed, along with disposable populations that have nothing meaningful to exploit, encamped life has always been situated within a much wider terrain of market-driven processes that give secondary consideration to surplus lives. What is more, as neoliberal governmentality faces a global crisis of its own making, we are in fact encountering a logical inversion to Agamben's modeling as the politically *included* are increasingly being forced into fortified compounds and gated protectorates that link together the nodal points of a privatized sovereignty within the global space of flows. Having said this, Agamben's insistence that biopolitical marks of separation reveal a distinct violence has merit. It is not, however, that the human condition needs violence in order to resolve its differences. Imposed universality takes hold of difference to produce a violent cartography of human separation.

It is often said that the days when intellectuals could live in an ivory tower are gone. While this is true (and is partly driven by the market's need to have a distinct intellectual identity), contemporary intellectuals, mirroring the world of which they are part, increasingly inhabit a radically interconnected world in which corporate-driven, networked, structured relations define how they mediate their relationship both to the university and the broader world of global flows. A number of critical scholars and academics have been dismayed by this development, as the pursuit of knowledge once central to the creation of epistemic communities gives way to various risk-based assessments. Others openly embrace the idea of "the gated intellectual."[19] Replicating the structural logic of privately owned, fortified strongholds evident in all global megacities, gated intellectuals—walled off from growing impoverished populations—are also cut loose from any ethical mooring or sense of social responsibility as understood in a reciprocal sense of the term. Instead they voice their support for what might be called gated or border pedagogy—one that establishes boundaries to protect the rich, isolates citizens from each other, excludes those populations considered disposable, and renders invisible young people, especially poor youth of color, along with others marginalized by class and race. Such intellectuals play no small role in legitimating what David Theo Goldberg has called a form of neoliberalism that promotes a "shift from the caretaker or pastoral state of welfare capitalism to the 'traffic cop' or 'minimal' state, ordering flows of capital, people, goods, public services and information."[20]

Gated intellectuals and the privately funded institutions or marketed forms of finance that support them believe in societies that stop questioning themselves, engage in a history of forgetting, and celebrate the progressive "decomposition and crumbling of social bonds and communal cohesion."[21] Policed borders, surveillance, state secrecy, targeted assassinations, armed guards, and other forces provide the imprimatur of dominant power and containment, making sure that no one can trespass onto gated property, domains, sites, protected global resources, and public spheres. On guard against any claim to the common good, the social contract, or social protections for the underprivileged, gated intellectuals spring to life in universities, news programs, print media, charitable foundations, churches, think tanks, and other cultural apparatuses, aggressively surveying the terrain to ensure that no one is able to do the crucial pedagogical work of democracy by offering resources and possibilities for resisting the dissolution of sociality, reciprocity, and social citizenship itself. Such guarded consolidation and retrenchment of positions does not entertain paranoiac entropy. It has already amassed an arsenal of preemptive intellectual strikes that allegedly document the demise of the public intellectual as an unfortunate side effect or collateral damage to a wider war effort into which we are all openly recruited. If gated communities are the false registers of safety, gated intellectuals have become the new registers of conformity.

The gated mentality of market fundamentalism has walled off, if not disappeared, those spaces where dialogue, critical reason, and the values and practices of social responsibility can be engaged. The armies of antipublic intellectuals who appear daily on television, radio talk shows, and other platforms work hard to create a fortress of indifference and manufactured stupidity. They ask that intellectualism remain a private affair. Public life is therefore reduced to a host of substanceless politicians, embedded experts, and gated thinkers who pose a dire threat to those vital public spheres that provide the minimal conditions for citizens who can think critically and act responsibly. Higher education is worth mentioning because, for engaged and public intellectuals, it is one of the last strongholds of democratic action and reasoning and one of the most visible targets along with the welfare state.

As is well known, higher education is increasingly being removed from the discourse of public values and the ideals of a substantive democracy at a time when it is most imperative to defend the institution against an onslaught of forces that are as anti-intellectual as they are antidemocratic in nature. Many of the problems in higher education can be linked to the evisceration of funding, the intrusion of the security apparatus of the state, the lack of faculty self-governance, and a wider culture that appears increasingly to view education as a private right rather than a public good. Within the wider sociopolitical environment, corporate power and interests are all too willing to define higher education as a business venture, students as consumers and investors, and faculty as a cheap source of labor. Left to the logic of the market, education is something that consumers and investors now purchase for the best price, deal, and profit. All of these disturbing trends, left unchecked, are likely to challenge the very meaning and mission of the university as a democratic public sphere.

Gated intellectualism points to new forms of intellectual violence—violence(s) that is/are markedly different from the old colonial pursuit of "redeeming savages" through brutalizing subservience, the suppression of women's rights, and the often violent attacks on homosexuals. Although it is fully appreciated that the outside can no longer be left to chance, the veritable distancing between the gated intellectual and his or her precarious surroundings points to a form of inclusive exclusion whose violence employs the preferred technologies of the time. Not only is drone violence the preeminent technology for contemporary forms of violence in which war is seldom declared, it is also the apt metaphor for the twenty-first-century intellectual violence of the gated intellectual.

Abandoning any attempts at making the world more enlightened, what takes its place is a short, sharp, and speedy intellectual attack that points to a purely immanent conception of thought. Such thinking has no time to reflect upon the significance of events. It has no patience for contested memories or excavating the complex histories that make our present. Neither does it entertain the possibility that the world may be thought and lived otherwise. What remains is a politically settled intellectual environment that deems everything alternative to be potentially hostile. There is nothing in this relationship that suggests any reciprocal attempt at establishing better ethical relations among the world of peoples. Instead, fully removed from the realities of contested political spaces, neoliberal risk assessment measures, along with their highly biotechnologized performance indicators, become the surest way to create alternative conditions of the real. This is nothing but simulacrum. It proposes nothing but a manufactured reality that is virtually conceived within the highly policed nodal protectorates of neoliberal governance without any concern to experience the world.

VIOLENCE TO MEMORY

History remains the biggest casualty of intellectual violence. The past is written so that the present course of action appears both natural and timeless. What is at stake here is the question of memorialization and how this relates to a politics of events. We have no concern here with those various speculative attempts at offering a definitive philosophical proof for the meaning of events in order to stupefy publics with another form of intellectual violence. There is no poetic joy to reading such hyperstructural technicism, whose language is akin to a perpetual motion machine whose only purpose is its own activity. Political events are now framed in order to debunk any notion of critical analyses on account of the fact that they break open what false semblance of peace exists to the creation of new ways of thinking and relating to the world. Not, of course, to suggest that the conditions that give rise to a revolutionary impetus cannot be critically understood as we seek to explain systemic oppression. But it is to acknowledge that political events have to be understood in terms of their own specificity, and that they forever appear *untimely* (to echo Nietzsche's claim) to us at their moment of arising. Who, for instance, could have anticipated the impact of Rosa Parks's simple yet profound disruption of elements that sent into permanent flux the conventional order of things? Or that the first visible signs of resistance to the New World Order would come from the Zapatistas—an incredibly poor indigenous population in an unknown land?

Our concern with intellectual violence brings us directly to the closing down of the historical space as the multiple experiences of political events are subsumed within the one "true" narrative. September 11, 2001, showed how imposing a uniform truth on the event represented a profound failure of the political imaginary. Judith Butler accounts for this in terms of the framing of the problem:

> The "frames" that work to differentiate the lives we can apprehend from those we cannot (or that produce lives across a continuum of life) not only organize visual experience but also generate specific ontologies of the subject. Subjects are constituted through norms which, in their reiteration, produce and shift the terms through which subjects are recognized.[22]

Importantly, for Butler, since what matters here is the subsequent production of certain truthful subjectivities out of the ashes of devastation, we must bring into question the framing of life as a seemingly objective ontological and epistemological fact:

> To call the frame into question is to show that the frame never quite contained the scene it was meant to limn, that something was already outside, which made the very sense of the inside possible, recognizable. The frame never quite determined precisely what it is we see, think, recognize, and apprehend. Something exceeds the frame that troubles our sense of reality; in other words, something occurs that does not conform to our established understanding of things.[23]

This call to break with the dominating content the time is more than an attempt to draw attention to the multiplicity of the experiences of events. It is to open up the space of the political by breaking apart the myth that there is a universal experience of truth. In the hours and days that followed the tragic events of September 11, 2001, the unfolding sense of trauma and loss drew people together in a fragile blend of grief, shared responsibility, compassion, and a newfound respect for the power of common purpose and commitment.[24] The translation of such events into acts of public memory, mourning, and memorializing are ambivalent and deeply unsettling. They offered no certainty. We must recall that they do not only bring about states of emergency and the suspension of civil norms and order: they can, and did, give birth to enormous political, ethical, and social possibilities. Yet, such enlightened moments proved fleeting. A society has to move with deliberate speed from the act of witnessing to the responsibility of just memorializing; put simply, to the equally difficult practice of reconfiguring what politics, ethics, and civic engagement should mean after 9/11. On the tenth anniversary of that tragic day, the struggle to remember and reclaim those moments in good faith was constantly challenged, and in ways that few of us would dare to have imagined a decade later. Public memory became the enemy of a state immersed in a culture of fear as dissent and civil liberties were sacrificed on the altar of security, and ethics and justice gave way from the state legitimation of torture under George W. Bush to the state's right, under President Obama, to murder those considered an enemy of the state, regardless of the due process of law.[25]

The events of 9/11 show how loss, memory, and remembrance share an uneasy, if not unsettled, embrace. Remembrance can become dysfunctional, erasing the most important elements of history and trivializing what survives of the event through either crass appeals to an untroubled celebration of patriotism or a crass commercialization of 9/11 as just another commodity for sale. But remembrance can also recover what is lost to this historical amnesia. It can both produce difficult thoughts, bringing forth not only painful memories of personal loss and collective vulnerability but also new understandings of how specific events infuse the present, and become a force for how one imagines the future, including, to quote Roger Simon, how "one imagines oneself, one's responsibility to others, and one's civic duty to a larger democratic polity and range of diverse communities."[26] Memory can be an instigator of both despair and hope, often in ways in which the division between desperation and hope becomes blurred. For instance, the spectacular shock and violence of 9/11 ruptured an arrogant and insular period in American history that had proclaimed the triumph of progress and the end of ideology, history, and conflict, all the while imposing an unbearable experience of loss, grief, sorrow, and shock on large segments of the world's population.

The collective fall from grace is now well known. Instead of being a threshold to a different future and a register for a restored democratic faith, the decade following 9/11 became an era of buried memories and monumentalization. Rather than initiating a period of questioning and learning, the war on terror morphed into a war without end, producing abuses both at home and abroad, all of which resembled an unending fabric of normalizing violence. America's particular status as a symbol of freedom that elicited worldwide respect was fatefully diminished, giving way to a culture of fear, mass hysteria, and state secrecy. At the same time that the Bush administration waged war overseas, it unleashed ruthless market forces at home, along with a virulent propaganda machine in which public issues collapsed into private concerns, and the future—like the futures market that drove it—was detached from any viable notion of ethical and social responsibility. Finance capital replaced human capital, economics was detached from ethics, youth were viewed as *a* risk rather than *at* risk, and the formative culture necessary for a democracy collapsed into a rampaging commercialism as citizens became defined exclusively as consumers and the notion of the social along with collaborative social bonds were viewed as a liability rather than as a public good central to any viable notion of civic engagement and democracy itself. Finance capital replaced the social debt—based on the obligations we owe to each other—with financial debt, in which creditors now savagely rule a generation of debtors chained to contractual relations marked by persistent deficits, hardships, surveillance, and subordination.[27]

Shared trauma of violence doesn't, however, necessarily translate into discourses of revenge. Counterviolence is simply the option most preferred by certain political ways of thinking. Undoubtedly the history of modern politics has been marked out by the normality of violence. Therefore, what the United States and its allies did in the immediate aftermath of 9/11 was not in any way exceptional. Doing nothing violent in response would have been exceptional. Instead, the response followed the all-too-familiar conventional norm of using violence to reason the world, serve justice, and avert future catastrophes. But it *must* be remembered that none of this is inevitable. Indeed, despite this violent weight of historical reasoning, at the human level it is increasingly clear that the experience of the tragedy was far more complex. What 9/11 made apparent is that memory as a moral, critical, and informed practice requires those elements of counter-memory that challenge the official narratives of 9/11 in order to recover the most valuable and most vulnerable elements of democratic culture too often sacrificed in tragedy's aftermath.

In the hours and days that bled out from the tragic events of 9/11, the unfolding sense of trauma and loss drew us together in a fragile blend of grief, shared responsibility, compassion, and a newfound respect for the power of common purpose and commitment. Hence, if we truly wished to honor the victims of 9/11, we should not be reluctant to engage in a public dialogue about both the legacy and the politics that precipitated and emerged from the events that took place on that tragic day. Such uncomfortable moments of consciousness provide the basis for a form of witnessing that refuses the warmongering, human rights violations, xenophobia, and violations of civil liberties that take shape under the banner of injury and vengeance. Simon Critchley dared to think the "impossible":

> What if the government had simply decided to turn the other cheek and forgive those who sought to attack it, not seven times, but seventy times seven? What if the grief and mourning that followed 9/11 were allowed to foster a nonviolent ethics of compassion rather than a violent politics of revenge and retribution? What if the crime of the Sept. 11 attacks had led not to an unending war on terror, but the cultivation of a practice of peace — a difficult, fraught and ever-compromised endeavour, but perhaps worth the attempt?[28]

Critchley's provocation offers more than a warning against the political ruination of violent responses. He is challenging us to think how we may have a political ethics adequate to such events. This shift toward a politics of forgiveness is no doubt a remarkable task. Perhaps that is the precise point. Ours remains a history marked by a violent humanism so often masquerading under the name of security, peace, and justice. Advocating a politics of forgiveness when faced with such crises is that which passes for something truly exceptional—an affirmative politics of real exceptionalism. Critchley's affinity with Derridean ethics is striking here. As Jacques Derrida maintained, an act of forgiveness worthy of the name must be offered in event of something altogether unforgiveable: "It *should not be* normal, normative, normalizing. It should remain exceptional and extraordinary, in the face of impossible: as if it interrupted the ordinary course of historical temporality."[29] This forgiveness as we currently see it presents itself as an aporia of the impossibility of forgiving unforgivable acts.

And yet, as Derrida reminds us, it is precisely when the aporetic moment arrives that it becomes both possible and necessary. He writes: "It only becomes possible from the moment that it appears impossible."[30] The fact that such a proposition still appears altogether impossible is indicative of the continuum of violence. And yet, the normalized alternative, so common to the history of modern life, illustrates with devastating and politically debilitating surety why Nietzsche was insistent that nihilistic behavior was tied to a spirit of revenge. Once we begin to act out of resentment, so the catastrophic cycle of violence continues to the evacuation of political alternatives. At a time when neoliberalism has turned governance into a legitimation for war, surveillance, and terror, the spirit of revenge and a culture of cruelty do more than permeate everyday lives; the discourse of revenge also reinforces the power of the national security state and contributes to the expansion of its punishing apparatuses, extending from the prison to the schoolroom. And increasingly, the punitive nature of the practices produced by the national security state bear down heavily on those intellectuals now labeled as whistle blowers, "unprivileged enemy belligerents," unpatriotic critical academics, and so on. In the midst of the production of such violence, collective fear serves to silence intellectuals, force them into gated and safe citadels where they do not have to fear being wiretapped, targeted, kidnapped, or subject to state of emergency laws such as the Patriot Act or the National Defense Authorization Act (NDAA). Or it seduces them into either silence or complicity with the rewards of power, regardless of how tainted ethically and politically such rewards might be.

RADICAL CRITICALITY

One of the consequences of thinking about threats in global terms has been the collapse of the space/time continuum that once held together the linear world of sovereign reasoning.[31] While we may rejoice, in part, at the breaking open of the former Westphalia semblance of peace that effectively served already established colonial powers by rewriting the rules in their favor, its displacement by a full-spectrum catastrophic imaginary of endangerment has been politically disastrous. As times of war and times of peace merge without any meaningful distinction, so there has been a collapse of the private into the public, the militaristic into the civic, and the authoritarian into the humanitarian. An intellectual casualty of this has been the merger between the radical and the fundamental. While each of these terms once retained a very distinct and oppositional meaning, their coming together is indicative of a social terrain that is violently hostile to political difference. Any thought that seeks to affirm alternative ways of thinking or service to the world is treated as either some immature posturing (the unreason of youth) or the surest indication of a pathological dysfunction (reasoned hostility). So our question therefore becomes, How may we reclaim the terms of radical criticality without succumbing to a violent reasoning that propels us to mimic dominant ways of thinking politics?

We need to learn to live with violence less through the modality of the sacred than through the critical lens of the profane. By this we mean that we need to appreciate our violent histories and how our subjectivities have been formed through a history of physical bloodshed. This requires more of a willingness to interrogate violence in a variety of registers (ranging from the historical and concrete to the abstract and symbolic) than it does a bending to the neoliberal discourses of fate and normalization. We need to acknowledge our own shameful compromises with the varied forces of violence. And we need to accept that intellectualism shares an intimate relationship with violence both in its complicity with violence and as an act of violence. There is an echo of the pornographic here not just in the ethical detachment that now accompanies state violence, particularly with drone technologies, but also in the recuperation of the pleasure principle in the increasing maximization of the spectacle of violence. We need then to reject what Leo Lowenthal has called the imperative to believe that "thinking becomes a stupid crime."[32] This does not require a return to the language of Benjamin's idea of divine violence as a pure expression of force regardless of its contestable claims to nonviolent violence.[33] We prefer instead to deploy the oft-abused term "critical pedagogy" as a meaningful political counter to vicissitudes of intellectual violence.

Intellectuals are continually forced to make choices (sometimes against our better judgments). The truth, of course, is that there are no clear lines drawn in the sand neatly separating what is left from what is right. And yet as Paulo Freire insisted, one is invariably drawn into an entire history of struggle the moment our critical ideas are expressed as force and put out into the public realm to the disruption of orthodox thinking. There is, however, a clear warning from history: our intellectual allegiances should be less concerned with ideological dogmatism. There is, after all, no one more micro-fascist or intellectually violent than the authenticating militant whose self-imposed vanguardism compels allegiance through the stupidity of unquestioning loyalty and political purity. To the charges here that critical pedagogy merely masks a retreat into cultural relativism, we may counter that there is no reciprocal relationship with that which doesn't respect difference while at the same time recognizing that pedagogy is an act of intervention. Pedagogy always represents a commitment to the future, and it remains the task of educators to make sure that the future points the way to a more socially just world, a world in which the discourses of critique and possibility in conjunction with the values of reason, freedom, and equality function to alter, as part of a broader democratic project, the grounds upon which life is lived. This is hardly a prescription for either relativism or political indoctrination, but it is a project that gives education its most valued purpose and meaning, which in part is "to encourage human agency, not mould it in the manner of Pygmalion."[34]

Critical pedagogy has a responsibility to mediate the tension between a respect for difference and the exercise of authority that is directive, that is, a mode of authority capable of taking a position while not standing still. Central to its understanding as a moral and political practice, pedagogy as a form of cultural politics contests dominant forms of symbolic production while constantly opening a space to question its own authority and the ever-present danger of fetishizing its own practices. An ethics of difference is central to such a pedagogy, especially at a historical conjuncture in which neoliberalism arrogantly proclaims that there are no alternatives. Within this regime of common sense, neoliberalism eliminates issues of contingency, struggle, and social agency by celebrating the inevitability of economic laws in which the ethical ideal of intervening in the world gives way to the idea that we "have no choice but to adapt both our hopes and our abilities to the new global market."

An ethics of difference, as Foucault critically maintained, requires waging an ongoing fight against fascism in all its forms: "not only historical fascism, the fascism of Hitler and Mussolini—which was able to use the desire of the masses so effectively—but also the fascism in us all, in our heads, and in our everyday behaviour, the fascism that causes us to love power, to desire the very thing that dominates and exploits us."[35] Or as Deleuze once put it, "In every modernity and every novelty, you find conformity and creativity; an insipid conformity, but also 'a little new music'; something in conformity with the time, but also something untimely—separating the one from the other is the task of those who know how to love, the real destroyers and creators of our day."[36]

Academics then are required to speak a kind of truth, but as Stuart Hall points out, "maybe not truth with a capital T, but . . . some kind of truth, the best truth they know or can discover [and] to speak that truth to power."[37] Implicit in Hall's statement is the awareness that to speak truth to power is not a temporary and unfortunate lapse into politics on the part of academics: it is central to opposing all those modes of ignorance, whether they are market-based or rooted in other fundamentalist ideologies that make judgments difficult and democracy dysfunctional. Our view is that academics have an ethical and pedagogical responsibility not only to unsettle and oppose all orthodoxies, to make problematic the commonsense assumptions that often shape students' lives and their understanding of the world, but also to energize them to come to terms with their own power as individual and social agents. Higher education, in this instance, as Pierre Bourdieu, Paulo Freire, Edward Said, Stanley Aronowitz, Susan Searls Giroux, and other intellectuals have reminded us, cannot be removed from the hard realities of those political, economic, and social forces that both support it and consistently, though in diverse ways, attempt to shape its sense of mission and purpose.[38] Politics is not alien to higher education but central to comprehending the institutional, economic, ideological, and social forces that give it meaning and direction. Politics also references the outgrowth of historical conflicts that mark higher education as an important site of struggle. Rather than the scourge of either education or academic research, politics is a primary register of their complex relation to matters of power, ideology, freedom, justice, and democracy.

Talking heads who proclaim that politics have no place in the classroom can, as Jacques Rancière points out, "look forward to the time when politics will be over and they can at last get on with political business undisturbed," especially as it pertains to the political landscape of the university.[39] In this discourse, education as a fundamental basis for engaged citizenship, like politics itself, becomes a temporary irritant to be quickly removed from the hallowed halls of academia. In this stillborn conception of academic labor, faculty and students are scrubbed clean of any illusions about connecting what they learn to a world "strewn with ruin, waste and human suffering."[40] As considerations of power, politics, critique, and social responsibility are removed from the university, balanced judgment becomes code, as C. Wright Mills suggests, for "surface views which rest upon the homogeneous absence of imagination and the passive avoidance of reflection. A vague point of equilibrium between platitudes."[41] Under such circumstances, the university and the intellectuals who inhabit it disassociate higher education from larger public issues, remove themselves from the task of translating private troubles into social problems, and undermine the production of those public values that nourish a democracy. Needless to say, pedagogy is always political by virtue of the ways in which power is used to shape various elements of classroom identities, desires, values, and social relations, but that is different from being an act of indoctrination.

Instead of accepting the role of the gated intellectual, there is an urgent need for public intellectuals in the academy, art world, business sphere, media, and other cultural apparatuses to move from negation to hope. Now more than ever we need reasons to believe in this world. This places renewed emphasis on forms of critical pedagogy that move across different sites—from schools to the alternative media—as part of a broader attempt to construct a critical formative culture in the Western world that enables citizens to reclaim their voices, speak out, exhibit ethical outrage and create the social movements, tactics, and public spheres that will reverse the growing tide of neoliberal fascism. Such intellectuals are essential to democracy, even as social well-being depends on a continuous effort to raise disquieting questions and challenges, use knowledge and analytical skills to address important social problems, alleviate human suffering where possible, and redirect resources back to individuals and communities who cannot survive and flourish without them. Engaged public intellectuals are especially needed at this time to resist the hollowing out of the social state, the rise of a governing-through-crime complex, and the growing gap between the rich and poor that is pushing all liberal democracies back into the moral and political abyss of the Gilded Age—characterized by what David Harvey calls the "accumulation of capital through dispossession," which he claims is "is about plundering, robbing other people of their rights" through the dizzying dreamworlds of consumption, power, greed, deregulation, and unfettered privatization that are central to a neoliberal project.[42]

Under the present circumstances, it is time to remind ourselves that critical ideas are a matter of critical importance. Ideas are not empty gestures, and they do more than express a free-floating idealism. Ideas provide a crucial foundation for assessing the limits and strengths of our senses of individual and collective agency and what it might mean to exercise civic courage in order to not merely live in the world but to shape it in light of democratic ideals that would make it a better place for everyone.

Critical ideas and the technologies, institutions, and public spheres that enable them matter because they offer us the opportunity to think and act otherwise, challenge common sense, cross over into new lines of inquiry, and take positions without standing still—in short, to become border-crossers who refuse the silos that isolate the privileged within an edifice of protections built on greed, inequitable amounts of income and wealth, and the one-sided power of neoliberal governance. Gated intellectuals refute the values of criticality. They don't engage in debates; they simply offer already rehearsed positions in which unsubstantiated opinion and sustained argument collapse into each other. Yet, instead of simply responding to the armies of gated intellectuals and the corporate money that funds them, it is time for critical thinkers with a public interest to make pedagogy central to any viable notion of politics. It is time to initiate a cultural campaign in which the positive virtues of radical criticality can be reclaimed, courage to truth defended, and learning connected to social change. The current attack on public and higher education by the armies of gated intellectuals is symptomatic of the fear that reactionaries have of critical thought, quality education, and the possibility of a generation emerging that can both think critically and act with political and ethical conviction. Our task is to demand a return to the political as a matter of critical urgency.

CHAPTER FIVE

On the Urgency for Public Intellectuals in the Academy

The university is a critical institution or it is nothing.

—Stuart Hall

I want to begin with the words of the late African American poet, Audre Lorde, a formidable writer, educator, feminist, gay rights activist, and public intellectual, who displayed a relentless courage in addressing the injustices she witnessed all around her. She writes:

> Poetry is not a luxury. It is a vital necessity of our existence. It forms the quality of the light within which we predicate our hopes and dreams toward survival and change, first made into language, then into idea, then into more tangible action. Poetry is the way we help give name to the nameless so it can be thought. The farthest horizons of our hopes and fears are cobbled by our poems, carved from the rock experiences of our daily lives.[1]

And although Lorde refers to poetry here, I think a strong case can be made that the attributes she ascribes to poetry can also be attributed to higher education—a genuine higher education.[2] In this case, an education that includes history, philosophy, all of the arts and humanities, the criticality of the social sciences, the world of discovery made manifest by natural science, and the transformations in health and in law wrought by the professions that are at the heart of what it means to know something about the human condition. Lorde's defense of poetry as a mode of education is especially crucial for those of us who believe that the university is nothing if it is not a public trust and social good: that is, a critical institution infused with the promise of cultivating intellectual insight, the imagination, inquisitiveness, risk-taking, social responsibility, and the struggle for justice. At best, universities should be at the "heart of intense public discourse, passionate learning, and vocal citizen involvement in the issues of the times."[3] It is in the spirit of such an ideal that I first want to address those larger economic, social, and cultural interests that threaten this notion of education, especially higher education.

As I have stated throughout this book, in spite of being discredited by the economic recession of 2008, market fundamentalism or unfettered free-market capitalism has once again become a dominant force for producing a corrupt financial service sector, runaway environmental devastation, egregious amounts of human suffering, and the rise of what has been called the emergence of "finance as a criminalized, rogue industry."[4] The Gilded Age is back with huge profits for the ultra-rich, banks, and other large financial service institutions while at the same time increasing impoverishment and misery for the middle and working classes. The American dream, celebrating economic and social mobility, has been transformed into not just an influential myth but also a poisonous piece of propaganda. One indication of the undoing of the American dream into an American nightmare can be seen in the fact that "the most striking change in American society in the past generation—roughly since Ronald Reagan was elected President—has been the increase in the inequality of income and wealth" and the concentration of wealth into fewer and fewer hands.[5]

I want to revisit the state of inequality in America because any discourse about the purpose of higher education and the responsibility of academics as public intellectuals has to begin with how matters of wealth and power are changing the purpose and meaning of education, teaching, and the conditions under which academics now labor. The current assaults on higher education cannot be removed from the war on youth, unions, students, public servants, and the public good. Moreover, the financial crisis of the last few years has become a cover for advancing the neoliberal revolution and assault on higher education. For example, when University of Texas at Austin president Bill Powers argues for what he calls a "business productivity initiative" to save money, he is not simply responding to a projected budget shortfall. Under the dictates of neoliberal austerity policies, he is changing the nature of education at UT by arguing that the research initiatives will be evaluated and deemed most profitable in terms of their benefits to various industries. Those academic courses and departments that are aligned with and provide potential profits for industry will receive the most funding. As Reihaneh Hajibeigi points out, "this means liberal arts majors and departments will be given minimal funding if the benefits of those studies aren't seen as being profitable to UT."[6]

The figures listed below point to a different kind of crisis, one that puts in peril the most basic and crucial institutions that make a democracy possible along with the formative culture and critical agents that support and protect it. We need to be reminded as part of the pedagogy of public memory that these figures matter, given their role as both flashpoints that signal a rupture from the increasingly lost promises of a democracy to come and a call to conscience in addressing the horrors of the growing antidemocratic tendencies that make clear the presence of an emerging authoritarianism in the United States. We live at a time of immense contradictions, problems, and antagonisms, and such figures offer us a way to both make visible disparities in power relations and to address the necessity of combining moral outrage with ongoing political struggles. If democracy needs a keen sense of the common good and a robust understanding of education as a public good, these statistics signify the death of both—a vanishing point at which the ideas, policies, and institutions that sustain democratic public life and civic education dissolve into the highest reaches of power, avarice, and wealth.

The United States now "has the highest level of inequality of any of the advanced countries."[7] One measure of the upward shift in wealth is evident in Joseph E. Stiglitz's claim that "in the 'recovery' of 2009–2010, the top 1% of US income earners captured 93% of the income growth."[8] The vast inequities and economic injustice at the heart of the mammoth gap in income and wealth become even more evident in a number of revealing statistics. For example, "the average pay for people working in U.S. investment banks is over $375,000 while senior officers at Goldman

Sachs averaged $61 million each in compensation for 2007."[9] In addition, the United States beats out every other developed nation in producing extreme income and wealth inequalities for 2012. The top 1 percent now owns "about a third of the American people's total net worth, over 40 percent of America' total financial wealth . . . and half of the nation's total income growth."[10] Andrew Gavin Marshall provides even more granular figures. He writes:

> Looking specifically at the United States, the top 1% own more than 36% of the national wealth and more than the combined wealth of the bottom 95%. Almost all of the wealth gains over the previous decade went to the top 1%. In the mid-1970s, the top 1% earned 8% of all national income; this number rose to 21% by 2010.[11]

In this instance, the absolute acceleration of the gap in income and especially wealth results in the quickening of misery, impoverishment, and hardship for many Americans while furthering what might be called a thin and failed conception of democracy. At the same time, political illiteracy and religious fundamentalism have cornered the market on populist rage, providing support for an escalating political and economic crisis.[12] Pointing to some of the ugly extremes produced by such inequality, Paul Buchheit includes the following: each of the right-wing, union-busting Koch brothers made $3 million per hour from their investments; the difference in hourly wages between CEOs and minimum-wage workers was "$5,000.00 per hour vs. $7.25 per hour," "The poorest 47% of Americans have no wealth," and "the 400 wealthiest Americans own as much wealth as 80 million families—62% of America."[13]

At the risk of being repetitious, I want to stress a range of statistics that may say little about cause and effect but that do, as Bauman notes, "challenge our all-too-common ethical apathy and moral indifference . . . they also show, and beyond reasonable doubt, that the idea of the pursuit of a good life and happiness being a self-referential business for each individual to pursue and perform on his or her own is an idea that is grossly misconceived."[14] While wealth and income are redistributed to the top 1 percent, the United States fails to provide adequate health and safety for its children and citizens. Both a 2007 UNICEF report and a 2009 OECD study ranked the United States near the bottom of the advanced industrial countries for children's health and safety and twenty-seventh out of thirty for child poverty. Median wealth for Hispanic and Black households has been reduced to almost zero as a result of the recession; young people are increasing unable to attend college because of soaring tuition rates, and those that do attend are increasingly strapped with unmanageable debts and few jobs that will enable them to pay off their loans. More than 50 million Americans lack health care and many will die as a result of state cutbacks in Medicaid programs. The justice system is racially and class bound and increasingly incarcerates large numbers of poor minorities of class and color while refusing to prosecute hundreds of executives responsible for billions of dollars lost due to fraud and corruption.[15]

It is important to note that the violence of unnecessary hardship and suffering produced by neoliberal ideology and values is not restricted to the economic realm. Neoliberal violence also wages war against the modernist legacy of "questioning the givens, in philosophy as well as in politics and art."[16] Ignorance is no longer a liability in neoliberal societies but a political asset endlessly mediated through a capitalist imaginary that thrives on the interrelated registers of consumption, privatization, and depoliticization. Manufactured ignorance is the new reigning mode of dystopian violence, spurred on by a market-driven system that celebrates a passion for consumer goods over a passionate desire for community affairs, the well-being of the other, and the principles of a democratic society.[17] As the late Cornelius Castoriadis brilliantly argues, under neoliberalism, the thoughtless celebration of economic progress becomes the primary legitimating principle to transform "human beings into machines for producing and consuming."[18]

Under such circumstances, many institutions of higher education are now committed almost exclusively to business values, such as preparing students for low-skilled jobs in the global economy while at the same time transforming faculty into an army of temporary subaltern labor—all done as part of an appeal to rationality, one that eschews matters of inequality, power, and ethical grammars of suffering.[20] Universities have not only strayed from their democratic mission, they also seem immune to the plight of students who have to face a harsh new world of high unemployment, the prospect of downward mobility, debilitating debt, and a future that mimics the failures of the past.

The question of what kind of education is needed for students to be informed and active citizens is rarely asked.[21] In the absence of a democratic vision of schooling, it is not surprising that some colleges and universities are not only increasingly opening their classrooms to the Defense Department and national intelligence agencies but also aligning themselves with those commanding apparatuses that make up the punishing state.[22] In the first instance, one cannot but be puzzled by Yale University's decision to allow the Department of Defense to fund the US Special Operations Command Center of Excellence for Operational Neuroscience—a program designed to "teach special operations personnel the art of 'conversational,' and 'cross cultural intelligence gathering, and pay volunteers from the community's vast immigrant population (mainly poor Hispanics, Moroccans and Iraqis) to serve as test subjects."[23] In other words, Yale would invite "military intelligence to campus to hone their wartime interrogation techniques on the local nonwhite population."[24] In another symptomatic instance of mission drift, Florida Atlantic University in Boca Raton attempted to put together a deal to rename its football stadium after the GEO Group, a private prison corporation "whose record is marred by human rights abuses, by lawsuits, by unnecessary deaths of people in their custody and a whole series of incidents."[25] One Mississippi judge called GEO "an inhuman cesspool."[26] And as Dave Zirin points out, GEO's efforts to spend $6 million "to rename the home of the FAU Owls was an effort to normalize their name: GEO Group, just another corporation you can trust, the Xerox of private prisons."[27] As a result of numerous protests by FAU students, faculty, and outside civil rights groups, the company withdrew its $6 million donation.[28] The "Stop Owlcatraz" campaign exposed not only the often poisonous links between corporations and universities but also the workings of a "deeply racist system of mass incarceration" that should be high on the list of issues faculty and students should be addressing as part of a broader campaign to connect the academy to public life.[29]

The antidemocratic values that drive free-market fundamentalism are embodied in policies now attempting to shape diverse levels of higher education all over the globe. The script has now become overly familiar and increasingly taken for granted, especially in the United

States. As I have mentioned throughout this book, shaping the neoliberal framing of public and higher education is a corporate-based ideology that embraces standardizing the curriculum, top-down governing structures, courses that promote entrepreneurial values, and the reduction of all levels of education to job training sites. For example, one university is offering a master's degree to students who commit to starting a high-tech company while another allows career advisers to teach capstone research seminars in the humanities. In one of these classes, the students were asked to "develop a 30-second commercial on their 'personal brand.'"[30]

Central to this neoliberal view of higher education is a market-driven paradigm that wants to eliminate tenure, turn the humanities into a job preparation service, and reduce most faculty to the status of part-time and temporary workers, if not simply a new subordinate class of disempowered educators. The indentured service status of such faculty is put on full display as some colleges have resorted to using "temporary service agencies to do their formal hiring."[31] Faculty in this view are regarded as simply another cheap army of reserve labor, a powerless group that universities are eager to exploit in order to increase the bottom line while disregarding the needs and rights of academic laborers and the quality of education that students deserve.

There is little talk in this view of higher education about shared governance between faculty and administrators, nor of educating students as critical citizens rather than potential employees of Walmart. There are few attempts to affirm faculty as scholars and public intellectuals who have both a measure of autonomy and power. Instead, faculty members are increasingly defined less as intellectuals than as technicians and grant writers. Students fare no better in this debased form of education and are treated either as consumers or as restless children in need of high-energy entertainment—as was made clear in the 2012 Penn State scandal. Nor is there any attempt to legitimate higher education as a fundamental sphere for creating the agents necessary for an aspiring democracy. This neoliberal, corporatized model of higher education exhibits a deep disdain for critical ideals, public spheres, knowledge, and practices that are not directly linked to market values, business culture, the economy, or the production of short-term financial gains. In fact, the commitment to democracy is beleaguered, viewed less as a crucial educational investment than as a distraction that gets in the way of connecting knowledge and pedagogy to the production of material and human capital. Such modes of education do not foster a sense of organized responsibility central to a democracy. Instead, they foster what might be called a sense of organized irresponsibility—a practice that underlies the economic Darwinism and civic corruption at the heart of American politics.

HIGHER EDUCATION
AND THE CRISIS OF LEGITIMACY

In the United States, many of the problems in higher education can be linked to low funding, the domination of universities by market mechanisms, the rise of for-profit colleges, the intrusion of the national security state, and the lack of faculty self-governance, all of which not only contradicts the culture and democratic value of higher education but also makes a mockery of the very meaning and mission of the university as a democratic public sphere. Decreased financial support for higher education stands in sharp contrast to increased support for tax benefits for the rich, big banks, the defense budget, and megacorporations. Rather than enlarge the moral imagination and critical capacities of students, too many universities are now wedded to producing would-be hedge fund managers, depoliticized students, and creating modes of education that promote a "technically trained docility."[32] Strapped for money and increasingly defined in the language of corporate culture, many universities are now "pulled or driven principally by vocational, [military], and economic considerations while increasingly removing academic knowledge production from democratic values and projects."[33] While there has never been a golden age when higher education was truly liberal and democratic, the current attack on higher education by religious fundamentalists, corporate power, and the apostles of neoliberal capitalism appears unprecedented in terms of both its scope and intensity. The issue here is not to idealize a past that has been lost but to reclaim elements of a history in which the discourses of critique and possibility offered an alternative vision of what form higher education might take in a substantive democratic society.

Universities are losing their sense of public mission, just as leadership in higher education is being banalized and stripped of any viable democratic vision. College presidents are now called CEOs and move without apology between interlocking corporate and academic boards. With few exceptions, they are praised as fundraisers but rarely acknowledged for the force of their ideas. In this new Gilded Age of money and profit, academic subjects gain stature almost exclusively through their exchange value on the market. It gets worse. In one egregious recent example, BB&T Corporation, a financial holdings company, gave a $1 million gift to Marshall University's business school on the condition that *Atlas Shrugged* by Ayn Rand (Paul Ryan's favorite book) be taught in a course. What are we to make of the integrity of a university when it accepts a monetary gift from a corporation or rich patron demanding as part of the agreement the power to specify what is to be taught in a course or how a curriculum should be shaped? Some corporations and universities now believe that what is taught in a course is not an academic decision but a market consideration.

Questions regarding how education might enable students to develop a keen sense of prophetic justice, utilize critical analytical skills, and cultivate an ethical sensibility through which they learn to respect the rights of others are becoming increasingly irrelevant in a market-driven and militarized university. As the humanities and liberal arts are downsized, privatized, and commodified, higher education finds itself caught in the paradox of claiming to invest in the future of young people while offering them few intellectual, civic, and moral supports.[34]

If the commercialization, commodification, and militarization of the university continue unabated, higher education will become yet another of a number of institutions incapable of fostering critical inquiry, public debate, acts of justice, and public values.[35] But the calculating logic of the corporate university does more than diminish the moral and political vision and practices necessary to sustain a vibrant democracy and an engaged notion of social agency. It also undermines the development of public spaces where critical dialogue, social responsibility, and social justice are pedagogically valued—viewed as fundamental to providing students with the knowledge and skills necessary to address the problems facing the nation and the globe. Such democratic public spheres are especially important at a time when any space that produces "critical thinkers capable of putting existing institutions into question" is under siege by powerful economic and political interests.[36]

Higher education has a responsibility not only to search for the truth regardless of where it may lead but also to educate students to be capable of holding authority and power politically and morally accountable, while at the same time sustaining "the idea and hope of a public culture."[37] Though questions regarding whether the university should serve *strictly* public rather than private interests no longer carry the weight of forceful criticism they did in the past, such questions are still crucial in addressing the purpose of higher education and what it might mean to imagine the university's full participation in public life as the protector and promoter of democratic values. Toni Morrison is instructive in her comment that "if the university does not take seriously and rigorously its role as a guardian of wider civic freedoms, as interrogator of more and more complex ethical problems, as servant and preserver of deeper democratic practices, then some other regime or ménage of regimes will do it for us, in spite of us, and without us."[38]

What needs to be understood is that higher education may be one of the few public spheres left where knowledge, values, and learning offer a glimpse of the promise of education for nurturing public values, critical hope, and a substantive democracy. It may be the case that everyday life is increasingly organized around market principles, but confusing a market-determined society with democracy hollows out the legacy of higher education, whose deepest roots are moral, not commercial. This is a particularly important insight in a society where not only is the free circulation of ideas being replaced by ideas managed by the dominant media, but also where critical ideas are increasingly viewed or dismissed as banal, if not reactionary. Celebrity worship and the commodification of culture now constitute a powerful form of mass illiteracy and increasingly permeate all aspects of the educational force of the wider cultural apparatus. But mass illiteracy does more than depoliticize the public; it also becomes complicit with the suppression of dissent. Intellectuals who engage in dissent and "keep the idea and hope of a public culture alive,"[39] are often dismissed as irrelevant, extremist, elitist, or un-American. We now live in a world in which the politics of dis-imagination dominates, such that any writing or public discourse that bears witness to a critical and alternative sense of the world is dismissed as having nothing to do with the bottom line. Imagine how this quote from the late and great public intellectual James Baldwin would be received today.

> You write in order to change the world knowing perfectly well that you probably can't, but also knowing that [writing] is indispensable to the world. The world changes according to the way people see it, and if you alter even by a millimeter the way people look at reality, then you can change it.[40]

In a dystopian society, utopian thought becomes sterile and even Baldwin's prophetic words are out of place, though more important than ever. In spite of the legacy and existence of public intellectuals that extend from Baldwin and C. Wright Mills to Naomi Klein and Barbara Ehrenreich, we live in a new and more dangerous historical conjuncture. Anti-public intellectuals now dominate the larger cultural landscape, all too willing to flaunt co-option and reap the rewards of venting insults at their assigned opponents while being reduced to the status of paid servants of powerful economic interests. But the problem is not simply with the rise of a right-wing cultural apparatus dedicated to preserving the power and wealth of the rich and corporate elite. As Stuart Hall recently remarked, the state of the Left is also problematic in that, as he puts it, "The left is in trouble. It's not got any ideas, it's not got any independent analysis of its own, and therefore it's got no vision. It just takes the temperature. . . . It has no sense of politics being educative, of politics changing the way people see things."[41]

The issue of politics being educative, of recognizing that matters of pedagogy, subjectivity, and consciousness are at the heart of political and moral concerns should not be lost on either academics or those concerned about not only what might be called writing in public but also the purpose and meaning of higher education itself. Democracy places civic demands upon its citizens, and such demands point to the necessity of an education that is broad-based, critical, and supportive of meaningful civic values, participation in self-governance, and demo-cratic leadership. Only through such a formative and critical educational culture can students learn how to become individual and social agents, rather than merely disengaged spectators, able both to think otherwise and to act upon civic commitments that "necessitate a reordering of basic power arrangements" fundamental to promoting the common good and producing a meaningful democracy.[42] This is not a matter of imposing values on education and in our classrooms. The university and the classroom are already defined through power-laden discourses and a myriad of values that are often part of the hidden structures of educational politics and pedagogy. A more accurate position would be, as Toni Morrison notes, to take up our responsibility "as citizen/scholars in the university to accept the consequences of our own value-redolent roles." She continues: "Like it or not, we are paradigms of our own values, advertisements of our own ethics—especially noticeable when we presume to foster ethics-free, value-lite education."[43]

DREAMING THE IMPOSSIBLE

Reclaiming higher education as a democratic public sphere begins with the crucial project of challenging, among other things, those market fundamentalists, religious extremists, and rigid ideologues who harbor a deep disdain for critical thought and healthy skepticism, and who look with displeasure upon any form of education that teaches students to read the word and the world critically. The radical imagination in this discourse is considered dangerous and a dire threat to political authorities. Needless to say, education is not only about issues of work and economics, but also about questions of justice, social freedom, and the capacity for democratic agency, action, and change, as well as the related issues of power, inclusion, and social responsibility.[44] These are educational and political issues, and they should be addressed as part of a broader effort to reenergize the global struggle for social justice and democracy.

Martin Luther King Jr. is instructive here because he recognized clearly that when matters of social responsibility are removed from matters of agency, the content of politics and democracy are deflated. He writes:

> When an individual is no longer a true participant, when he no longer feels a sense of responsibility to his society, the content of democracy is emptied. When culture is degraded and vulgarity enthroned, when the social system does not build security but induces peril, inexorably the individual is impelled to pull away from a soulless society.[45]

If young people are to develop a respect for others, social responsibility, and keen sense of civic engagement, pedagogy must be viewed as the cultural, political, and moral force that provides the knowledge, values, and social relations to make such democratic practices possible. If higher education is to characterize itself as a site of critical thinking, collective work, and public service, educators and students will have to redefine the knowledge, skills, research, and intellectual practices currently favored in the university. Central to such a challenge is the need to position intellectual practice "as part of an intricate web of morality, rigor and responsibility"[46] that enables academics to speak with conviction, use the public sphere to address important social problems, and demonstrate alternative models for bridging the gap between higher education and the broader society. Connective practices are crucial in that it is essential to develop intellectual practices that are collegial rather than competitive, refuse the instrumentality and privileged isolation of the academy, link critical thought to a profound impatience with the status quo, and connect human agency to the idea of social responsibility and the politics of possibility.

Connection also means being openly and deliberately critical and worldly in one's intellectual work. Increasingly, as universities are shaped by a culture of fear in which dissent is equated with treason, the call to be objective and impartial, whatever one's intentions, can easily echo what George Orwell called the official truth or the establishment point of view. Lacking a self-consciously democratic political focus, teachers are often reduced to the role of a technician or functionary engaged in formalistic rituals, unconcerned with the disturbing and urgent problems that confront the larger society or the consequences of one's pedagogical practices and research undertakings. In opposition to this model, with its claims to and conceit of political neutrality, I argue that academics should combine the mutually interdependent roles of critical educator and active citizen. This requires finding ways to connect the practice of classroom teaching with the operation of power in the larger society and to provide the conditions for students to view themselves as critical agents capable of making those who exercise authority and power answerable for their actions. Such an intellectual does not train students solely for jobs but also educates them to question critically the institutions, policies, and values that shape their lives, relationships to others, and connections to the larger world.

I think Stuart Hall is on target here when he insists that educators also have a responsibility to provide students with "critical knowledge that has to be ahead of traditional knowledge: it has to be better than anything that traditional knowledge can produce, because only serious ideas are going to stand up."[47] At the same time, he insists on the need for educators to "actually engage, contest, and learn from the best that is locked up in other traditions," especially those attached to traditional academic paradigms.[48] Students must be made aware of the ideological and structural forces that promote needless human suffering while also recognizing that it takes more than awareness to resolve them. This is the kind of intellectual practice that Zygmunt Bauman calls "taking responsibility for our responsibility,"[49] one that is attentive to the suffering and needs of others. At the very least, such responsibility means rejecting what Irving Howe calls the honored place that capitalism has found for intellectuals who now speak for power rather than for the truth and consider themselves noble guardians of the status quo.[50]

Education cannot be decoupled from what Jacques Derrida calls a democracy to come, that is, a democracy that must always "be open to the possibility of being contested, of contesting itself, of criticizing and indefinitely improving itself."[51] Within this project of possibility and impossibility, education must be understood as a deliberately informed and purposeful political and moral practice, as opposed to one that is either doctrinaire, instrumentalized, or both. Moreover, a critical pedagogy should be engaged at all levels of schooling. Similarly, it must gain part of its momentum in higher education among students who will go back to the schools, churches, synagogues, and workplaces in order to produce new ideas, concepts, and critical ways of understanding the world in which they live. This is a notion of intellectual practice and responsibility that refuses the insular, overly pragmatic, and privileged isolation of the academy. It also affirms a broader vision of learning that links knowledge to the power of self-definition and to the capacities of students to expand the scope of democratic freedoms, particularly those that address the crisis of education, politics, and the social as part and parcel of the crisis of democracy itself.

In order for critical pedagogy, dialogue, and thought to have real effects, they must advocate the message that all citizens, old and young, are equally entitled, if not equally empowered, to shape the society in which they live. This is a message we heard from the brave students fighting tuition hikes and the destruction of civil liberties and social provisions in Quebec and to a lesser degree in the Occupy Wall Street movement.

These young people who are protesting against the 1 percent recognize that they have been written out of the discourses of justice, equality, and democracy and are not only resisting how neoliberalism has made them expendable, they are also arguing for a collective future very different from the one on display in the current political and economic systems in which they feel trapped. These brave youth are insisting that the relationship between knowledge and power can be emancipatory, that their histories and experiences matter, and that what they say and do counts in their struggle to unlearn dominating privileges, productively reconstruct their relations with others, and transform, when necessary, the world around them.

If educators are to function as public intellectuals, they need to listen to young people who are producing a new language in order to talk about inequality and power relations, attempting to create alternative democratic public spaces, rethinking the very nature of politics, and asking serious questions about what democracy is and why it no longer exists in the United States. Simply put, educators need to argue for forms of pedagogy that close the gap between the university and everyday life. Their curricula need to be organized around knowledge of those communities, cultures, and traditions that give students a sense of history, identity, place, and possibility. More importantly, they need to join students in engaging in a practice of freedom that points to new and radical forms of pedagogies that have a direct link to building social movements in and out of the colleges and universities.

Although there are still a number of academics such as Noam Chomsky, Angela Davis, John Ralston Saul, Bill McKibben, Germaine Greer, and Cornel West who function as public intellectuals, they are often shut out of the mainstream media or characterized as marginal, unintelligible, and sometimes unpatriotic figures. At the same time, many academics find themselves laboring under horrendous working conditions that either don't allow for them to write in a theoretically rigorous and accessible manner for the public because they do not have time—given the often intensive teaching demands of part-time academics and increasingly of full-time, nontenured academics as well. Or they retreat into a kind of theoreticism in which theory becomes lifeless, detached from any larger project or the realm of worldly issues. In this instance, the notion of theory as a resource—if not theoretical rigor itself—is reduced to a badge of academic cleverness, shorn of the potential to advance thought within the academy or to reach a larger audience outside their academic disciplines.

Consequently, such intellectuals often exist in hermetic academic bubbles cut off from both the larger public and the important issues that impact society. To no small degree, they have been complicit in the transformation of the university into an adjunct of corporate and military power. Such academics have become incapable of defending higher education as a vital public sphere and unwilling to challenge those spheres of induced mass cultural illiteracy and firewalls of jargon that doom to extinction critically engaged thought, complex ideas, and serious writing for the public. Without their intervention as public intellectuals, the university defaults on its role as a democratic public sphere capable of educating an informed public, a culture of questioning, and the development of a critical formative culture connected to the need, as Cornelius Castoriadis puts it, "to create citizens who are critical thinkers capable of putting existing institutions into question so that democracy again becomes society's movement."[52]

Before his untimely death, Edward Said, himself an exemplary public intellectual, urged his colleagues in the academy to directly confront those social hardships that disfigure contemporary society and pose a serious threat to the promise of democracy. He urged them to assume the role of public intellectuals, wakeful and mindful of their responsibilities to bear testimony to human suffering and the pedagogical possibilities at work in educating students to be autonomous, self-reflective, and socially responsible. Said rejected the notion of a market-driven pedagogy, one that created cheerful robots and legitimated organized recklessness and illegal legalities. In opposition to such a pedagogy, Said argued for what he called a pedagogy of wakefulness and its related concern with a politics of critical engagement. In commenting on Said's public pedagogy of wakefulness, and how it shaped his important consideration of academics as public intellectuals, I begin with a passage that I think offers a key to the ethical and political force of much of his writing. This selection is taken from his memoir, *Out of Place*, which describes the last few months of his mother's life in a New York hospital and the difficult time she had falling to sleep because of the cancer that was ravaging her body. Recalling this traumatic and pivotal life experience, Said's meditation moves between the existential and the insurgent, between private pain and worldly commitment, between the seductions of a "solid self" and the reality of a contradictory, questioning, restless, and at times, uneasy sense of identity. He writes:

> "Help me to sleep, Edward," she once said to me with a piteous trembling in her voice that I can still hear as I write. But then the disease spread into her brain—and for the last six weeks she slept all the time—my own inability to sleep may be her last legacy to me, a counter to her struggle for sleep. For me sleep is something to be gotten over as quickly as possible. I can only go to bed very late, but I am literally up at dawn. Like her I don't possess the secret of long sleep, though unlike her I have reached the point where I do not want it. For me, sleep is death, as is any diminishment in awareness. . . . Sleeplessness for me is a cherished state to be desired at almost any cost; there is nothing for me as invigorating as immediately shedding the shadowy half-consciousness of a night's loss than the early morning, reacquainting myself with or resuming what I might have lost completely a few hours earlier. I occasionally experience myself as a cluster of flowing currents. I prefer this to the idea of a solid self, the identity to which so many attach so much significance. These currents like the themes of one's life, flow along during the waking hours, and at their best, they require no reconciling, no harmonizing. They are "off" and may be out of place, but at least they are always in motion, in time, in place, in the form of all kinds of strange combinations moving about, not necessarily forward, sometimes against each other, contrapuntally yet without one central theme. A form of freedom, I like to think, even if I am far from being totally convinced that it is. That skepticism too is one of the themes I particularly want to hold on to. With so many dissonances in my life I have learned actually to prefer being not quite right and out of place.[53]

Said posits here an antidote to the seductions of conformity, a disciplinarily induced moral coma, and the lure of corporate money. For Said, it is a sense of being awake, displaced, caught in a combination of diverse circumstances that suggests a pedagogy that is cosmopolitan and imaginative—a public-affirming pedagogy that demands a critical and engaged interaction with the world we live in, mediated by a responsibility for challenging structures of domination and for alleviating human suffering. That is, a pedagogy that writes the public. As an ethical and political practice, a public pedagogy of wakefulness rejects modes of education removed from political or social concerns, divorced from history and matters of injury and injustice. Said's notion of a pedagogy of wakefulness includes "lifting complex ideas into the public space," recognizing human injury inside and outside of the academy, and acting on the assumption that there is more hope in the world when we can use theory to question what is taken for granted and change things.[54] This is a pedagogy in which academics are neither afraid of controversy or the willingness to make connections that are otherwise hidden, nor are they afraid of making clear the connection between private issues and broader elements of society's problems.

For Said, being awake becomes a central metaphor for defining the role of academics as public intellectuals, defending the university as a crucial public sphere, engaging how culture deploys power, and taking seriously the idea of human interdependence while at the same time always living on the border—one foot in and one foot out, an exile and an insider for whom home was always a form of homelessness. As a relentless border-crosser, Said embraced the idea of the "traveler" as an important metaphor for engaged intellectuals. As Stephen Howe, referencing Said, points out, "It was an image which depended not on power, but on motion, on daring to go into different worlds, use different languages, and 'understand a multiplicity of disguises, masks, and rhetorics. Travelers must suspend the claim of customary routine in order to live in new rhythms and rituals . . . the traveler crosses over, traverses territory, and abandons fixed positions all the time.'"[55] And as a border intellectual and traveler, Said embodied the notion of always "being quite not right," evidenced by his principled critique of all forms of certainties and dogmas and his refusal to be silent in the face of human suffering at home and abroad.

Being awake meant refusing the now popular sport of academic-bashing or embracing a crude call for action at the expense of rigorous intellectual and theoretical work. On the contrary, it meant combining rigor and clarity, on the one hand, and civic courage and political commitment, on the other. A pedagogy of wakefulness meant using theory as a resource, recognizing the worldly space of criticism as the democratic underpinning of public-ness, defining critical literacy not merely as a competency but as an act of interpretation linked to the possibility of intervention in the world. It pointed to a kind of border literacy in the plural, in which people learned to read and write from multiple positions of agency; it also was indebted to the recognition forcibly stated by

Hannah Arendt, "Without a politically guaranteed public realm, free-dom lacks the worldly space to make its appearance."[56]

For those brave academics such as Said, Pierre Bourdieu, Ellen Willis, and others, public intellectuals have a responsibility to unset-tle power, trouble consensus, and challenge common sense. The very notion of being an engaged public intellectual is neither foreign to nor a violation of what it means to be an academic scholar but central to its very definition. According to Said, academics have a duty to enter into the public sphere unafraid to take positions and generate contro-versy, functioning as moral witnesses, raising political awareness, making connections to those elements of power and politics often hidden from public view, and reminding "the audience of the moral questions that may be hidden in the clamor and din of the public debate."[57] At the same time, Said criticized those academics who retreated into a new dogmatism of the disinterested specialist that separates them "not only from the public sphere but from other professionals who don't use the same jargon."[58] This was especially unsettling to him at a time when complex language and critical thought remain under assault in the larger society by all manner of antidemocratic forces. But there is more at stake here than a retreat into convoluted discourses that turn theory into a mechanical act of academic referencing and a deadly obscurantism, there is also the retreat of intellectuals from being able to defend the public values and democratic mission of higher education. Or, as Irving Howe put it, "intellectuals have, by and large, shown a painful lack of militancy in defending the rights which are a precondition of their existence."[59]

The view of higher education as a democratic public sphere commit-ted to producing young people capable and willing to expand and deepen their sense of themselves, to think about the world critically, "to imagine something other than their own well-being," to serve the public good, and to struggle for a substantive democracy has been in a state of acute crisis for the last thirty years.[60] When faculty assume, in this context, their civic responsibility to educate students to think critically, act with conviction, and connect what they learn in classrooms to important social issues in the larger society, they are often denounced for politicizing their class-rooms and for violating professional codes of conduct, or, worse, labeled as unpatriotic.[61] In some cases, the risk of connecting what they teach to the imperative to expand the capacities of students to be both critical and socially engaged may cost academics their jobs, especially when they make visible the workings of power, injustice, human misery, and the alterable nature of the social order. What do the liberal arts and humanities amount to if they do not teach the practice of freedom, especially at a time when training is substituted for education? Gayatri Spivak provides a context for this question with her comment: "Can one insist on the importance of training in the humanities in [a] time of legitimized violence?"[62]

In a society that remains troublingly resistant to or incapable of questioning itself, one that celebrates the consumer over the citizen and all too willingly endorses the narrow values and interests of corporate power, the importance of the university as a place of critical learning, dialogue, and social justice advocacy becomes all the more imperative. Moreover, the distinctive role that faculty play in this ongoing pedagogical project of democratization and learning, along with support for the institutional conditions and relations of power that make it possible, must be defended as part of a broader discourse of excellence, equity, and democracy.

Despite the growing public recognition that market fundamentalism has fostered a destructive alignment among the state, corporate capital, and transnational corporations, there is little understanding that such an alignment has been constructed and solidified through a neoliberal disciplinary apparatus and corporate pedagogy produced in part in the halls of higher education and through the educational force of the larger media culture. The economic Darwinism of the last thirty years has done more than throw the financial and credit systems into crisis; it has also waged an attack on all those social institutions that support critical modes of agency, reason, and meaningful dissent. And yet, the financial meltdown most of the world is experiencing is rarely seen as part of an educational crisis in which the institutions of public and higher education have been conscripted into a war on democratic values. Such institutions have played a formidable, if not shameless, role in reproducing market-driven beliefs, social relations, identities, and modes of understanding that legitimate the institutional arrangements of cutthroat capitalism. William Black calls such institutions purveyors of a "criminogenic environment"—one that promotes and legitimates market-driven practices that include fraud, deregulation, and other perverse practices.[63] Black claims that the most extreme pedagogical expression of such an environment can be found in business schools, which he calls "fraud factories" for the elite.[64]

There seems to be an enormous disconnect between the economic conditions that led to the devastating financial meltdown and the current call to action by a generation of young people and adults who have been educated for the last several decades in the knowledge, values, and identities of a market-driven society. Clearly, this generation will not solve this crisis if they do not connect it to the assault on an educational system that has been reduced to a lowly adjunct of corporate interests and the bidding of the warfare state.

Higher education represents one of the most important sites over which the battle for democracy is being waged. It is the site where the promise of a better future emerges out of those visions and pedagogical practices that combine hope, agency, politics, and moral responsibility as part of a broader emancipatory discourse. Academics have a distinct and unique obligation, if not political and ethical responsibility, to make learning relevant to the imperatives of a discipline, scholarly method, or research specialization. If democracy is a way of life that demands a formative culture, educators can play a pivotal role in creating forms of pedagogy and research that enable young people to think critically, exercise judgment, engage in spirited debate, and create those public spaces that constitute "the very essence of political life."[65]

Finally, I want to suggest that while it has become more difficult to imagine a democratic future, we have entered a period in which young people all over the world are protesting against neoliberalism and its pedagogy and politics of disposability. Refusing to remain voiceless and powerless in determining their future, these young people are organizing collectively in order to create the conditions for societies that refuse to use politics as an act of war and markets as the measure of democracy. They are taking seriously the words of the great abolitionist Frederick Douglass, who bravely argued that freedom is an empty abstraction if people fail to act, and "if there is no struggle, there is no progress."[66] Their struggles are not simply aimed at the 1 percent but also at the 99 percent as part of a broader effort to get them to connect the dots, educate themselves, and develop and join social movements that can rewrite the language of democracy and put into place the institutions and formative cultures that make it possible. Stanley Aronowitz is right in arguing:

The system survives on the eclipse of the radical imagination, the absence of a viable political opposition with roots in the general population, and the conformity of its intellectuals who, to a large extent, are subjugated by their secure berths in the academy. [At the same time,] it would be premature to predict that decades of retreat, defeat and silence can be reversed overnight without a commitment to what may be termed "a long march" though the institutions, the workplaces and the streets of the capitalist metropoles.[67]

The protests that began in 2011 in the United States, Canada, Greece, and Spain make clear that this is not—indeed, *cannot be*—only a short-term project for reform but a political movement that needs to intensify, accompanied by the reclaiming of public spaces, the progressive use of digital technologies, the development of public spheres, the production of new modes of education, and the safeguarding of places where democratic expression, new identities, and collective hope can be nurtured and mobilized. A formative culture must be put in place pedagogically and institutionally in a variety of spheres extending from churches and public and higher education to all those cultural apparatuses engaged in the production and circulation of knowledge, desire, identities, and values.

Clearly, such efforts need to address the language of democratic revolution rather than the seductive incremental adjustments of liberal reform. This suggests calling for a living wage, jobs programs (especially for the young), the democratization of power, economic equality, and a massive shift in funds away from the machinery of war and big banks, as well as building a social movement that not only engages in critique but also makes hope a real possibility by organizing in order to seize power. We need collective narratives that inform collective struggles. In this instance, public intellectuals can play a crucial role in providing theoretical resources and modes of analyses that can help to shape such narratives along with broader social movements and collective struggles. There is no room for failure here because failure would cast us back into the clutches of authoritarianism—which, while different from previous historical periods, shares nonetheless the imperative to proliferate violent social formations and a death-dealing blow to the promise of a democracy to come.

Given the urgency of the problems faced by those marginalized by class, race, age, and sexual orientation, I think it is all the more crucial to take seriously the challenge of Derrida's provocation that "We must do and think the impossible. If only the possible happened, nothing more would happen. If I only I did what I can do, I wouldn't do anything."[68] We may live in dark times, as Hannah Arendt reminds us, but history is open and the space of the possible is larger than the one on display. Academics in their role as public intellectuals can play a crucial part in raising critical questions, connecting critical modes of education to social change, and making clear that the banner of critical independence and civic engagement, "ragged and torn though it may be, is still worth fighting for."[69]

CHAPTER SIX

The Promise of Education in Difficult Times

Reading against Fascism in the Age of Trump

The Marxist cultural critic Walter Benjamin once argued that every rise of fascism bears witness to a failed revolution. Benjamin was not only addressing elements of a failed political revolution, but also the failure of language, values, courage, vision, and a critical consciousness. In the midst of a moment when an older social order is crumbling and a new one is struggling to define itself, there is always a moment of confusion and danger. We have arrived at such a moment in which two worlds are colliding. First, there is the harsh and crumbling worlds of neoliberal globalization and its mobilizing passions that fuel a US–style fascism.[1] Second, there are countermovements with their search for a new politics that can rethink, reclaim, and invent a new understanding of democratic socialism, untainted by capitalism.[2] In the midst of this struggle, a new political movement and social order will be born, though one without guarantees. What is clear at the present historical moment is that something sinister and horrifying is happening to liberal democracies all over the globe. The global architecture of democracy is giving way to authoritarian tyrannies. As alarming as the signs may be, the public cannot look away and allow the terrors of the unforeseen to be given free rein. Consequently, those who believe in a radical democracy cannot allow the power of dreams to turn into nightmares.

It is hard to imagine a more urgent moment for developing a language of critique and possibility that would serve to awaken our critical and imaginative senses and help free us from the tyrannical nightmare that has descended upon the United States under the rule of Donald Trump. In an age of social isolation, information overflow, a culture of immediacy, consumer glut and spectacularized violence, reading critically and thinking analytically become essential pedagogical practices. This is especially true if we are to take seriously the notion that a democracy cannot exist or be defended without informed and engaged citizens. This is particularly true at a time when denial has become a national pastime matched only by the increasing normalization of one of the most alarming administrations ever to take hold of the US presidency.

Against a numbing indifference, despair, and withdrawal into the private orbits of the isolated self, there is a need to create those formative cultures that are humanizing, foster the capacity to hear others, and sustain complex thoughts and engage social problems. We have no other choice if we are to resist the increasing destabilization of democratic institutions, the assault on reason, the collapse of the distinction between fact and fiction, and the taste for brutality that now spreads across the United States like a plague. Under the Trump administration, there is a merging of abject criminality, massive corruption, unchecked stupidity, a culture of cruelty, and a pathological disdain for democracy. Utopian visions, powerful social movements, and new forms of politics are undercut by a culture shaped by militarism, illegal legalities, social atomization, and the surrender of liberal freedoms and social rights for security and safety. Shared fears have replaced shared responsibilities, fueled by an apocalyptic populism that feeds off misdirected anger and outrage that has become a petri dish for a fascist politics.

Neoliberal fascism feeds on manufactured ignorance by undermining reason, logic, and evidence. By emphasizing emotion over reason and collapsing the lines between fiction and reality, it becomes more difficult for the larger public to critically understand and engage the conditions that shape their everyday lives. At work here is a form of pedagogical terrorism whose aim is to undermine the opportunity for individuals to read the world critically, to think analytically, and to be able to imagine a future that does not mimic the present. As the institutional, temporal, discursive, and spatial markers that support a democratic culture disappear, the promise of the social imagination gives way to spectacles of violence, insipid modes of entertainment, and modes of governance in which massive suffering becomes normalized and a hatred of the other becomes a defining feature of politics. Against this attack on the democratic imaginary, there is the urgent challenge to create the conditions for individuals to learn how to be knowledgeable, informed, and critical citizens; there is also the need to keep alive in the public realm a recognition of how crucial the act of translation is as a political resource for developing a critical and engaged sense of agency. In this instance, language becomes not only valuable as a form of translation, but also, as George Steiner observes, as "the main instrument of [people's] refusal to accept the world as it is."[3]

The pedagogical lesson here is that fascism begins with language, hateful words, the demonization of others considered disposable, and moves to an attack on ideas, the burning of books, the disappearance of intellectuals, and the emergence of the carceral state and the horrors of detention jails and camps. As Jon Nixon suggests, knowing how to read the word, image, and diverse worlds of representation is a form of critical education that "provides us with a protected space within which to think against the grain of received opinion: a space to question and challenge, to imagine the world from different standpoints and perspectives, to reflect upon ourselves in relation to others, and, in so doing, to understand what it means to 'assume responsibility.'"[4] Under such circumstances, thinking against the grain offers opportunities for people to break out of their own experiences at a time when neoliberal ideology not only constrains our imaginations but also imprisons them in almost impenetrable orbits of self-interest and hyper-individualism.

Trump's presidency is symptomatic of the long decline of liberal democracy in the United States; yet its presence and authoritarian reach signifies one of the gravest challenges, if not dangers, the country has faced in over a century. A formative culture of lies, ignorance, corruption and violence is now fueled by a range of orthodoxies shaping US life, including social conservatism, market fundamentalism, apocalyptic nationalism, religious extremism, and white nationalism—all of which occupy the centers of power at the highest levels of government. Historical memory and moral witnessing have given way to a bankrupt nostalgia that celebrates the most regressive moments in US history. Trump's view of American history is one marked by the Gilded Age of massive inequality, a racist state, an embrace of whiteness as a site of universal privilege, and a full-fledged assault on the rights of minorities of color, ethnicity, gender, and religion. Trump's world is not based on the liberal democratic model of Abraham Lincoln and Franklin D. Roosevelt but on the racist ideologies of Andrew Jackson and the late Senator Strom Thurmond.

Fantasies of absolute control, racial cleansing, unchecked militarism and class warfare are at the heart of a US social order that has turned lethal. This is a dystopian social order soaked in hollow words, an imagination pillaged of any substantive meaning, a politics cleansed of compassion and used to legitimate the notion that alternative worlds are impossible to entertain. What we are witnessing is an abandonment of democratic institutions and values and a full-scale attack on dissent, thoughtful reasoning, and the radical imagination. Trump has degraded the office of the president and has elevated the ethos of political corruption, hyper-masculinity, and lying to a level that leaves many people numb and exhausted. Under such circumstances, the United States is moving into the dark shadows of a present that bears a horrifying resemblance to an earlier period of fascism with its language of racial purification, hatred of dissent, systemic violence, intolerance, and its "glorification of aggressive and violent solutions to complex social problems."[5]

The history of fascism offers an early warning system and teaches us that language, which operates in the service of violence, desperation, and the troubled landscapes of hatred, carries the potential for resurrecting the darkest moments of history. It erodes our humanity, and makes many people numb and silent under the glare of ideologies and practices that mimic and legitimate hideous and atrocious acts. A language that eliminates the space of plurality, glorifies walls and borders, hates differences that do not mimic a white public sphere, and makes vulnerable populations—even young children—superfluous as human beings. Trump's language, like that which characterized older fascist regimes, mutilates contemporary politics, disdains empathy and serious moral and political criticism, and makes it more difficult to criticize dominant relations of power. His toxic language also fuels the rhetoric of war, a supercharged masculinity, anti-intellectualism, and a resurgent white supremacy. However, it is not his alone. This language of nascent fascism has been brewing in the United States for some time. It is a language that is comfortable viewing the world as a combat zone, a world that exists to be plundered, and one that views those deemed different because of their race, ethnicity, religion, or sexual orientation as a threat to be feared, if not eliminated. When Trump uses the toxic rhetoric of "animals," "infest," "vermin," he is doing more than using ugly epithets, he is also materializing such discourse into policies that rip children from their mother's arms, puts young children in cages, and forces children as young one year old to appear before immigration judges.[6]

Moreover, while there is no perfect mirror, it has become all the more difficult for many people not to recognize how the "crystalized elements" of totalitarianism have emerged in new forms in the shape of a US–style fascism. In part, this may be because history is no longer treated seriously, especially at a time when the need for instant pleasure and the language of tweets overrides the necessary discipline and potential pleasure that comes with the slowing down of time and the hard work of imaginative contemplation. Moreover, as Leon Wieseltier observes we live in an era in which "words cannot wait for thoughts [and] patience is a . . . liability."[7] In age of instant gratification, history has become a burden to be treated like a discarded relic that no longer deserves respect. The past is now either too unpleasant to contemplate or is delegated to the abyss of willful ignorance and consigned to the memory hole. However frightening and seemingly impossible in a liberal democracy, neither history nor the ghost of fascism can be dismissed because Trump has not created concentration camps or engineered plans for genocidal acts, though he has caged children and denied immunity to immigrants many of whom, if forced to return to their countries, face an almost certain death.

Fascism is hardly a relic of the past or a fixed political and ideological system. Fascist ideologies, values, and social relations never exist entirely in the past and can be found in a range of ideas, attitudes, and social relations articulated by the Trump administration and other authoritarians across the globe. The essential educational issue here is what fascist politics, principles, and ideas have become manifest in the present and how they herald a possible model for the future. Where are the ideological, political, economic, and pedagogical fault lines that should be setting off alarm bells and warning signs about the United States' descent into authoritarianism?

Renowned historian of modern Germany Richard Evans observes the Trump administration may not replicate all the features of Germany and Italy in the 1930s, but the legacy of fascism is important because it echoes a dangerous "warning from history" that cannot be written off.[8] Fascism is not static; nor does it exist entirely in the repository of history. Moreover, the protean elements of fascism always run the risk of crystallizing into new forms. The ghosts of fascism should terrify us, but most importantly, the horrors of the past should educate us and imbue us with a spirit of civic justice and collective courage in the fight for a substantive and inclusive democracy. Historical consciousness is a crucial tool for unravelling the layers of meaning, suffering, search for community, the overcoming of despair, and the momentum of dramatic change, however unpleasant this may be at times. No act of the past can be deemed too horrible or hideous to contemplate if we are going to enlarge the scope of our imaginations and the reach of social justice, both of which might prevent us from looking away, indifferent to the suffering around us.

The rise of a fascist politics under the Trump administration suggests the need for rethinking the importance of historical memory, civic literacy, and education as essential acts and pedagogical practices that are central to what it means to be an informed and critical citizen willing fight for the ideas, values, and institutions that make a democracy possible. Rather than dismiss the notion that the organizing principles and fluctuating elements of fascism are still with us, a more appropriate response to Trump's rise to power is to raise questions about what elements of his government signal the emergence of a fascism suited to a contemporary and distinctively US political, economic, and cultural landscape. Surely, his ongoing lawlessness, attacks on the media, racism, his nativist discourse, xenophobic politics, and his National Emergency declaration to build a wall on the US–Mexican border (a symbol of nativism) speak to echoes of a history that was built around hatred, bigotry, war, and violence.

In an age when memory is under attack, critical thinking and critical pedagogy become both a source of hope and a tool of resistance. A critical pedagogy that relates power and knowledge and learning to social change offers the opportunity to connect the past to the present and to view the present as a window into those horrors of a history that must never be repeated. The notion of critical pedagogy as a form of moral witnessing and historical memory is particularly important as the US is sinking into the abyss of fascism. The signs are all around us, and we cannot afford to ignore them. A critical reading of history provides us with a vital resource that helps inform the ethical ground for resistance—an antidote to Trump's politics of disinformation, division, diversion, and fragmentation. Memory as a form of critical consciousness is crucial in developing a form of historical and social responsibility to offset a willful ignorance that reinforces the American nightmare.[9] In the face of this nightmare, thinking and judging must be connected to our actions.[10] At the very least, thinking critically, reading contemplatively, slowing time down, and refusing the commodified emotional management produced by the pedagogical apparatuses in the service of neoliberalism provide the opportunity and space for people to say no and refuse "to settle for fast solutions, easy answers [and] formulaic resolutions."[11] As I have said elsewhere, "Historical learning is not about constructing a linear narrative but about blasting history open, rupturing its silences, highlighting its detours, acknowledging the events of its transmission, and organizing its limits within an open and honest concern with human suffering, values, and the legacy of the often un-representable or misrepresented."[12]

If education is to be seen as being at the center of politics in the shaping of consciousness, identities, values, and social relations then it is important to understand the inextricable and mutually related ways in which education and politics inform each other. In opposition to dominant instrumental views of education, progressive educators and others must argue for a notion of education that is viewed as inherently political—one that relentlessly questions the kinds of labor, practices, research, and modes of evaluation that are enacted in higher education. As my late colleague Roger Simon observed, pedagogy is "an introduction to, preparation for, and legitimation of particular forms of social life and always presupposes a vision of the future [and] represents a version of our own dreams for ourselves, our children, and our communities. But such dreams are never neutral; they are always someone's dreams and to the degree that they are implicated in organizing the future for others they always have a moral and political dimension."[13] While such a pedagogy does not offer guarantees, it defines itself as a moral and political practice that is always implicated in power relations because it offers particular versions and visions of civic life and how we might construct representations of others, our physical and social environment, and ourselves. Neutral, objective education is an oxymoron. It does not exist outside of relations of power, values, and politics. Education is inextricably connected to the related issues of power, inclusion, and social responsibility. Ethically, educators need to cast a critical eye on those forms of knowledge and social relations that define themselves through a conceptual purity and political innocence that clouds the fact that the alleged neutrality on which they stand is already grounded in ethico-political choices. In order to prevent the depoliticization of education, educators and others must challenge the image of education as neutral and removed from the related realms of power and politics.

This is particularly important if we are to define pedagogy as the practice of freedom, one that arises from the conviction that educators and other cultural workers have a responsibility to unsettle power, trouble consensus, and challenge common sense. This is a view of pedagogy that should disturb, inspire, and energize a vast array of individuals and publics. Such pedagogical practices should enable students to interrogate common sense understandings of the world, take risks in their thinking, however difficult, and be willing to take a stand for free inquiry in the pursuit of truth, multiple ways of knowing, mutual respect, and civic values in the pursuit of social justice.

We live at a time when the corruption of discourse has become a defining feature of politics, reinforced largely by an administration and a conservative media apparatus that does not simply lie, but also work hard to eliminate the distinction between fantasy and fact. As Hannah Arendt has argued, at issue here is the creation of modes of agency that are complicit with fascist modes of governance. She writes in *The Origins of Totalitarianism*: "The ideal subject of totalitarian rule is not the convinced Nazi or the convinced Communist, but people for whom the distinction between fact and fiction (i.e., the reality of experience) and the distinction between true and false (i.e., the standards of thought) no longer exists."[14]

Under the Trump administration, the role of education in cultivating a critical citizenry capable of participating in and shaping a democratic society is being undermined, if not lost. Lost also is an educational vision that takes people beyond the world of common sense, functions as a form of provocation, teaches them to be creative, exposes individuals to a variety of great traditions, embraces the arts, and creates the pedagogical conditions for individuals to expand the range of human possibilities. Under the influence of corporate power and a growing authoritarianism in the United States, education in multiple informal and formal platforms operates increasingly in the service of lies, racism, unchecked market values, and a full-fledged assault on critical consciousness and public values. Moreover, higher education is now dominated by a neoliberal discourse that removes it from its role as a democratic public sphere. Instead, it has become a financial investment and another workstation whose goal "is to ensure that young people and society generally, can compete in a global economy."[15] As Stefan Collini observes, this neoliberal view no longer conceives of "universities as places of education; they are conceived of simply as engines of economic prosperity and as agencies for equipping future employees to earn higher salaries."[16] Under such circumstances, education becomes vocationalized, democracy is cast as the enemy of freedom, and politics turns dark.

Under the reign of a hyperactive global neoliberalism, time and contemplation have become a burden, subject to an "excess of stimuli, information, and impulses [that] radically changes the structure and economy of attention. Perception becomes fragmented and scattered."[17] The contemplative attention central to thinking and reading the world critically and listening attentively now give way to a hyperactive flow of information in which speed, compulsion, sound bites, fragments of information, and a relentless stream of disruptions overcome thinking. There is a type of violence in which the fragmented mind undercuts the capacity to think dialectically, undermining the ability to make connections, imagine capaciously, and develop comprehensive maps of meaning.[18] At work here is a form of depoliticization that leaves individuals isolated, exhausted, ignorant of the forces that bear down on their lives, and susceptible to a high-charged culture of stimulation.

The terror of the unforeseen—those unanticipated actions— becomes even more ominous when history is used to hide rather than illuminate the past, when it becomes difficult to translate private issues into larger systemic considerations, and people willingly allow themselves be both seduced and trapped into spectacles of violence, cruelty, and authoritarian impulses. Thinking and reading the world critically is the precondition for intervening in the world. That is why critical thinking and reading critically are so dangerous to Trump, his acolytes, and those who hate democracy. Democracy can only survive with a public attentive to the power of language, ideas, media-based representations, books, and texts that matter. It can only survive when we refuse to engage the power to think otherwise in order to act otherwise. Higher education provides a special target for fascists who view its critical function as dangerous, its civic role as reinforcing the importance of public service and equal rights, and its claim to pedagogical practices that teach not just the truth but "the practice of freedom to a general public."[19] Higher education, particularly when it presses the claim for economic and social justice, is viewed by conservatives as particularly dangerous, especially in a time of legitimized state violence.

The crisis of neoliberalism with its financial ruin for millions, its elimination of the welfare state, its deregulation of corporate power, its unchecked racism and its militarization of society, has yet to be matched by a crisis of ideas—one that embraces historical memory, rejects the normalization of fascist principles, and opens a space for an imagining that alternative worlds can be brought into being. While the long-term corrosion of politics and the emerging fascism in the US will not end by simply having people learn how to think and read critically, the spaces opened by such pedagogical practices create a bulwark against cynicism and fosters a notion of hope that can be translated into forms of collective resistance. That is why reading and thinking critically is so dangerous and is so necessary. Thinking critically and acting courageously in dark times is not an option, but a necessity.

Higher education, in spite of its increasing corporatization, is still one of the few spaces left where critical thought, knowledge, and informed dialogue is possible. It is still one of the few spheres in which education is central to creating informed students capable of mastering acts of translation which is not only about mastering diverse forms of linguistic plurality, but also contains the potential of engaging public scripts, narratives, discourses, and ideologies by reconfiguring and rewriting them as part of a larger emancipatory project. Though under siege by a brutal neoliberal ideology, it is still one of the few places that can function as a center of humane critique, teach students how to think differently, provide a breadth of knowledge, and enable students to think hard about important social and political issues.

Thinking critically is often viewed as dangerous by the Trump administration because it not only points to the critical function and mission of higher education as a democratic public sphere, but it also illuminates its mission to produce civically literate and engaged critical citizens. What is most feared by conservatives and ideological fundamentalists is that higher education also holds the promise of linking learning to social change. Higher education poses a threat to the apostles of neoliberalism because it still contains, at least in spirit, a refusal to be defined exclusively by "the discipline of the market."[20] Of course, what is missed in the neoliberal view of education is that educating young people is not a matter of profit, but social responsibility, especially since the survival of any substantive democracy depends on cultivating in young people a set of dispositions, sensibilities and habits at the heart of a formative culture essential to secure it.[21] But that noble ideal and promise is under attack in an age ruled by manufactured ignorance and mass inequities in wealth, power, and income.

Within the current neoliberal historical moment, ignorance rules America. Not the simple, if somewhat innocent ignorance that comes from an absence of knowledge, but a malicious ignorance forged in the arrogance of refusing to think hard about an issue. We most recently saw this exemplified in Donald Trump's disingenuousness 2019 State of the Union address in which he lied about the quantity of drugs streaming across the southern border, demonized the immigrant community with racist attacks, misrepresented the facts regarding the degree of violence at the border, and employed an antiwar rhetoric while he has repeatedly threatened war with Iran and Venezuela. Willful ignorance reached a new low when Trump, in the face of two years of malicious tweets aimed at his critics, spoke of the need for political unity.

Willful ignorance often hides behind the rhetoric of humiliation, lies, and intimidation. Trump's reliance upon threats to impose his will took a dangerous turn given his ignorance of the law when he used his speech to undermine the Special Council investigation into Russian interference in the 2016 election. He did so with his hypocritical comment, "and the only thing that can stop [the economic miracle] are foolish wars, politics, or ridiculous partisan investigations. If there is going to be peace and legislation, there cannot be war and investigation." According to Trump, the Democrats had a choice between reaching legislative deals or pursuing "ridiculous partisan investigations." Clearly the country could not do both. William Rivers Pitt is right in claiming that in one moment he tied "the ongoing Robert Mueller investigation inextricably to terrorism, war, and political dysfunction."[22] As Mike DeBonis and Seung Min Kim point out, House Speaker Nancy Pelosi, added to this criticism by "accusing Trump of an all-out threat to lawmakers sworn to provide a check and balance on his power."[23] It gets worse. In the aftermath of the Mueller investigation, the Trump administration has refused, in response to congressional subpoenas, to turn over the president's tax returns and an unredacted version of the Mueller report. In doing so, the administration has used the power of executive privilege to rebuke every attempt at congressional oversight. While the issue of whether the latter amounts to a constitutional crisis is up for debate, what is frightening is the willingness of Trump to hold onto power regardless of the cost. Frank Rich touches on this issue by referring to the possibility of Trump losing the 2020 election and what Trump might do in response. He writes:

> In any case, . . . the wholesale White House effort to bury the unre-
> dacted Mueller report, resist subpoenas, and shut down all testimony

by administration officials could drag on for months, if not years. But in a way this may be the least of the country's problems, as Trump stops at nothing to hold on to power. As Jerry Nadler and Nancy Pelosi have said, we are in "a constitutional crisis." But even constitutional crises are relative. The ultimate crisis may arrive, as Pelosi has been warning, when Trump, if defeated, attacks the legitimacy of the 2020 election. If his loss is narrow (and perhaps even if it isn't), the imagination reels at picturing what havoc he and his riled-up base, a third of the country, might sow to extend his rule.[24]

Trump revels in a culture of fear, threats of violence, and endless crises. This is all the more dangerous given how it is reinforced by a culture of manufactured illiteracy, fake news, and "alternative facts." Opinion divorced from evidence or even a paltry of facts now trumps reason and evidence-based arguments. News has become entertainment and echoes reality rather than interrogating it. Popular culture revels in the spectacles of shock and violence.[25] Defunded and corporatized, many institutions of higher education have been all too willing to make the culture of business the business of education, and the transformation has corrupted their mission. As a result, many colleges and universities have been McDonaldized as knowledge is increasingly viewed as a commodity resulting in curricula that resemble fast-food menus.[26] In addition, faculty are subjected increasingly to a Wal-Mart model of labor relations; students fare no better and are now relegated to the status of clients, if not commodities. Fear has become an organizing principle of American society and is important because it can be easily transformed into policies that put people behind walls.

On a larger scale, the educational force of the culture's disimagination machines have been transformed into a spectacle for violence, trivialized entertainment, and a tool for legitimating ignorance. As education becomes pivotal to politics itself, it removes democratic values and a compassion for the other from the ideology, policies, and institutions that now control American society. Other threats to higher education come from conservative think tanks, far-right groups, and right-wing pundits who are monitoring faculty syllabi, calling for universities to teach the Great Books model of humanities education, and urging legislators and college administrators to eliminate tenure and academic institutes that address major social issues such as poverty and voter registration. In some cases, alt-right and neo-Nazi groups are issuing death threats against faculty who speak out against racism and other volatile social issues.

EDUCATION AS A DEMOCRATIC PUBLIC GOOD

How might we imagine education as a dominant element of politics whose task is, in part, to create a new language for students, one that is crucial to reviving a radical imagination, a notion of social hope, and the courage to collectively struggle? How might higher education and other cultural institutions address the deep, unchecked nihilism and despair of the current moment? How might higher education be persuaded to not abandon democracy, and take seriously the need to create cognizant citizens capable of fighting what Walter Benjamin once called the "illumination" of fascism and its swindle of fulfillment? As Christopher Newfield argues, "democracy needs a public," and higher education has a crucial role to play in this regard as a democratic public good rather than defining itself through and primarily within the culture of business and the values of the financial elite.[27]

Current discourses about fascism often point to the assumptions that drive its politics in its present and diverse forms. What is not often mentioned is the formative culture that gives it meaning, creates the subjects who identify with its toxic worldview, and shapes the desires it mobilizes as part of a larger set of assumptions about the future and who shall inherit it. If we are to expand these important considerations, it is crucial to address how culture and education are intimately connected with social relations rooted in diverse class, racial, economic, and gender formations. To do so we must connect the domains of meaning and representation with the development and functioning of institutional forms of power, especially what might be called the rise of commanding cultural apparatuses that mark a distinctive form of public pedagogy in the current historical moment. Moreover, we need to rethink how culture is not only marked by different sites of struggle, but also how such struggles take place around and over language, values, and social relations within the institutions that organize them, extending from public and higher education to the mainstream media to the expansive world of digital culture.

In what follows, I want to look at the relationship between culture and power and its relationship to politics through a broader understanding of education as deeply rooted in a politics often divorced from any understanding of the wider neoliberal and formative pedagogical assumptions that drive it. I am particularly interested in fleshing out the role of understanding as a crucial element of any viable notion of education and its relationship to politics.

Marx was certainly right in arguing that the point is not to understand the world but to change it, but what he underemphasized was that the world could not be transformed if one does not understand what is to be changed. As Terry Eagleton rightly notes, "Nobody has ever changed a world they didn't understand."[28] Moreover, the lack of mass resistance to oppression signals more than apathy or indifference, it also suggests that we do not have an educated and energizing vision of the world for which we want to struggle.[29] Political struggle is dependent on the political will to change, which is central to any notion of a critical education, collective agency, and the willingness to address the radical and pragmatic issues of our time. In addition to understanding the world, students and learned public must connect what they know and learn to the central task of bringing their ideas to bear on society as a whole. This means that a critical consciousness must be matched by a fervent willingness to take risks, and challenge the destructive narratives that are seeping into public realm and becoming normalized. In this instance, higher education has a crucial role to play in combining the role of the educator as for both a scholar and engaged critical citizen. Any dissatisfaction with injustice necessitates that educators combine the demands of moral witnessing with the pedagogical power of persuasion and the call to address the tasks of emancipation. The institutions of higher education need to enable the pedagogical conditions for producing individuals and social movements willing to disturb the normalization of a fascist politics and other anti-democratic populist forces while willing to oppose various forms of racist, sexist, and neoliberal orthodoxy.

As Robin D. G. Kelley observes, we cannot confuse catharsis and momentary outrage for a radical restructuring of society.[30] In a time of increasing tyranny, resistance in many quarters appears to have lost its usefulness as a call to action. At the same time, the pedagogical force of civic ignorance and illiteracy has morphed into a national ideal. Tyranny and ignorance feed each other in a theater of corporate controlled media ecosystems and functions more as a tool of domination than as a pedagogical outlet in pursuit of justice and the practice of freedom. Under such circumstances, when education is not viewed as crucial to politics, resistance withers in the faux language of privatized struggles and fashionable slogans.[31]

For instance, the novelist Teju Cole has argued that "'resistance' is back in vogue, and it describes something rather different now. The holy word has become unexceptional. Faced with a vulgar, manic, and cruel regime, birds of many different feathers are eager to proclaim themselves members of the Resistance. It is the most popular game in town."[32] Cole's critique appears to be borne out by the fact that the most unscrupulous of liberal and conservative politicians such as Madeleine Albright, Hillary Clinton, and even James Clapper, the former director of national intelligence, are now claiming that they have joined the resistance against Trump's fascist politics. Even Michael Hayden, the former National Security Agency chief and CIA director under George W. Bush, has joined the ranks of Albright and Clinton in condemning Trump as a proto-fascist. Writing in the *New York Times*, Hayden, ironically, chastised Trump as a serial liar and in doing so quoted the renowned historian Timothy Snyder, who stated in reference to the Trump regime that "post-truth is pre-fascism."[33] The irony here is hard to miss. Not only did Hayden head Bush's illegal warrantless wiretapping program while the head of the NSA, he also lied repeatedly about his role in Bush's sanction and implementation of state torture in Afghanistan and Iraq.

This tsunami of banal resistance and its pedagogical architecture was on full display when an anonymous member of the Trump's inner circle published an op-ed in the *New York Times* claiming that he or she and other senior officials were part of "the resistance within the Trump administration."[34] The author was quick to qualify the statement by insisting such resistance had nothing to do with "the popular 'resistance' of the left." To prove the point, it was noted by the author that the members of this insider resistance liked some of Trump's policies such as "effective deregulation, historic tax reform, a more robust military and more."[35] Combining resistance with the endorsements of such reactionary policies reads like fodder for late-night comics. Education in the wider cultural and political sphere has been reduced to the logic of conformity parading as resistance. At the same time, the institutions of higher education in the age of Trump appear to offer little resistance to the ongoing dismantling of civic culture and democratic public spheres. In part, higher education has been corporatized, becoming an adjunct of the culture of business. Under such circumstances, education as a form of political intervention in the best civic and critical sense is undermined and poses a threat to faculty and students who attempt to embrace education as tool of liberation. Education is linked to the logic of efficiency and instrumentalized to become a depoliticizing force largely used to produce students who are incapable of holding power accountable.

RE-ENERGIZING COLLECTIVE AGENCY

If resistance to a growing authoritarianism in both the larger society and higher education is to make a difference for the better, it has to embrace civic courage, mount a defense of human dignity, and take on the challenge of not only bearing witness to the current injustices but struggle to overcome them. Of course, the issue is not to disavow resistance as much as to redefine it as inseparable from fundamental change that calls for the overthrow of capitalism itself. Neoliberalism has now adopted almost as a badge of honor the language of racial cleansing, white supremacy, white nationalism, and fascist politics. Unapologetic for the widespread horrors, gaping inequality, destruction of public goods, and a re-energizing of the discourse of hate and culture of cruelty, neoliberalism has joined hands with a toxic fascist politics painted in the hyper-patriotic colors of red, white, and blue. As I have noted elsewhere [also see conclusion]:

> Neoliberalism's hatred of democracy, the common good, and the social contract has unleashed generic elements of a fascist past in which white supremacy, ultra-nationalism, rabid misogyny and immigrant fervor come together in a toxic mix of militarism, state violence, and a politics of disposability. Modes of fascist expression adapt variously to different political historical contexts assuring racial apartheid-like forms in the post-bellum U.S. and overt encampments and extermination in Nazi Germany. Fascism with its unquestioning belief in obedience to a powerful strongman, violence as a form of political purification, hatred as an act of patriotism, racial and ethnic cleansing, and the superiority of a select ethnic or national group has resurfaced in the United States. In this mix of economic barbarism, political nihilism, racial purity, economic orthodoxy, and ethical somnambulation a distinctive economic-political formation has been produced that I term neoliberal fascism.[36]

While the call to resist neoliberal fascism is to be welcomed, it has to be interrogated rather than aligned with individuals and ideological forces that helped put in place the racist, economic, religious, and educational forces that helped produce it. What many liberals and conservative calls to resistance have in common is an opposition to Trump rather than to the conditions that created him. In some cases, liberal critics such as Christopher R. Browning, Yascha Mounk, and Cass R. Sunstein document insightfully America's descent into fascism but are too cautious in refusing to conclude that we are living under a fascist political regime.[37] They all share the notion that fascism cannot come to the United States because of the strength of liberal institutions such as the courts and the independent media. Unfortunately, these institutions can be subverted and used to reinforce rather than challenge authoritarian power relations. We have too many historical and contemporary examples of this type of surrender to fascist politics with the most recent being the colonizing of the judicial system by the right wing in Brazil.[38] This is more than a retreat from political courage, it is a refusal to name how liberalism itself with its slavish alignment with the financial elite has helped create the conditions that make a fascist politics possible.[39]

Trump's election, the Kavanaugh supreme court nomination affair, and his reckless and dangerous use of declared national emergency on the Mexico border to boost his nativist credentials make clear that what is needed is not only a resistance to the established order of neoliberal capitalism but a radical restructuring of society itself. That is not about resisting oppression in its diverse forms but overcoming it—in short, changing it.[40] The Kavanaugh hearings and the liberal response was a telling example of what might be called a politics of disconnection. At the same time, as progressive politicians such as Bernie Sanders and Representative Alexandria Ocasio-Cortez push for policies such as free higher education, a Green New Deal, and Medicare for all, the Wall Street wing of the Democratic Party along with liberals such as Thomas Friedman shriek in horror over connecting personal and political rights to economic rights. Any call to dismantle the death-dealing machinery of inequality turns liberals into arch defenders of the worst elements of neoliberalism along with a resuscitation of "Third Way" politics, all the while hiding behind the claim that they are the only party resisting Trump's ideology of letting neoliberal capitalism bury all but the rich.[41]

While it is crucial to condemn the Trump administration for its blatant disregard for the constitution, expressed hatred of women, and its symbolic expression and embrace of white privilege and power, it is necessary to enlarge such a criticism to include the political, social, economic, and educational system that made the Trump administration possible. Trump represents not only the deep-seated rot of misogyny but also, as Grace Lee Boggs has stated, "a government of, by, and for corporate power."[42] We need to look beyond the white nationalists and neo-Nazis demonstrating in the streets in order to recognize the terror of the unforeseen, the terror that is state sanctioned, and hides in the shadows of power, particularly the power of global elites and their new political formations. Such a struggle for educators and other cultural workers means more than analyzing and challenging material relations of power or the economic architecture of neoliberal fascism, it also means addressing and using the tools and tactics necessary to rethink and create the conditions for producing an up-to-date notion of individual and collective agency as the basis for a new kind of democratic socialist politics. Educators and other cultural workers need to develop a comprehensive politics and view of education that brings together various single-issue movements, so that the threads that connect them become equally as important as the particular forms of oppression that define their singularity. They need to make power visible and address how it works, help the oppressed understand the world in order to change it, and create discourses and modes of communication that speak to people in a way that is engaging, understandable, and energizing. Identity and agency are crucial sources of politics and must be addressed as important pedagogical issues regarding what it means to bring ideas to bear on society as a whole and to rethink the very nature of politics. In addition, there is a need for public intellectuals to combine intellectual complexity and theoretical rigorousness with accessibility, take matters of argument and persuasion seriously as part of a politics of identification, and cross disciplinary borders in order to theorize and speak with what Rob Nixon calls the "cunning of lightness" and a "methodological promiscuity" that keeps language attuned to pressing the claims for justice.[43]

Outside of those intellectuals who write for *CounterPunch, Truthout, Truthdig, Rise Up Times, Salon,* and a number of other critical media outlets, there are too few intellectuals, artists, journalists willing to challenge the rise of an American version of neoliberal fascism. It is not enough to report in an alleged "balanced fashion" on Trump's endorsement of violence against journalists, the massive levels of inequality produced under neoliberalism, the enactment by the Trump administration of savage policies of racial cleansing aimed at undocumented immigrants, and the emergence of a police state armed with terrifying new technologies aimed at predictive policing. The real challenge is to tie these elements of oppression together and to recognize how the threads of state violence, white supremacy, and fascist politics point to the emergence of a distinctive new political order, one that bodes badly for higher education.

Shock, outrage, and resistance in the midst of a fascist politics are undermined by the mainstream press which is always on the hunt for higher ratings and an increase in their bottom line. Rather than talk about fascism, they focus on the threat to or strength of liberal institutions. Rather than report on the mounting state violence and its relationship to the increased violence of neo-fascist thugs such as the Proud Boys, they talk about spectacularized acts of violence such as mass shootings. Rather than raise questions about the dangerous conditions at work in a society in which more and more people seem to prefer authoritarian rule over democracy, they talk about Trump's eccentric behavior or keep tabs on his endless lying. This is not helpful, and it misses the nature of the true threat to democracy, its genesis, and the power of a corporate elite who are now comfortable with the fascist politics that Trump embodies.

Trump is a master at understanding not only how language shapes the way individuals think, but also how to turn words into weapons. He also "has a strong instinct to repeat his most outrageous claims, and this allows him to put the press to work as a marketing agency for his ideas."[44] Trump drives the news cycles knowing full well that neoliberal capitalism is about the uninhibited and unchecked search for profits and that the mainstream media is all too willing to faithfully transmit his ideas and insidious ideology so as to reach the largest audience. That is why Trump's daily Twitter bombs drive the mainstream media. The mainstream media amplifies Trump's lies and in doing so they become complicit with legitimating his falsehoods, his weaponization of language in the service of violence, and his demonization of critics and entire cultures. In addition, the press reproduces a news cycle filled with a steady stream of shlock that makes profits for the owners of big capital.

An iPsos poll found that "a surprising 26 percent of all Americans, and 43 percent of Republicans, agree with the statement that the president "should have the authority to close news outlets engaged in bad behavior."[45] In addition, a majority of Americans across the ideological spectrum—72 percent—think "it should be easier to sue reporters who knowingly publish false information."[46] Couple this with the fact that Trump has recently stated privately to his aids that he regrets reversing his policy of separating children from their parents at the border and you have a mix of fascist principles coupled with a dangerous demagogue who cannot bring the country fast enough to the fascist abyss.[47] While it is true that the United States under Trump is not Hitler's Germany, Trump has tapped into America's worst impulses and, as Jason Stanley and others remind us, his ultra-nationalism, white supremacist views, and racist diatribes, coupled with his attack on immigrants, the media, African Americans, and Muslims, are indicative of a politics right out the fascist playbook.[48] If the public and media keep denying this reality, the endpoint is too horrible to imagine. If we are to understand the current resurgence of right-wing populist movements across the globe, economic factors alone do not account for the current mobilizations of fascist passions.

Reiterating a central theme of this book, it is crucial to recognize as Pierre Bourdieu once put it, "the most important forms of domination are not only economic but also intellectual and pedagogical, and lie on the side of belief and persuasion."[49] He goes on to state that educators and left intellectuals have underestimated the symbolic and pedagogical dimensions of struggle and have not always forged appropriate weapons to fight on this front."[50] In part, this means that educators and others must make matters of culture and pedagogy an organizing principle of politics in order to address people's needs and struggles. And they should do so in a language that is both rigorous and accessible. Matters of culture and consciousness in the Gramscian sense are central to the meaning of politics and only when the left can address that issue will there be any hope for massive collective resistance in the form of a broad-based movement.

Many of the great peace activists of the twentieth century extending from Mahatma Gandhi and Paulo Freire to Jane Addams and Martin Luther King Jr. shared a passion for education not as a methodology but as a democratic project. They emphasized producing individuals who believed in education as both a public good and a practice of freedom for inspiring and energizing people to assume a degree of civic courage, social responsibility, and critical agency. Refusing to view education as neutral or reducing it to the instrumental practice of training, they sought to reclaim education as part of a wider struggle to deepen and extend the values, social relations, and institutions of a substantive democracy.

They argued passionately that in the merging of politics and education there was a moment of truth in which education could not be removed from the demand for justice and progressive social change. Education for these pillars of moral courage and intellectual vitality meant that universities stood as center of human critique, addressed society's most pressing problems, viewed pedagogy a moral and political practice, and education as matter of "social responsibility, not as a matter of profit."[51] They understood that tyranny and authoritarianism are not just the product of state violence and repression, but also thrive on popular docility, mass apathy, and a flight from moral responsibility. Each wrote during times of momentous political revolutions when democracy was under siege. In doing so, they recognized and made real a moment of truth about education and its ability to transform how people understand themselves, their relations to others, and the larger world. In the face of massive injustice and indignity, these prophetic voices refused to look away from human suffering, and embraced the possibility for resistance fueled by courage, compassion, and the ability to think otherwise in order to act otherwise.

One of Martin Luther King's great insights lies in his recognition that education provided a bulwark against both ignorance and indifference in the face of injustice. Like Gandhi, he warned people over and over again not to remain silent in the face of racism, militarism, and extreme materialism and argued that "He who accepts evil without protesting against it is really cooperating with it." Of the civil rights era, King warned that "History will have to record that the greatest tragedy of this period of social transition was not the strident clamor of the bad people, but the appalling silence of the good people. . . . In the end, we will remember not the words of our enemies, but the silence of our friends." These advocates of civic courage and compassion echoed in their words and actions what King called the "fierce urgency of now," reminding us that "tomorrow is today" and that "there is such a thing as being too late." Gandhi also spoke to this issue when he stated that "The future depends on what we do in the present." Let us hope that in the midst of our witness to the current revolt against democracy across the globe, higher education will neither remain silent nor be too late.

We live in an age when the horrors of the past are providing the language and politics of illiberal democracies all over the globe. This is a world where dystopian versions of a catastrophic, misery producing neoliberalism merge with unapologetic death-dealing visions of a fascist politics. We live in an era that testifies to the horrors of a past struggling to reinvent itself in the present, and which should place more than a sense of ethical and political responsibility on those of us bearing witness to it. As my friend Brad Evans notes, under such circumstances, we live in a time "that asks us all to continually question our own shameful compromises with power," and to act with others to overcome our differences in order to dismantle this assault on human rights, human dignity, economic justice, equality, and democracy itself.[52] If higher education is to take up the fight against fascism it will have to rethink the meaning of education as a practice of freedom enabled through pedagogical practices that produce hard thinking, embodied compassion, and a commitment to a life that is publicly and politically engaged. At the same time, it will have to create spaces that produce an intellectual wakefulness, a critical attentiveness to how power works in the service of inequality and injustice, and a commitment to a view of education that in part defines itself as part of an ongoing struggle against authoritarianism in all of its forms.

One of the challenges facing the current generation of educators, students, and others is the need to address the question of what education should accomplish in a society at a historical moment when it is slipping into the dark night of authoritarianism. What work do educators have to do to create the economic, political, and ethical conditions necessary to endow young people and the general public with the capacities to think, question, doubt, imagine the unimaginable, and defend education as essential for inspiring and energizing the citizens necessary for the existence of a robust democracy? What kind of language is necessary for higher education to redefine its mission, one that enables faculty and students to work toward a different future than one that echoes the present, to confront the unspeakable, to recognize themselves as agents, not victims, and to muster up the courage to act in the service of a substantive and inclusive democracy? In a world in which there is an increasing abandonment of egalitarian and democratic impulses, what will it take to educate young people and the broader polity to challenge authority and hold power accountable?[53]

CHAPTER SEVEN

Higher Education, Neoliberalism, and the Politics of Disposability

INTRODUCTION

The question of what the role of higher education is in a time of tyranny has to be situated within the current historical moment when neoliberal fascism is on the march and has produced a wide-ranging shift in the economy, ideology, power, culture, and politics. Ways of imagining society through the lens of democratic ideals, values, and social relations have given way to narratives that substitute cruelty for compassion, greed for generosity, and nativism for social bonds rooted in human rights. In an age in which authoritarianism is emerging across the globe, the language of disposability and cultural and biological pollution have become the new mantra not just for an assault on human rights but also as a warning and unapologetic forecast of the horrors of state power and its turn to a politics of social and racial cleansing. In the current era, education, reason, and informed judgment and their relationship to democracy face a number of growing challenges. One such challenge is obvious in that the formative cultures necessary to ensure the production of knowledgeable and critical citizens necessary for a democracy are collapsing under the weight of the powers of the financial elite and big corporations. We live at a time when fascism is on the table and has become a driving, if not commanding, force in American politics.

The utopian visions that support the promise of a radical democracy and prevent the dystopian nightmare of a fascist politics are disappearing in the United States, Brazil, Hungary, and a number of other countries.[1] The viciousness of the Trump administration and the cruelty imposed by neoliberalism now mutually inform each other. Trump's policies range from stripping food stamps and health care from poor children to caging immigrant children in some god-forsaken prison in Texas and allowing thousands of Puerto Ricans to live for more than a year without electricity, safe water, and decent shelter. Such policies are matched by an ongoing, if not relentless, discourse of dehumanization and objectification aimed at those considered vulnerable and disposable. Notions of the public good are held in disdain matched only by laws and policies that defund public schools, higher education, and other social services in a maelstrom of privatization, deregulation, and corruption. Across the globe, torturers, military dictators, white supremacists, and other political monsters have upended any notion of democracy in the popular imagination.

The deep grammar of violence now shapes all aspects of cultural production and becomes visceral in its ongoing production of domestic terrorism, mass shootings, the mass incarceration of people of color, and the war on undocumented immigrants. Not only has it become more gratuitous, random, and in some cases trivialized through the monotony of repetition, it also has become the official doctrine of the Trump administration in shaping its domestic and security policies. Trump's violence has become both promiscuous in its reach and emboldening in its nod to right wing extremist groups. The mix of white nationalism and expansion of policies that benefit the rich, big corporations, and the financial elite are increasingly legitimated and normalized in a new political formation that I call throughout this book *neoliberal fascism*.[2] This new historical conjuncture emerges through a fusion of discredited eugenicist discourses (e.g., Trump's notion you have to be born with the right genes)[3] and a rebooted melange of mythic notions of meritocracy (objective measures of individual quality), scientific racism (pseudoscience that supports racial hierarchies), Horatio Alger fables (anyone can work hard and become rich and successful), and a sheer contempt for the "losers" who are viewed as alien to a white public sphere supported by Trump and his minions.[4]

The dual logics of disposability and pollution have become central to a punishing state that both legitimates the denigration of human life and too often unleashes state violence upon immigrants, people of color, poor people, and anyone else considered a threat to the belief that the public sphere is exclusively for whites. Under the Trump administration, the discourses of disposability and pollution are increasingly visible when applied to undocumented immigrants or those marginalized by ethnicity and race—whom those in power place in the same categories as contaminants and toxins. Those individuals considered disposable often meet a more violent end. This is visible in the current criminalization of immigrant children on the southern border who are forcibly separated from their parents and deposited in child migrant detention centers largely run by for-profit businesses that are making close to a billion dollars in profits.[5] Some children have died while in these internment centers and many of them suffer from a range of abuses, including allegations of sexual abuse.[6] The logic of disposability also fuels, throughout the United States, the modeling of public schools after armed camps, and the targeting of poor Black and Brown youth as objects of control and harassment by the criminal justice system, particularly through the expansion of the school-to-prison pipeline.[7]

Obsessed with race, Donald Trump has weaponized and racialized the culture wars by using racially charged language to legitimate white supremacist ideologies and pit his supporters against protesting Black athletes, undocumented Latinx immigrants, dark-skinned immigrants, and other people of color whom he routinely insults and punishes through race-based policies. Trump has claimed that "laziness is a trait in Blacks," and called for "a total and complete shutdown of Muslims entering the United States." Meanwhile he stated in December 2015 that a "judge hearing a case about Trump University was biased because of the judge's Mexican heritage." Moreover, he frequently criticizes African Americans for being unpatriotic, ungrateful, and disrespectful. These comments are a small sampling of Trump's racist remarks.[8]

Racism runs deep not only in Trump's base but also in a Republican Party that, as Paul Krugman points out, engages in extreme gerrymandering, voter suppression, voter purges, "deliberating restriction of minority access to the polls," and the ongoing subversion of state legislatures.[9] This is the party that gave us "Strom Thurmond, George

H. W. Bush's Willie Horton campaign, and Ronald Reagan's 1980 campaign speech in favor of 'states rights' in a Mississippi town adjacent to the site where three civil-rights workers had been murdered in 1964."[10] In the era of Trump, Frank Rich goes further and argues, "The Republican Party has proudly and uninhibitedly come out of the closet as the standard-bearer for white supremacy in the Trump era."[11] George Packer adds to this signaling the emerging fascist politics that now engulfs the Republican Party. He argues that simply smug ideological fundamentalists and political purists such as Barry Goldwater, Phyllis Schlafly, Ronald Reagan, and Newt Gingrich no longer define the Republican Party. He writes:

> It is now a party that has chosen power over democracy and in doing so has become "meaner and madder and crazier" . . . , more grotesque than ever: paranoia and conspiracy thinking; racism and other types of hostility toward entire groups; innuendos and incidents of violence. The new leader is like his authoritarian counterparts abroad: illiberal, demagogic, hostile to institutional checks, demanding and receiving complete acquiescence from the party, and enmeshed in the financial corruption that is integral to the political corruption of these regimes.[12]

What we are witnessing at the current moment is not only the emergence of dangerous illiberal, anti-democratic ideologies that mimic the legacy of white nationalism but also the resurgence of a powerful affective and educational culture nurtured by false promises, anger, feelings of repulsion, hatred, and the spectacularization of violence. What is alarming about this culture of intolerance, bigotry, and violence is its alignment with the Nazi obsession with notions of cultural and biological pollution and their systemic efforts to purge society of those deemed contaminated. This language is not unlike Trump's characterization of asylum seekers as vermin, who will bring "large-scale crime and disease" to the United States.[13]

UNMASKING LANGUAGE OF DISPOSABILITY

Rather than being a historical relic of a horrible past, the language of pollution and disposability has remerged under the Trump administration to an unusual extent. This is a language rooted in what Thomas Mann once called "the archaic shudder," one that opens the door to the rhetoric of racial purity, social cleansing, and the glorification of violence.[14] This merging of white nationalism and policies aimed at racial cleansing are buttressed by the cruel architecture of neoliberalism, which creates landscapes of unabashed misery, violence, and terror. Neoliberalism offers little hope for economic and social justice while claiming ironically that it is not only a moral beacon and force for the good but also perniciously that there is no realistic alternative to it.

This toxic ideology is further solidified in the assumption that the connective social bonds that make a democracy possible should be viewed with disdain and replaced with a notion of individualism in which all problems and the means to address them be placed solely at the feet of individuals.[15] Under such circumstances, fear and economic anxiety produced by massive inequality, the dismantling of the welfare state, precarious employment, eroding white privilege, demographic changes, and the collapse of the social contract are redirected to those human beings considered "losers," "outsiders," and "excess."

The merging of neoliberalism and elements of a fascist playbook are now anchored firmly in the language of disposability and pollution. This rhetoric is part of a representational crisis marked by the increasing attraction of and growth of architectures of meaning and proliferating digital platforms and cultural apparatuses engaged in the production of modes of desire, identifications, and values that fuel a right wing or apocalyptic populism. The current historical conjuncture is marked by a new era of politics and way of thinking about place, community, rootlessness, and identity. The once dominant narratives about critical agency, truth, justice, and democracy are collapsing. Fascist terror is no longer fixed in the past or ephemeral to the twenty-first century. Under the Trump administration, malice, lies, and unrelenting cruelty have become official policy and fraught with dangerous risks. Fascist politics avoids reason, maligns the truth, and appeals to a pathological nationalism. In doing so it creates a mythic past that either denigrates or excludes those considered at odds with its notions of white supremacy and racial purity. What emerges is a celebration of the brutality of the 1930s, which becomes a signpost for imagining a present under what Trump nostalgically codes in the slogans "America First" and "Make America Great Again." Culture now becomes integral to a politics deeply rooted in an antidemocratic ethos.

Under neoliberalism, a new political formation has developed in which a racialist worldview merges with the economic dictates of a poisonous form of casino capitalism. Echoes of the past can be heard in Trump's and his associates' repeated use of a language boiling over with terms such as "vermin," "animals," "stupid," and "losers," to name only a few of the toxic expressions crucial to a politics of social cleansing, racial purity, and violent forms of exclusion. The current language of disposability and pollution carries powerful affective overtones that "transform the noble concept of a common humanity into a disdainful sneer," if not worse.[16]

The language of pollution is used to treat some groups as not simply inferior but also as a threat to the body politic, and is closely aligned with the language of camps and extermination. More than an ostentatious display of power on the part of the Trump administration, the language of pollution and disposability functions as a performative language designed to dramatize and reenact national identity, one that defines itself in white nationalist assumptions. Assigned to the dumping ground of social and political abandonment, those individuals or families considered noxious and superfluous are now associated with a rootlessness that bears a close resemblance to the Nazi notion of blood and soil. Looking back at the Nazi era, the dangers of the language of disposability and pollution become terrifying given how they were deployed in the interest of unimaginable horrors. Professor Richard A. Etlin provides a glimpse of the logic and effects of the discourse of pollution and its morphing into policies of disposability and eradication. He writes:

> From propaganda posters to problems in mathematics textbooks for schoolchildren, Germans were repeatedly asked, once the Nazis had come to power, to ponder the economic costs of maintaining the lives of the handicapped and mentally ill. Forced sterilization of people considered "hereditarily ill" had been decreed in July 1933; compulsory abortions, in 1935. The legalized secret killing of deformed and [mentally impaired] children began in 1939, as did plans for the murder of Germany's adult mental patients, both programs "planned and administered by medical professionals" involving "some of Germany's oldest and most highly respected hospitals." The utilitarian calculation of the cost of sustaining life for these so-called unproductive members of German society does not account for the full reasoning behind such measures. Rather, one must look to an altered moral outlook best represented by the notion of the "Vernichtung lebensunwerten Lebens," that is, the "destruction" or "extermination," of "lives not worth living."[17]

The politics of disposability is no longer a discourse limited to the historical memory of totalitarian governments, internment camps, and extermination policies. As both a state-legitimated ideology and established policy, it now exists at the highest levels of the US government and is central to the creation of a death-saturated age. Fantasies of absolute control, racial cleansing, unchecked militarism, and class warfare are at the heart of an American imagination that has turned lethal. This dystopian mindset is marked by hollow words and lethal actions; similarly, its dreamscape is pillaged of any substantive meaning, cleansed of compassion, and used to legitimate the notion that alternative worlds are impossible to entertain.

In this worldview, the present creates nightmares parading as dreams in which the future is imagined "by way of a detour through a mythic past."[18] There is more at stake here than shrinking political horizons and the aligning of the existing moment with echoes of a fascist past.[19] What we are witnessing is a mode of governing fueled by fantasies of exclusion accompanied by a full-scale attack on morality, thoughtful reasoning, and collective resistance rooted in democratic forms of struggles. We are also witnessing an unprecedented assault on the mainstream media and the fundamental necessity in a democracy for independent, critical journalism.

Trump's threat to use "libel laws," his labeling critical news outlets as "fake news," and his notion of the media as the "enemy of the American people"—a term linked to authoritarian regimes—are key warning signs of a fascist politics.[20] He has normalized the unthinkable, legitimated the inexcusable, and defended the indefensible. Pollution in its biological, ecological, and material forms has become the centerpiece of Trump's endorsement of a fascist politics that is at the heart of a growing right-wing populism across the globe and is bolstered by his support.

Trump has also expanded the discourse of pollution and disposability to enact a full-fledged attack on the environment.[21] As the editorial board of the *New York Times* put it, "Trump imperils the planet" with his corporate-friendly, retrograde policies.[22] Not only has he appointed cabinet members who harbor a deep disdain for environmental regulations to head the Environmental Protection Agency (EPA), the Department of the Interior, and other agencies whose purpose is to serve the public good, but he has also enacted policies utterly destructive to the environment and human life. For example, the Trump administration is lifting federal protections for thousands of waterways and wetlands, compromising the safety of water for millions of Americans. The Department of the Interior will allow oil drilling on millions of previously protected acres including the establishment of oil and gas production wells in federally controlled waters of the US Artic. The EPA will lift restrictions on carbon emissions from new coal plants and has proposed weakening greenhouse gas emissions and fuel standards for light-duty vehicles.[23] The Trump administration has weakened the Endangered Species Act and the Bureau of Safety and Environmental Enforcement as part of its "energy dominancy" agenda, to eliminate safety rules for offshore oil and natural gas drilling platforms.[24] Responding to a government report that predicted dire consequences to the United States from climate change, Trump stated, "I don't believe it."[25]

Trump's astonishingly irrational response is not simply about his own ignorance regarding scientific studies or the validity of science itself, it is primarily about pandering to the major corporations who make big profits in plundering the environment. Trump is simply echoing the inhumane and ethically irresponsible ethos and pragmatism at the heart of a sordid capitalism that thrives on economic shock doctrines. He, along with many in the established political parties, refuse to acknowledge that the emerging disasters overtaking the planet call into question the very foundations of a predatory global capitalism, which divorces economic activity from social costs, and embraces a death-dealing notion of progress at any price.[26]

Wealth extraction, exploitative low wages and employment contingency, manufactured inequality, brutal forms of labor discipline, and engineered suffering are the defining characteristics of the neoliberal capitalism now driving Trump's policies. Ted Steinberg is right in arguing, "Flirtation with disaster is in a sense the essence of neoliberal capitalism, a hyperactive form of [an] exploitative economic order that seems to know no limits."[27] It is important to note that Trump's environmental rollbacks do more than increase the profits of plundering corporations; they also endanger the lives of millions. For instance, a Harvard University study by professors David Cutler and Francesca Dominici calculated that repealing the Clean Power Plan Rule would "lead to an estimated 36,000 deaths each decade and nearly 630,000 cases of respiratory infection in children alone."[28] Moreover, the authors estimate that the repeal of emission requirements for heavy trucks alone "could lead to as many as 41,000 premature deaths per decade and 900,000 cases of respiratory tract symptoms."[29] They conclude with this sobering warning:

> Overall, an extremely conservative estimate is that the Trump environ-mental agenda is likely to cost the lives of over eighty thousand U.S. residents per decade and lead to respiratory problems for many more than one million people. This sobering statistic captures only a small fraction of the cumulative public health damages associated with the full range of rollbacks and systemic actions proposed by the Trump administration.[30]

BEYOND A POLITICS OF OBJECTIFICATION

We live in an age in which the welfare of children is no longer a measure of the degree to which public and higher education, if not society itself, lives up to its democratic ideals. In an age of growing fascism, those in power no longer view children as the promise of a future but as a threat to the present. In particular, poor Black and Brown children are being treated as what Teju Cole calls "unmournable bodies."[31] Rather than being educated, many are being imprisoned; rather than living in communities that are safe and clean, many are relegated to cities where the water is poisoned and the police function as an occupying army. In the age of Trump, children of undocumented workers are stripped of their humanity, caged in internment camps, sometimes sexually abused, and subjected to the unethical grammars of state violence. Sometimes they lose their lives, as did two children from Guatemala who died while in custody of Customs and Border Protection: seven-year-old Jakelin Caal and eight-year-old Felipe Gomez. In this way the dual logic of disposability and pollution becomes the driving force of a machinery of social death.

Undocumented children occupy a ruthless space of social and po-litical abandonment beyond the reach of human rights. This is a zone in which moral numbness becomes a central feature of politics, power, and governance. How else to explain Republican congressman Peter King re-sponding to the deaths of these two children by praising ICE's "excellent record," stating that since there are "only two children that have died," the death count is a testament to how competent organizations like ICE actually are.[32] This is a fascist discourse marked by the rhetorical tropes of hate, demonization, and violence.

As a form of domestic terrorism—defined as terrorist violence perpetrated by American citizens against its own people—the state produces and legitimates in both its policies and its alignment with corporate controlled media forms of material and symbolic violence in which people are rendered less than human, treated as excess, and subjected to zones of social abandonment and terminal exclusion. Such terrorism is at the heart of the Trump administration and is evident in its anti-immigration policies, its militarization of the southern border, its expansion of the surveillance state, and its war on Muslims. It is also evident in its defense of mounting police violence against Black youth, its revocation of DACA, its attack on workers' rights and safety protections, its creation of internment camps near the US–Mexico border, its scorn for reproductive rights, and its elevation of the police state as a central force for organizing society to name only a few examples.

Disposable populations now labor under what Richard Sennett has called the "spectre of uselessness" and are catapulted out of the moral universe central to any notion of humanity. Such populations have their children forcibly taken away from them by immigration officials, are chased out of their homes, forced into exile, pushed into homelessness and poverty, excluded from the rights that grant them full-fledged citizenship. Too many of the poor and other vulnerable populations are frequently left to fend for themselves in the face of often devastating political and social costs caused by the financial elite and exploitative corporations such as the pharmaceutical companies partly responsible for the opioid crisis in the United States. These vulnerable populations are also removed from their material goods, crucial social provisions, and lack control over their bodies. Such populations under the reign of neoliberalism are viewed with scorn, disdain, and have a social death forced upon them in lieu of a real death.

Disposability, pollution, and dispossession have another lethal register in that they attempt, through a range of cultural, social, and pedagogical apparatuses, to make people unknown to themselves as potentially critical and engaged citizens. As public spheres increasingly become sites where politics thrive on the energies of a racially coded fascist politics, critical modes of subjectivity and identification are under siege. That is, new powerful cultural pathways work to choke democratic values, modes of agency, and social relations normally rooted in the virtues of social and economic justice, compassion for others, and also the public goods and institutions that make such values and relationships possible. Critical thinking, civic courage, and collective resistance are diverted into the private orbit of therapy, the isolated space of emotional management, the atomizing logic of willful self-change, and a landscape of fractured identities.

This assault on democratic modes of agency and values is particularly aggressive and widespread under a political formation that merges neoliberal ideology and the structures of white supremacy. One consequence is that the public sphere now becomes a phantom empty space, a barren presence that further underscores neoliberalism's celebrated ethos of unbridled privatization. Neoliberal fascist politics is strengthened through the domestic machineries of inscription that extend from schools and the social media to the world of celebrity culture and corporate-controlled sports events. The corporate dominated circuits of culture depoliticize people by defining them as both consumers and as isolated individuals for whom all the problems they face are both self-induced and only subject to change through the register of individual freedom rather than collective responsibility.

This narrative of individual freedom and responsibility is constructed through the false notion of unlimited choices delusionally detached from any realistic material constraints. As such, this fictional idea of individual freedom is both overburdening and politically debilitating given its refusal to provide a language for individuals to be able to translate private problems into broader social and systemic considerations.[33]

It is in the midst of a culture steeped in a growing plague of social atomization, loneliness, and a race-based right-wing populist nationalism that the false dreamscape of a fascist politics gains ascendency. This false dreamscape provides individuals with a misleading sense of community, simple answers to complex problems, and mobilizes elements of legitimate anger against the ruins created by a neoliberal global economy into modes of identification that feed on resentment, the longing for a strong man, and totalitarian impulses. In this instance, agency becomes unmoored from democratic communal relations and disconnected from a legitimate critique of existing power relations. Immiserization on both the material and psychic levels along with a state sanctioned culture of fearmongering and bigotry are producing political and pedagogical landscapes that mobilize the highly charged emotive appeals of a fascist politics. This is a politics, as the writer Ian Hughes points out, that is embraced by tyrants who function as entrepreneurs of hate. He writes:

> For each of these tyrants, their first goal was to exacerbate the feelings of separateness and otherness felt towards their chosen target out-group, whether they were Jews, *kulaks*, "capitalist railroaders" or other "enemies of the people." Their second goal was to inflame feelings of anger and fear towards that out-group. And their third goal was to spread stories that explained, in false and simple terms, why that outgroup was a deserving target of people's hate. These stories varied widely but they had certain elements in common: "the enemy is repulsive in looks and habits"; "the enemy is contaminated and is spreading disease;" "the enemy is part of a conspiracy seeking to control us"; "the enemy is a criminal"; "the enemy is a seducer and a rapist"; "the enemy is an animal, an insect or a germ"; "the enemy is the enemy of God"; "the enemy is a murderer who delights in killing"; "the enemy is standing in the way of our making our country great again."[34]

This tale of turning a "fabricated enemy" into an object has a long heritage in both the horrors of genocide against Native Americans, the reign of terror and disposability during the period of American slavery, and the apartheid system of incarceration that repudiates the claim that the reign of white supremacy and fascist politics is safely interred in the past.

Trump's relentless racism and xenophobia are also monumentally evident in his call for funding a border wall and his ongoing threat of a partial shutdown of the US government as a bargaining chip to have Congress meet his racist demands. Trump has not only attempted to justify the wall by demonizing undocumented immigrants, he has criminalized an entire culture of women, men, and children most of whom are seeking asylum in the United States. His defense for building the wall rests on a series of fabrications. According to Trump, the US faces an "invasion" of illegal immigrants who largely consist of criminals, gangs, human traffickers, drug smugglers, and other alleged dangerous individuals. As Bill Blum observes:

> In truth, in terms of illegal immigration and drug smuggling, there is no crisis along the U.S.-Mexico frontier. Undocumented immigra-

tion has dropped to the lowest levels in decades, and the vast majority of drug contraband—heroin, methamphetamine, cocaine and fentanyl—crosses into the U.S. at ports of entry rather than through unfenced areas of the border.[35]

The real crisis is not at the border but at home. Trump's self-serving fictional political crisis has created a major crisis at home for thousands of children whose families were held hostage to his 2019 partial government shutdown. While the press often cited that eight hundred thousand people would not be paid as a result of the shutdown, the reality is that these workers have spouses, children, and other members of their families who faced a severe financial crisis and as a result endured a great deal of misery and suffering. The shutdown was an attack first and foremost on human rights, justice, and democracy and is part of larger war on people of color, children, and others who are deemed throwaways. The border wall began as a throwaway crowd pleaser for Trump; it is now a symbol of the disposability, pollution, and exclusion that is at the core of a neoliberal fascist politics.

This discourse of disposability is designed not only to segregate and exclude, but also to create a culture divided between winners and losers, friends and enemies. In doing so, it has produced a social order in which all that is left is fear, uncertainty, and anxiety for those who are the victims of state terrorism. In addition, it reinforces a self-serving notion of anxiety and hatred on the part of those whites who falsely imagine themselves as victims menaced by the increasing presence of those whom they falsely deem threatening contaminants by virtue of their race, class, religion, gender, and ethnicity. This language of objectification operates in the service of a toxic politics that, as Hannah Arendt puts it, "guide[s] the behavior of its subjects [as] a preparation to fit each of them equally well for the role of executioner and the role of victim."[36]

Repeated endlessly by the Trump administration and the political parties of the post-1980s era, the logic of objectifying the precariat by means of notions such as that of disposability became a tool of violence used against the marginalized other and a rhetorical weapon used by those whose racial, class, and gender privilege were viewed as at risk of losing power. Disposability as weapon of objectification and social exclusion has not only been used to undermine the bodies, capacities, and modes of identification crucial to creating engaged, well-versed, critical citizens, it has also become normalized as a story of victimhood. As the false promises of neoliberal capitalism become clear failures, the fear of powerlessness fuels a sense of victimization among many poor and middle-class whites who feel displaced in a demographically changing world. Written out of the discourse of social and economic mobility and security, the vulnerable accept with blind faith the dominant culture's seductive and venomous affirmation of hatred, white supremacy, and white nationalism.

In this instance, the rhetoric of objectification by way of pollution and disposability has a doubling function in that it both creates real victims while reinforcing the false assumption on the part of right-wing populists that those considered other "pollute" the United States and pose a threat to white Americans. Here, the rhetoric of pollution names those considered a threat to an alleged white public sphere and feeds the fantasies of an apocalyptic nationalism. If Trump has proven adept at one thing, it is stoking the fears of those white Americans who comfortably inhabit mythic tales of race-based conspiracy theories of victimhood. The relentlessly asinine Fox News host Tucker Carlson echoed these sentiments when he claimed that immigration makes the US "poorer and dirtier."[37] Many liberal commentators were quick to condemn Tucker's racist rhetoric, but they did acknowledge it as a tactic to further legitimate the fear and anger that often erupts in violence against those considered disposable.

FASCIST NEOLIBERALISM THRIVES ON DEPOLITICIZATION

The footprints of a fascist politics are now found not only in the registers of racial purity, the chants of blood and soil, and a culture of cruelty, but also in the neoliberal stress on unchecked individualism, the collapse of social obligations, the uprooting of civic culture, and the effects of social atomization, all of which work to depoliticize and render agency susceptible to modes of agency that embrace shared fears and hatreds rather than shared values and social obligations. Exclusion is no longer simply an economic issue that reinforces class divisions between workers and capitalists. On the contrary, it is more capacious under neoliberal fascism and is about not allowing more and more people the right to both enter the United States and participate in public life. The latter issue is most evident in Trump's claim that "he intends to issue an executive order that would end birthright citizenship for children born in the United States to undocumented immigrants."[38] Trump's disregard for the constitutionality of birthright citizenship says as much about his racism as it does about his repeated disregard for the law.

In the current historical moment, agency is being emptied of its democratic possibilities in a neoliberal order in which identities and desires are defined through a market logic that enshrines consumerism, unending competition, unbridled individualism, a survival-of-the-fittest ethos, and the celebration of unbridled self-interest. All of these forces are a breeding ground for unleashing a hatred for the common good, the social contract, and democracy itself. Within this new social and political formation, the people-objectifying discourses of disposability and pollution are aligned with the resonant discourse of bigotry, nativism, and misogyny and configured as part of a condition for the production of accommodating and unquestioning modes of identification and self-hood. In this instance, isolation and loneliness, as Hannah Arendt once argued, become crucial to the production of tyranny and are grounded in perpetuating the conditions for powerlessness and the inability of individuals to act as critical and educated participants in shaping the forces that bear down on their lives.[39] Of course, there is more at work here than an existential crisis of agency and the depoliticizing experience of loneliness that strengthens the appeal of a fascist politics to the masses, there is also the fear of and suppression of resistance on the part of the financial and corporate elites.[40]

Neoliberal ideology becomes a justification for lawlessness when responsibility is shifted to the most vulnerable individuals, with women being disproportionally burdened as they are also marginalized by class and race. Even though the problems faced by the dispossessed are not of their own making, the poisoned discourse of neoliberalism insists that their fate is a product of personal issues ranging from weak character, bad choices, or simply a moral deficiency. Isolation breeds political impotence, fear, and intimidation, which work to instill toxic convictions and also "to destroy the capacity to form any."[41] In this discourse, everyone is defined as an island and all connective forms of economic and social justice vanish from the public imagination giving a free reign to the forces of lawlessness, brutality, cruelty, and misery.

As misfortune is emptied of any broader political, economic, and social content, it is indeed depoliticized and viewed as a weakness, hence making it all the easier for the punishing state to criminalize social problems. As the late Frankfurt School theorist Leo Lowenthal once noted, terror functions as a form of dehumanization and "fate itself becomes so enigmatic as to lose all meaning. . . . The creative faculties of fantasy, imagination, memory become meaningless and tend to atrophy where they can no longer bring about any desired change in the individual's fate."[42] One consequence is that those individuals who are relatively powerless to address broader social issues are forced to partake in a system that encourages them to embrace their own oppression as though it were a normal part of their everyday existence.

Operating under the false assumption that there are only individual solutions to socially produced problems, the atomization of the individual thus becomes normalized rendering human beings numb and fearful, immune to the demands of economic and social justice, increasingly divorced from matters of politics, ethics, and social responsibility. This amounts to a form of domestic terrorism, evident as individuals descend into a moral stupor, susceptible to political shocks, and seduced by the pleasure of the manufactured spectacle. In this instance not only does the political become relentlessly personal, it also reinforces the ongoing process of depoliticization. In this case, agency is reduced to a dystopian narrative limited to how to survive, dumbs down the notion of autonomy to acts of consumption, allowing any aspirations that regain some sense sovereignty to be hijacked by right-wing parties and populist movements.

Against the erosion of democratic ideals of equality and popular sovereignty, right wing populists produce narratives in which democracy is removed from the discourse of equality and is wedded "to nationalistic authoritarian forms of neoliberalism that, in the name of recovering democracy, in fact drastically restrict it."[43] Underlying this regressive notion of populism are pedagogical practices in which the desire on the part of people to gain control over their lives "has been captured by right-wing populist parties that have managed to construct the people through a xenophobic discourse that excludes immigrants, considered as a threat to national prosperity."[44]

Within this new fascist neoliberal populist political formation, language functions to repress any sense of moral decency, connection to others, and as a result personal communication rooted in democratic values loses all meaning. Individuals are pressured increasingly to act exclusively in their own self-interest, and in doing so are reduced to "ruthless seekers after their own survival, psychological pawns and puppets of a system that knows no other purpose than to keep itself in power."[45] All vestiges of critical agency now dissolve into a form of political regression and infantilism—not unlike what we see in many of the individuals and groups who give Trump undying and unquestioned loyalty.

This is a politics in which the ongoing process of depoliticization makes it easier for the financial elite and other right-wing extremists to argue that the objectifying logic of disposability and the curse of pollution mutually reinforce each other, making it easier to believe in the words of Oxford economic historian Avner Offer that "those who suffer deserve to suffer."[46] As the connections are loosened between language and the common good, education and democracy, politics and civic responsibility, and truth and fiction, fascist terror reasserts itself as part of the largely unquestioned neoliberal diktat that there is no alternative to the current state of affairs. This speaks to both a crisis of agency, representation, education, and politics itself.

A WAVE OF RESISTANCE AGAINST NEOLIBERAL APPROACHES TO EDUCATION

Hannah Arendt once argued that "thinking itself is dangerous to all creeds, convictions, and opinions." In the current political climate, the institutions that nurture critical thinking are similarly seen as dangerous and threatening to our increasingly authoritarian social order. These institutions include public and higher education along with almost any form of progressive media. As a result, purveyors of neoliberal ideology and policy have been working relentlessly to undermine public education in order to define it in strictly economic terms. Taking an instrumentalist approach obsessed with measurement and quantification, they have aggressively attempted to turn education into a business, faculty into devalued clerks, and students into consumers. Fortunately, teachers and students are refusing to participate in the destruction of American education. The historic strike initiated on January 14, 2019 by thirty-three thousand teachers in Los Angeles—the nation's second-largest school district—is evidence of a nationwide trend in which public school teachers and students have increasingly gone on strike and engaged in walkouts. Soon after the Los Angeles strike, strikes followed in Oakland, California, and West Virginia.[47]

This wave of resistance has emerged to counter the neoliberal market-driven approach to education, which historically has cut across mainstream party lines. Market-driven reforms have been supported since the Reagan administration by every president and by every established political faction since the 1970s. Refusing to promote the relationship between education and democracy, critical thinking and active citizenship, and rejecting the connection between education and social and political change, the advocates of neoliberalism have weakened the power of teachers, attacked teachers' unions, reduced teaching to training, and implemented a full-fledged attack on the imagination through methods such as teaching for the test and cutting back on funding for the most basic necessities of schooling. Public schools have been transformed into charter schools or sites that aid in the criminalization of poor Black and Brown students. Neoliberal leaders have moreover sought to strip schools of their anti-authoritarian and egalitarian potential to teach students to live as critical and enlightened citizens in a democracy.[48]

The striking teachers in Los Angeles are not only fighting for smaller classes, more funding, regulation of charter schools, and higher salaries. They're also fighting for more services, less testing, full-time nurses in every school (80 percent of the LA schools do not have nurses), social workers, and more counselors, librarians, and psychologists. The teachers and students in LA strongly reject the crude neoliberal assertion that education is strictly about the pursuit of the practical or should be valued as the ultimate economic investment. They are also challenging how political power is concentrated at the top of school systems and fighting how formal education is overly influenced by billionaires such as Eli Broad and Reed Hastings who "spent an unprecedented 9.7 million in the spring of 2017 to ensure the election of a pro-privatization majority [to] the [Los Angeles] school board." This strike also echoes the fight educators are waging against big corporations and right-wing legislators who aggressively work to defund public education. In doing so, they are rejecting market and business values as the defining principles of education in favor of the broader considerations that focus on civic literacy, public values, and critical thinking. They are also rejecting forms of pedagogical terrorism that aim to remove students from addressing important social problems, if not from politics itself.

What has become clear to educators across the country is that neo-liberalism has not only achieved dominance over the economy, it has also become a fundamental organizing principle for shaping all aspects of education. At the public school level, it trains students in workplace discipline, lowers expectations and kills the imagination; at the level of higher education, it replaces nourishing students' critical capacities with training them for careers and limiting their willingness to believe in something larger than themselves. At the level of higher education, meagerly compensated adjuncts replace tenured faculty; services are outsourced, the salaries of administrators have soared; and students are viewed as customers.

The struggle against neoliberalism has to begin with a struggle for education as a democratic public good and the recognition that education is a moral and political practice that constitutes a struggle over knowledge, identities, agency, and a particular notion of the future. If teachers do not have control over the conditions of their labor, and if students lack the ability to address how knowledge is related to power, morality, social responsibility, and justice, they will have neither the power nor the language necessary to engage in collective forms of struggle against society's efforts to write them out of the script of democracy. They will have no language to recognize the rise of authoritarianism in the governing institutions of society and in their own values. If conservatives see pedagogy as the transmission of lifeless skills, striking teachers view pedagogy as the grounds by which students learn how knowledge is related to power, matters of self-definition, and the basis for intervening in the world. Public school teachers and faculty in higher education are refusing to be complicit with educational institutions that insist on the importance of training and mind-numbing forms of teaching in a time of widespread legitimized violence. This is a crucial point—one that teachers across the country are beginning to understand and act upon. Not only do these teachers see education as deeply political, they also see it as a form of organized resistance.

Democracy's gravediggers were long at work before the appearance of Donald Trump. Forces such as Republican Party extremists, right-wing billionaires, the financial elite, conservative media, nativists, white supremacists, and right-wing evangelicals have done everything they could to consolidate control of the commanding institutions of American life in order to undermine the rule of law and to separate issues of freedom and political power from the democratic traditions of equality and rule by the public. Neither Trump's rise nor the emergence of right-wing populism happened in a vacuum. Trump built on a longstanding neoliberal project buttressed by an anti-democratic formative culture in which educational institutions have been used to shape market-based identities, modes of agency and collective subjects bound together by the notion that there is no alternative to an unfair and pernicious capitalist social order.

In response to this argument, the late radical blogger Mark Fisher coined the term "capitalist realism." As he explains in his book on that topic, the term describes, "the widespread sense that not only is capitalism the only viable political and economic system, but also that it is now impossible even to imagine a coherent alternative to it."[49] For Fisher, capitalist realism functioned less as a crude form of quasi-propaganda than as a pedagogical, social, and cultural machine that produces "a pervasive atmosphere, conditioning not only the production of culture but also the regulation of work and education, and acting as a kind of invisible barrier constraining thought and action."[50] Hidden behind an unquestioned anonymity, neoliberalism appears less as an ideology than as a market-based rationality that by default rightly rejects any inquiry into its goal of governing all of social life. Neoliberalism's unforgiving logic of globalization attempts to make its own power invisible while making people prisoners of its privatizing, commodifying, mutilating ode to self-interest and hyper-individualism.

THE NORMALIZING OF NEOLIBERAL IDEOLOGY

As neoliberal ideology, values, and social relations become normalized, they become more successful and difficult to name, understand, and challenge. For instance, even as more and more people revolt in the current historical conjuncture against this dystopian project, neoliberal ideology and elements of a fascist politics merge to contain, distract, and misdirect the anger that has materialized in many instances out of legitimate grievances against both the government, controlling privileged elites, and the massive hardships caused by neoliberal capitalism. In this instance, capitalist realism has asserted itself, especially among Trump's followers, in a mix of blind faith and sheer exhaustion, one that has led to the need for simplistic solutions and the comfort offered by the strongman willing to relieve everyone of any sense of political and social responsibility in order to solve the problems that haunt the current period.

For instance, Trump fuels a racist antidemocratic authoritarian populism in his call for building a wall on the southern border. He does so by stoking fear. For the last two years, he has equated the culture of immigrants with the culture of crime, argued that undocumented workers are the main source of a terrorist threat in the United States, and stated that they constitute a humanitarian crisis. What he refuses to acknowledge is that, rather than being a threat, many immigrants at the southern border are trying to seek asylum. At the same time, without any sense of irony, Trump claimed in his televised address from the Oval Office, that his proposed wall is some sort of humanitarian priority. As John Cassidy in the *New Yorker* points out, Trump tried to frame the wall as "a solution to a humanitarian crisis on the southern border, rather than what it is and has been all along: the holy grail of a nativist political movement that he has nurtured and cultivated ever since he came down the escalator in Trump Tower."[51]

Trump has used, both in his campaign and presidency, the language of pollution to describe undocumented Brown people as "thugs," "rapists," and "murderers." Human suffering is not something he intends to end—it is something he produces en masse on a number of fronts, both domestic and foreign. Neoliberalism thrives on the power to distract. The mainstream press supports this strategy of distraction by focusing on Trump's shifting claims about whether the wall will be made of concrete or steel. What is missing from these arguments, as Sam Fulwood III points out, is that "The wall is symbolic. It exists solely for the purpose of allowing the president to continually promulgate a steady stream of racist, xenophobic, and anti-immigrant fearmongering."[52]

Trump's own racism is not only evident in his demonizing of people of color, immigrants, and others, it is also obvious in his giving a pardon to the notorious racist Joe Arpaio, the former Arizona sheriff, who made a career of demonizing and cracking down on immigrants.

Trump's silence speaks for itself with regards to racist statements made by Representative Steve King in a *New York Times* interview in which King said, "White nationalist, white supremacist, Western civilization—how did that language become offensive? Why did I sit in classes teaching me about the merits of our history and our civilization?"[53] Andrew Anglin, the founder of the neo-Nazi *Daily Stormer*, has referred to King, "basically [as] an open white nationalist at this point."[54] Michael Cohen, Trump's former attorney, appearing before the House Oversight and Reform Committee, stated

> He is a racist. . . . The country has seen Mr. Trump court white supremacists and bigots. You have heard him call poorer countries "shitholes.". . . In private, he is even worse. He once asked me if I could name a country run by a Black person that wasn't a "shithole." This was when Barack Obama was president of the United States. [Offering more evidence, Cohen observed,] while we were once driving through a struggling neighborhood in Chicago, he commented that only Black people could live that way.[55]

While some Republican Party members have roundly condemned King for his remarks and ignored Cohen's, they have failed to apply the same criticism to either Trump or their own policies, which extend from voter suppression to their support for heinous and morally repulsive border policies. Tellingly, when Trump was asked about King's racist remarks on the south lawn of the White House, he replied, "I don't—I haven't been following it. I really haven't been following it," even though the story had dominated the news. All the while Trump has continued to make racist comments of his own about undocumented workers. For instance, as CNN writer Maegan Vazquez observes, in the midst of the King affair, Trump had no reservations in quoting a flagrantly white nationalist column written by Pat Buchanan, the former communications director for president Ronald Reagan. Buchanan wrote: "The more multiracial, multiethnic, multicultural, multilingual America becomes—the less it looks like Ronald Reagan's America—the more dependably Democratic it will become. The Democratic Party is hostile to white men, because the smaller the share of the U.S. population that white men become, the sooner that Democrats inherit the national estate."[56]

This is neoliberal fascism embracing the discourse of a white supremacy and ultra-nationalism while sometimes hiding behind a language of humanitarianism and human rights. The willingness of a large segment of the US public to succumb to Trump's embrace of what Wendy Brown calls, "fomented nationalism, racism, xenophobia and desire for authoritarian rule" has its roots in a neoliberal culture of social disintegration.[57] In this context, neoliberal reason hides the effects of its racist and toxic economic, social, and political arrangements within a form of capitalist realism that undermines any hope for reclaiming a democratic project defined through the empowering logics of freedom, equality, and self-rule.

What Fisher wisely understood was that any resistance to neoliberal capitalism would have to engage education as a central feature of politics, especially as a way to challenge neoliberal common sense and the pedagogical apparatuses that produce it. Borrowing from the work of Antonio Gramsci, Raymond Williams, C. Wright Mills, and others, Fisher addressed this issue by expanding the meaning of education far beyond the notion of established schooling and pointed to popular culture, the arts, science, film, journalism, social media, and other sites of cultural production as the lens through which to both imagine an alternative to global capitalism and to mobilize individual and collective forms of resistance to it. In this instance, culture, if not the very notion of populism, becomes a site of struggle rather than a terrain grounded exclusively in the grip of domination. In the current situation, as Chantal Mouffe observes, it is crucial to discard the notion that populism is simply another form of demagogy. On the contrary, she writes, "it is a way of doing politics which can take various forms, depending on the periods and the places. It emerges when one aims at building a new subject of collective action—the people—capable of reconfiguring a social order lived as unfair," and in need of a defense of freedom, social justice, and equality.[58]

What does it mean to challenge the pedagogical assumptions that inform neoliberalism, who are the agents to do so, where will such struggles take place, and what form will the language of criticism and hope take if it is to address the everyday lives of people caught in the grip of neoliberal common sense? Neoliberalism has created a crisis of agency, representation, and resistance, and all of these elements must be addressed in terms of how they both function in a neoliberal order to undermine democracy and what it would mean to develop a language and mode of analysis capable of evaluating these issues as part of a comprehensive understanding of politics and collective struggles. We must also ask how the right wing and demagogue politicians were able to colonize populist aspirations to regain some control over the political process and why the left failed. Shaming those who follow Trump is a failing political strategy, especially since many of his followers have suffered under neoliberal globalization and while confused politically, are not in agreement with the neoliberal project. Rather than demonize Trump and his followers, a new political strategy suggests reclaiming the promise of a radical democracy, and exploring how such an ideal is undermined and attacked in a neoliberal order in which everything is privatized, commodified, deregulated, and organized as part of the culture of commercialism and subject to the dictates of finance capital.

Such a challenge would demand developing modes of education and critical analysis that examine in accessible and rigorous modes of expression how power is used by the ruling elite to exploit, exclude, dehumanize, and undermine any viable mode of critical agency. It would call into question the methods through which the state, corporations, and the financial elite use power to remove from peoples' lives essential services such as health care, public transportation, free quality education, housing, a social wage, healthy environment, and other services that enable people to expand their capacities as critically engaged, joyful agents. I am not suggesting that all conservative politicians, including right-wing elements of the Democratic Party such as the Clinton/Obama wing, support the same reactionary policies embraced by Trump and his followers. In fact, Democratic Party politicians from Clinton and Obama to Feinstein and Pelosi actually profess to be a counterforce to Trump—often labeling themselves as the party of resistance—but in the long run, they end up supporting policies and power relations that favor the ruling elites. Under such circumstances, these alleged "liberal" politicians, not unlike the German socialists in the Weimer Republic, turned their backs on the needs of workers, the poor, minorities of class and color, and in doing so helped to create a populist revolt that supported the anti-elitist, anti-government discourse on which Trump ran his presidential campaign.[59]

This raises further questions about how neoliberalism—disguised as the "liberal order"—became an incubator for the rise of Trump and an updated version of fascist politics. There is more at work here than the failure of liberalism to address the soaring issue of inequality in wealth and power. Or, for that matter, its failure to address more radical issues such as the democratization of the workplace and a strong commitment to not just political and personal rights but also economic and social rights in the form of a vigorous welfare program. The absence of access to economic and cultural resources undercuts the ability of the poor to exercise political and personal rights in a meaningful way. As Zygmunt Bauman points out, without social rights, "*political* rights will remain an unattainable dream, a useless fiction or a cruel joke."[60] The writer Pankaj Mishra considers these issues in his critique of the established liberal order. He writes:

> The obvious answer is that [the] much-cherished liberal order was the incubator for Trumpism and other authoritarianisms. It made human beings subordinate to the market, replacing social bonds with market relations and sanctifying greed. It propagated an ethos of individual autonomy and personal responsibility, while the exigencies of the market made it impossible for people to save and plan for the future. It burdened people with chronic debt and turned them into gamblers in the stock market. Liberal capitalism was supposed to foster a universal middle class and encourage bourgeois values of sobriety and prudence and democratic virtues of accountability. It achieved the opposite: the creation of a precariat with no clear long-term prospects, dangerously vulnerable to demagogues promising them the moon. Uncontrolled liberalism, in other words, prepares the grounds for its own demise.[61]

Following up on Mishra's comments, it is crucial to rethink how capitalist institutions limit human agency, along with most people's capacity to be critical and imagine the unimaginable as part of the collective struggle for a democratic future. This would suggest challenging neoliberal regimes of discipline, control and conformity with a pedagogical discourse in which it becomes clear that personal and political rights have to be matched by social and economic rights for any democracy to work. We need to tie the struggle for economic and social justice to new configurations of power and to new ways of understanding that are capable of recognizing and utilizing power in order to create a democratic socialist society.

Any viable notion of politics has to consider working through a variety of cultural apparatuses to activate a public imagination willing to fight for institutions and public goods capable of revitalizing social bonds, social responsibility and the capacity for experiences that go beyond the narrow notions of individualism and self-interest celebrated in the neoliberal worldview. It is both a political and pedagogical issue to imagine a future in which human needs take precedent over market considerations, while making clear how capitalism with its concentration of wealth and power in few hands produces modes of inequality and human misery. The agents and modes of resistance necessary for defeating capitalism and constructing a democratic socialist order will not emerge without the production of a formative culture that provides the knowledge, ideas, values, and social relations central to creating engaged citizens.

Sites of such struggle include not only higher education, but also public education, the arts, social services, the social media, religious institutions, and those other domains of cultural production capable of utilizing the voices and work of public intellectuals. At stake here is the challenge for educators and other cultural workers to own up to the complexity of the problems capitalism produces, to write and speak to people in a narrative that they can understand and identify with, and to address what it means to make knowledge, images, and ideas meaningful in order to make them critical and emancipatory.

CREATING A PEDAGOGY OF "PROFANE ILLUMINATION"

At stake here also is another pedagogical challenge rooted in the necessity to turn common senses into what Walter Benjamin once called "profane illumination," a process by which the dominant common sense assumptions of a capitalist hegemony are subject to the process of denaturalization, critical analysis, and the shock of new forms of recognition. This is a practice of making the familiar unfamiliar by treating it as a source of astonishment. Such a project is imperative if the pedagogical task of raising consciousness is to be successful in challenging neoliberalism's most powerful weapon—its claim that its worldview is self-evident and that any analysis of it is irrelevant. This is particularly important under a regime of neoliberalism in which the public collapses into the private, and personal experiences are removed from wider social forces, "thereby turning social uncertainty into a personal failure that is divorced from any collective cause or remedy."[62]

In addition to employing Benjamin's notion of "profane illumination," a radical cultural politics must insist that rational thinking is not enough. The left and other progressives also need a new way of thinking about the misery and suffering faced by many people. Such thinking must be sensitive to rejecting any hint of moral righteousness and the colonizing stance of preaching the gospel to vulnerable populations. Dispossessed populations must not be denied the tools and spaces to narrate their own stories. We need an array of tools and platforms to consider and unmask how dominant power works and impacts on peoples' lives. At the same time, these tools must do justice to the everyday experiences, events, emotions, modes of identification, and investments that people inhabit and experience in their daily lives. Radical pedagogical practice should take its cue from C. Wright Mills's *The Sociological Imagination*, in which he called for intellectuals and cultural workers to write, talk, and act in ways that make connections between private troubles and public issues, systemic structures and the production of particular modes of agency. This suggests a pedagogical exercise in the service of joint recovery and dialogue, and entering into a politics, language, and way of thinking that fully engages concrete everyday events—what Tracy K. Smith has described as "vulnerabilities . . . and actual ordeals life doles out to real people in fragile bodies."[63]

Central to challenging the objectifying language of pollution and disposability is the need to develop an alternative way of speaking, knowing, and thinking, one in which "language becomes a felt thing, a terrain to be crossed . . . a shifting and malleable possibility" capable of addressing a diverse audience.[64] This is very different from the turgid prose and disembodied language used by many academics, a language that is reductively abstract and functions as a "dead-on-delivery-prose," incapable of speaking to people who would be central to developing a left populism.[65]

Too much academic discourse functions largely as a form of verbal camouflage, or what C. Wright Mills once called "confused verbiage," creating barriers between universities and their public mission, and signals a retreat from public life.[66] By so doing, this conventional academic language runs the risk of becoming complicitous with a neoliberal logic that reduces governance, faculty, and students to the reductive axioms of a culture of business, financial gain, and professional insularity. This type of jargon often prevents academics from becoming border crossers, moving outside of their disciplines, and reaching across diverse forms of media in order to engage in the high-stakes pedagogical terrain of persuasion and belief to change the ways in which people see things. Arcane prose and reductive notions of professionalism also work to separate hard thinking and rigorous scholarship from being relevant to addressing pressing social problems and a wider array of publics.

Dylan Moore is right in reminding us that "the first casualties of to-talitarianism are the minds that would oppose it,"[67] which suggests all the more importantly the need for academics, writers, journalists, artists and others to connect their work to the public and to expose the workings of lies, power, and the reifying politics of disposability and pollution. Making language accessible and rigorous in order to address concrete social problems for a wider audience is crucial if cultural workers in diverse sites are to address the crisis of representation and agency that is at the heart of neoliberal authoritarianism. To raise public consciousness, the symbolic weapons of persuasion, passion, and beliefs must be integrated into a politics of recognition and identification in which people can be moved to not only think critically, but to be passionate and energized about their ability to change the world in which they find themselves. The left needs a political language infused with a deeply moral commitment to democracy, equality, and justice, especially at a time when violence, corruption, and lawlessness have become normalized, opening the door for the emergence of a fascist politics in America.

The issue of how ordinary Americans can be motivated to be self-reflective, moved by democratic values while embracing relationships marked by shared responsibilities, begins with a language in which people can be moved emotionally to analyze their problems and their relationship to broader social forces. One task of such a language is to awaken people's capacity to align themselves with collective identities steeped in communal bonds, develop a compassion for others, and identify with the public good. Such a language has to replace state-sanctioned fear with a radical notion of what Ronald Aronson describes in his book *We: Reviving Social Hope* as "social hope"—a hope that moves people not only to imagine a different future but to individually and collective act on it.[68]

The current crisis of agency, representation, values, and language demands a discursive shift that can call into question and defeat the formative culture and ideological scaffolding through which a savage neoliberal capitalism reproduces itself. Culture has become a war zone, which under Trump has been aggressively militarized and commercialized. As civic culture collapses, the crisis of democracy in the United States is growing, power becomes more concentrated in the hands of ruling elites, and casino capitalism is put on steroids. Trump has put the government in a shutdown, and mainstream media outlets are focused on discussions of Trump's wall, political infighting among Republicans, and the takeover of the House of Representatives by the Democrats.

Meanwhile nothing is being said about economic inequality, a government run by the ultra-rich, unrestrained corporate power, and a military budget that is as outsized as it is unethical. The ongoing assault on the body politic by extensive privatization, deregulation, and economic growth disguised as progress as it destroys the planet proceeds at breakneck speed. And it does so just as historical memory has been undermined and the social fabric has been put at risk in the face of racism, white nationalism, repression, and censorship. The space between crisis and catastrophe is closing and has terrifying implications for the future.

Since the 1980s, and particularly under Trump's reign, a new political formation has come into fruition, which echoes the horrors of a fascist past and is fueled by the toxic rhetoric of disposability and pollution. The mechanisms of power and ideology though which this emerging fascist politics asserts itself must be first challenged with a language that connects capitalism and human exploitation, exclusion, and the destruction of the planet. Crucial to the task of pressing the claim for economic and social justice is the need to make clear that capitalism and democracy are not synonymous. We need to reverse the neoliberal claim that politics and democracy are the enemy of freedom. Moreover, any notion of resistance must rethink the process of democratization as a matter of fundamental systemic change that embraces a radical restructuring of society.

The deep-seated problems of capitalism are too severe, bottomless, and profoundly destructive to be simply amended. They can only be challenged by a strong anti-capitalist mass movement. As Mark Fisher pointed out, Americans are in "a landscape . . . littered with ideological rubble," and in response, we must offer an effective rival to capitalism rather than a reaction to it.[69] Under the rule of neoliberalism, ideological repression works by stealth through forms of manufactured illiteracy produced by right-wing echo chambers and other cultural apparatuses that work aggressively to depoliticize people and make them complicitous with their own oppression. The endpoint is the withering of civic attachments, the decline of public life, and the evisceration of any notion of shared citizenship, all of which embolden a fascist politics. Defenders of a radical democracy need to argue with great energy and passion that "freedom" under capitalism has nothing to do with democracy and everything to do with entrapping millions in a web of reductive and punishing ideological and institutional constraints.

For a start, neoliberal ideology, public pedagogy, and its assault on democratic institutions can be further challenged, in part, by combining Benjamin's task of "profane illumination" and analytic rigor with what A. K. Thompson calls "premonitions," which speak to the need to place isolated events within broader sets of connections that allow us to think in terms of a comprehensive politics and notion of totality. Thompson is worth repeating on this issue. He writes:

> Premonitions are similar to illuminations and reflections in that, as forms of extrapolative reasoning, they reveal how a thing or event can be made to alert us to the broader social process from which it derives. The major difference is that, whereas Benjamin's concepts placed emphasis on the resolution of accumulated tensions, "premonitions" direct our attention toward the future that will obtain should present dynamics be left undisturbed. [70]

If the left and other progressives are to build on the failures of neoliberalism and create a new coalition of political agents, we need a new language, political story and understanding of politics in which a new socialist democratic order can be both imagined and struggled over. This means getting beyond the reductive notion that capitalism can only be understood as an economic system.

The economic crisis produced under neoliberalism has not been matched by a crisis of ideas. This suggests that at the heart of neoliberal capitalism and its fascist politics is a crisis of representation, agency, and memory. In part, this crisis was captured by the phrase attributed to Fredric Jameson or Slavoj Žižek that "it is easier to imagine the end of the world than it is to imagine the end of capitalism."[71] This dystopian assessment challenges us to redefine and rethink the politics that produced it. Doing so would require not only interrogating the current crisis of neoliberal fascism, but also thinking about the promise of a radical democracy.

At the heart of any viable theory of resistance is the need to develop a language of critique that makes visible neoliberalism's largely unchallenged narrative about how social life should be governed by market relations. Those concerned about education in a time of tyranny need a language that exposes neoliberalism's celebration of a disembodied individualism, its elevation of the ethos of competition to a national ideal, and also its war against the welfare state, the environment, and social bonds. This antidemocratic narrative cannot be simply written out of political struggles. At the very least, educators need to create new stories that become integral to how we imagine our society, enabling us to open up rather than close down the future.

The famed abolitionist Frederick Douglass understood the need for stories that went beyond reform, stories that inspired people to think and act outside of the old politics of the time. His words are as relevant today as they were when he first wrote them down. They speak to a generation of youth, teachers, educators and progressives who refuse to dream the future within the stifling confines of the present. Douglass wrote:

> It is not light that is needed, but fire; it is not the gentle shower, but thunder. We need the storm, the whirlwind, the earthquake. The feeling of the nation must be quickened; the conscience of the nation must be roused; the propriety of the nation must be startled; the hypocrisy of the nation must be exposed; and its crimes against God and man must be proclaimed and denounced.[72]

Antonio Gramsci remarked in his *Prison Notebooks*, "The crisis consists precisely in the fact that the old is dying and the new cannot be born; in this interregnum a great variety of morbid symptoms appear."[73] What is clear is that the morbid symptoms have arrived, but at the same time as they produce despair, they also present new challenges and the opportunity for revitalized struggles. This presents both a challenge and an opportunity for those who believe in the civic power of public and higher education to address the nature of the crisis as part of a crisis of education, memory, agency, values, power, and democracy itself.

What needs to be stressed here, as John Dewey, Václav Havel, and others have long warned us against, is a simplistic faith that the stability of the institutions in which a democracy is grounded, such as the courts, will automatically prevent the emergence of authoritarianism. Authoritarian societies are not just the result of bad governance; they also emerge from a more fundamental deformation in the culture itself. That is, democracy's survival depends on a formative culture whose strength lies in a set of habits and dispositions rooted in a civic culture and literacy capable of sustaining it. The deep-seated habits of cruelty, greed, consumerism, racism, and unchecked individualism at the heart of neoliberal fascism are eroding the social fabric that makes a democracy possible. Coercion, fear, intimidation, and repression are not the only tools used by authoritarian societies. Matters of value, identity, agency, and the habits of solidarity when in crisis are as threatening to a democracy as are the forces of repression. Education, once again, becomes an organizing principle of politics when it becomes obvious that fascism returns first in language and people's consciousness; that is, "democracy is only as strong as the men and women [and nonbinary people] who inhabit it."[74] Ignorance is the brick and mortar of fascism. Politics follows culture and this means that a knowledgeable public is central to any democracy. In addition, being informed means creating a culture and institutions in which individuals have access to diverse forms of historical and contemporary bodies of knowledge so that they can function both as critics and cultural producers. They should also be exposed to pedagogical practices that provide creative, fashion appropriate citizen-based skills that enable them to be reflective, analytical, and engaged in dialogue with others. Such capacities point not only to the need to create a society marked by a democratization of access, intelligence, and opportunity, it also points to a society that, if it is going to take seriously the promise of democracy to come, has to eliminate the massive inequality that characterizes American society. Inequities in wealth and power under the reign of neoliberalism breed and legitimate a logic of privatization and self-interest that are toxic and inimical to embracing higher education as a public good. This stranglehold on a democratic conception of the public and the common—and the institutions that enable it—demands of educators and others a radical rethinking of both the need for public funding and the understanding of pedagogy as the practice of freedom. Moreover, without a massive shift in thinking away from the privatization of everything, higher education will fail as a public trust and be relegated to an adjunct of corporate power. The great challenge facing higher education in a time of neoliberal and political tyranny is to reimagine and struggle for the university as a public good, one that takes seriously the challenge of addressing how the habits of democracy as part of a broader understanding of education and the institutions that sustain it can be both produced and protected. We have no time to waste.

Higher Education and the Threat of Neoliberal Fascism[1]

MARK KARLIN INTERVIEWS HENRY A. GIROUX

MARK KARLIN: WHY IS IT IMPORTANT TO HAVE AN HISTORICAL UNDERSTANDING OF FASCISM TO SHED LIGHT ON THE AGE OF TRUMP?

Henry A. Giroux: The conditions leading to fascism do not exist in some ethereal space outside of history. Nor are they historically precise or fixed in a static moment in the past. As Hannah Arendt reminds us, the protean elements of fascism always run the risk of crystallizing into new forms. Historical memory is a prerequisite to the political and moral witnessing necessary to successfully counter the fascism growing in the United States today. As Richard Evans, the renowned historian of modern Germany, observes, the Trump administration may not replicate all the features of Germany and Italy in the 1930s, but the legacy of fascism is important because it points to the horrors of a past that cannot be dismissed. What historians such as Evans, Timothy Snyder, and others have suggested is that it is crucial to examine history to understand what tyranny and authoritarianism look like and how we can use the past to fight against such forces. While the United States under Trump may not be an exact replica of Hitler's Germany, the mobilizing ideas, policies, passions, and ruthless social practices of fascism, wrapped in the flag and

193

discourses of racial purity, ultra-nationalism, and militarism, are at the center of power in the Trump administration. When selected elements of history are suppressed and historical consciousness and memory no longer provide insights into the workings of repression, exploitation, and resistance, people are easily trapped in forms of historical and social amnesia that limit their sense of perspective, their understanding of how power works, and the ways in which the elements of fascism sustain themselves in different practices. Fascism is not unvarying and expresses its most fundamental attacks on democracy in different arrangements, which is all the more reason for people to develop what Snyder calls "an active relationship to history" in order to prevent a normalizing relationship to authoritarian regimes such as the United States under Trump's rule. Surely, a critical understanding of history would go a long way in enabling the American people to recognize the elements of a fascist discourse in much of Trump's racist Tweets, speeches, and policies.

History unexpurgated provides us with a vital resource that helps inform the ethical ground for resistance, an antidote to Trump's politics of disinformation, division, diversion, and fragmentation. Moreover, history reminds us that in the face of emerging forms of authoritarianism, solidarity is essential. If there is one thing that the important lessons of history in the work of writers such as George Orwell have taught us, it is that we must refuse to be complicit in the mockery of truth. This is especially crucial in the current historical moment given the way the Trump administration along with far-right media giants such as Infowars, Sinclair Broadcast Group, Fox News, and Breitbart News Network work to aggressively propagate a vast disimagination machine. With the death of historical memory comes the nightmare we had thought was no longer possible to witness again. The lessons of history are crucial because they can readily be put to use in identifying present-day abuses of power and corruption. History not only grounds us in the past by showing how democratic institutions rise and fall, it is also replete with memories and narratives of resistance that pose a dangerous threat for any fascist and authoritarian system. This is particularly true today given the ideological features and legacies of fascism that are deeply woven into Trump's rhetoric of retribution, intolerance, and demonization; its mix of shlock pageantry, coercion, violence, and impunity; and the constant stoking of ultra-nationalism and racial agitation. Memory as a form of historical consciousness is essential in repaying our burden to the dead and the current victims by holding accountable those who remain mute and assume what Samantha Hill calls "a stance of deliberate blindness," and retreat from any sense of moral responsibility in the in the face of their reprehensible actions, if not crimes. Given the danger of right-wing populism and the incendiary rise of fascism in our time, Hannah Arendt is useful in reminding us that thinking and judging must be connected to our actions. Moreover, such thinking must grasp the underlying causes of the economic and political crisis at hand while acting collectively to fight neoliberal fascism and its embrace of white supremacy, social and economic inequality, and its hatred of democracy. That is why historical memory as a register of critical thinking is so dangerous to Trump and his acolytes. As Hill observes drawing from the work of Arendt, "The lessons of history are a crucial reminder that "blindness and silence are not options. In dark times, one must choose to think and judge."

MK: HOW ARE STATE VIOLENCE AND WHITE NATIONALISM RELATED?

HAG: Under the Trump regime, state violence and white nationalism are two sides of the same register of white supremacy and domestic terrorism. Trump's call to "Make America Great Again," his slogan "America First," and his emphatic call for a law-and-order regime are shorthand for legitimating state violence against Blacks, Muslims, undocumented immigrants, and those "others" who do not fit into his racist notion of ultra-nationalism and his attempts to resuscitate a white public sphere as emblematic of American white supremacy. Ta-Nehisi Coates is right in stating that "Trump's ideology is white supremacy." The merging of state sanctioned racism and state violence is the ideological signpost that informs Trump's notion of white Christian nationalism, which allows him to assemble a broad coalition of bigots, white supremacists, super-patriots, apocalyptic populists, and militarists. Under Trump, identity politics has surfaced with a revenge as the Republican Party unabashedly embraces itself as the white people's party. Under such circumstances, Trump's supportive response to incidents of violence by white supremacists in Charlottesville, Virginia, should surprise no one given the history of racism in the United States in general, and in the Republican Party (and Democratic Party as well) in particular. This is a racist legacy that extends from Nixon's Southern strategy and George W. Bush's treatment of the Black victims of Hurricane Katrina to Clinton's welfare and law-and-order policies to current Republican efforts at expanding the carceral state and suppressing the voting rights of Blacks. Trump not only embraces white supremacy, he elevates it. How else to explain his administration's announcement that it would no longer "investigate white nationalists, who have been responsible for a large share of violent hate crimes in the Unites States?" How else to explain his willingness to lift restrictions imposed by the Obama administration on local police departments' acquisition of military surplus equipment such as armored vehicles, bulletproof vests, and grenade launchers? How do we explain the endless tsunami of racist tweets and comments that he relentlessly produces with gleeful relish? Clearly, such actions deliver on Trump's Jacksonian approach to law and order, escalate racial tensions in cities that are often treated like combat zones, and reinforce a war culture and notions of militarism over community-building among police officers.

Such behaviors do more than reinforce Trump's endorsement of white nationalism; they send a clear message of support for a system of violence, amounting to acts of domestic terrorism. Moreover, they indicate a resounding contempt for the rule of law, and an endorsement not just of racist ideology but also of institutional racism and the primacy of the racially based incarceration state. Trump's law-and-order regime represents a form of domestic terrorism because it is a policy of state violence designed to intimidate, threaten, harm, and instill fear in particular communities. His relentless rhetoric of bigotry, racism, and demonization of selected groups not only plays to his white-nationalist base, it also normalizes support for state violence and signals an official position regarding racialized assaults against immigrants, especially Latin Americans. In addition, Trump's conduct emboldens right-wing extremists, giving them the green light to support profoundly intolerant legislation and ideologies and in some cases engage in acts of violence against those who oppose their racist views. Trump's overt racism and militant views have also inspired a number of white supremacists and neo-Nazis to run for public office. Trump's nod to right-wing extremists and neo-Nazis is evident in his deportation policies, his cruel law-and-order polices that separate children from their immigrant parents, his renewed call for racial profiling, his silence in the face of voter suppression in a number of states, and his endorsement of white nationalists and overt racists running for public office.

MK: HOW HAVE WE DEVOLVED INTO A NATION OF CIVIC ILLITERACY?

HAG: Donald Trump's ascendancy in American politics has made visible a plague of deep-seated civic illiteracy, a corrupt political system and a contempt for reason that has been decades in the making. It also points to the withering of civic attachments, the undoing of civic culture, the decline of public life and the erosion of any sense of shared citizenship. As market mentalities and moralities tighten their grip on all aspects of society, democratic institutions and public spheres are being downsized, if not altogether disappearing. As these institutions vanish—from public schools and alternative media to health care centers—there is also a serious erosion of the discourse of community, justice, equality, public values, and the common good. At the same time reason and truth are not simply contested or the subject of cognizant arguments as they should be, but wrongly vilified—banished to Trump's poisonous world of fake news. Under the Trump administration, language has been pillaged, truth and reason disparaged, and words and phrases emptied of any substance or turned into their opposite, all via the endless production of Trump's Twitter storms and the ongoing clown spectacle of Fox News. This grim reality points to a failure in the power of the civic imagination, political will, and open democracy. It is also part of a politics that strips the social of any democratic ideals and undermines any understanding of education as a public good. What we are witnessing is not simply a political project to consolidate power in the hands of the corporate and financial elite but also a reworking of the very meaning of literacy and education as crucial to what it means to create a critically informed citizenry and democratic society. In an age when literacy and thinking become dangerous to the anti-democratic forces governing all the commanding economic and cultural institutions of the United States, truth is viewed as a liability, ignorance becomes a virtue, and informed judgments and critical thinking demeaned and turned into rubble and ashes. Under the reign of this normalized architecture of alleged common sense, literacy is regarded with disdain, words are reduced to data, and science is confused with pseudoscience. Traces of critical thought appear more and more at the margins of the culture as ignorance becomes the primary organizing principle of American society.

Under the forty-year reign of neoliberalism, civic culture has been commodified, shared citizenship eroded, self-interest and a survival-of-the-fittest ethos elevated to a national ideal. In addition, language has been militarized, handed over to advertisers, game show idiocy, and a political and culturally embarrassing anti-intellectualism has been sanctioned by the White House. Couple this with a celebrity culture that produces an ecosystem of babble, shock, and tawdry entertainment. Add on the cruel and clownish anti–public intellectuals such as Jordan Peterson who defend inequality, infantile forms of masculinity, and define ignorance and a warrior mentality as part of the natural order, all the while dethroning any viable sense of agency and the political.

The culture of manufactured illiteracy is also reproduced through a media apparatus that trades in illusions and the spectacle of violence. Under these circumstances, illiteracy becomes the norm and education becomes central to a version of neoliberal zombie politics that functions largely to remove democratic values, social relations, and compassion from the ideology, policies, and commanding institutions that now control American society. In the age of manufactured illiteracy, there is more at work than simply an absence of learning, ideas, or knowledge. Nor can the reign of manufactured illiteracy be solely attributed to the rise of the new social media, a culture of immediacy, and a society that thrives on instant gratification. On the contrary, manufactured illiteracy is a political and educational project central to a right-wing corporatist ideology and set of policies that work aggressively to depoliticize people and make them complicitous with the neoliberal and racist political and economic forces that impose misery and suffering upon their lives. There is more at work here than what Ariel Dorfman calls a "felonious stupidity," there are also the workings of a deeply malicious form of twenty-first-century fascism and a culture of cruelty in which language is forced into the service of violence while waging a relentless attack on the ethical imagination and the notion of the common good. In the current historical moment, illiteracy and ignorance offer the pretense of a community in the form of a right-wing populism which provides a gift to the dark cloud of fascism that has descended upon the United States.

MK: HOW DOES CAPITALISM SUPPRESS AN EDUCATIONAL SYSTEM THAT NURTURES A ROBUST DEMOCRACY?

HAG: Increasingly, neoliberal regimes across Europe and North America have waged a major assault on higher education and those faculty and students who view it as crucial to producing the modes of learning and formative cultures necessary in the struggle for a strong and healthy democracy. For instance, in the United States, higher education is being defunded, devalued, and privatized while access to it by working and lower middle-class students is also being restricted. Those underprivileged students who do have access to some form of post-secondary education are too frequently burdened with crippling financial debts. Increasingly universities are being turned into accountability factories designed to mimic the values of casino capitalism. Disciplines and courses that are not organized around market principles are either being underfunded, cut, or refigured to serve market values. Disciplines such as women's studies, African American studies, labor studies, and Latino studies have lost much of their funding, have been closed, or have been marginalized while at the same time the humanities and liberal arts increasingly disappear or are marginalized. The attack on higher education has a long history. Since the 1980s the democratic principles of the university have been under assault by right-wing billionaires such as the Koch brothers, a select financial elite and big corporations, "leading to a blurring of the lines between the university and the corporate world." Increasingly, the object of higher education is the individual consumer rather than the public good.

Under such circumstances, power is concentrated in the hands of a managerial class that too often views education simply through the lens of a market-driven culture that harnesses matters of governance, teaching, and learning to the instrumental needs of the economy. Evidence of the corporate takeover of higher education is manifest in the emergence of governing structures that mimic the culture of business and modes of leadership defined almost entirely in entrepreneurial terms. Not only are these structures hierarchical and disempowering for faculty and students but also they produce massive levels of inequality among different faculty, staff, and students in regards to salaries, resources, and choices. Everything about education that matters appears to be absorbed into the discourse of business, metrics, and a reductionist notion of efficiency. Research is increasingly shaped, valued, and rewarded to the degree that it reflects corporate inter-ests and is defined in measurable terms. Academic rewards, promotions, and access to power are now tied to getting grants or outside corporate funding. Numerical signifiers and commercial values shape policies and practices at almost all levels of university life. For instance, university ser-vices are increasingly outsourced, students are defined as entrepreneurs, and the culture of education is morphed into the culture of business. In this instance, the distinction between knowledge and information, ideas and data diminish under the economic imperative to value knowledge in instrumental terms and to devalue ideas that serve the common good.

In addition, faculty in public universities have lost much of their power and autonomy and have been relegated to the role of part-time laborers, defined largely by the same type of workplace logic that char-acterizes Walmart and other service industries. The latter is designed, as Noam Chomsky points out, "to reduce labor costs and to increase labor servility." This casualization of faculty also functions to undercut academic freedom and free expression as many part-time and adjunct faculty are rightly afraid to speak out and address important social is-sues in and out of their classrooms for fear of being fired. Judith Butler is right in stating that faculty have increasingly lost the "financial and institutional support" along with "the guarantee and the conditions upon which freedom—both academic freedom and freedom of political expression—relies." Many adjunct faculty not only have few job protec-tions in such a precarious environment, they are also reduced to wages that in some cases force them to seek welfare and food assistance. As the university succumbs to an audit culture, it increasingly weds itself to a market-driven notion of customer satisfaction, metrics, and performance measures that represses a genuine critical education, not to mention any viable notion of dissent. As critical education is subordinated to the task of reproducing and benefiting the corporate order, education collapses into training and the role of faculty is instrumentalized and devoid of any democratic vision. The attack on higher education as a democratic public good and faculty as public and engaged intellectuals has a long history in the United States.

Under this market-driven notion of governance, faculty lose their power and autonomy. Under the reign of neoliberalism, students are often saddled with high tuition rates and a future predicated on ongoing uncertainty, economic instability, and ecological peril. In addition, as democratic visions are removed from higher education they are replaced by an obsession with a narrow notion of job-readiness and a cost accounting instrumental rationality. This bespeaks the rise of what theorists such as the late Stuart Hall called an audit or corporate culture, which serves to demoralize and depoliticize both faculty and students, often relieving them of any larger values other than those that reinforce their own self-interest, and retreat from any sense of moral and social responsibility. More specifically, as higher education both denies and actively abandons its role as a democratic public sphere, it tends to provide an education in which the citizen is transformed into a consumer, thereby laying the foundation for the development of self-seeking agents, who inhabit crippling orbits of privatization and are indifferent to the growth of despotic power around them. Under such circumstances, education collapses into training, and the only learning that is valued is reduced to that which is measurable.

One of the challenges facing the current generation of educators, students, and others is the need to address the question: what is the role and mission of education in a time of tyranny? What should it attempt to accomplish in a society at a historical moment when society is slipping over into an abyss of fascism? Central to such a challenge is the question of what education should accomplish in a democracy. What will it take for higher education not to abandon its role as a democratic public sphere? What work do educators have to do to create the economic, political, and ethical conditions necessary to endow young people and the general public with the capacities to think, question, doubt, imagine the unimaginable, and defend education as essential for inspiring and energizing the citizens necessary for the existence of a robust democracy? What kind of language is necessary for higher education to redefine its mission, one that enables faculty and students to work toward a different future than one that echoes the present, to confront the unspeakable, to recognize themselves as agents, not victims, and to muster up the courage to act in the service of a substantive and inclusive democracy? In a world in which there is an increasing abandonment of egalitarian and democratic values and impulses, what will it take to educate young people and the broader polity to challenge authority and hold power accountable?

MK: WHAT IS THE "CULTURE OF CRUELTY IN TRUMP'S AMERICA" AND WHY IS IT IMPORTANT TO ANALYZE?

HAG: The United States has a long history in which the culture of cruelty has undermined and challenged its professed claims to the democratic principles of equality, freedom, compassion, and justice. The hardening of the culture and the emergence of a social order driven by a collapse of ethics, an unchecked celebration of self-interest, a collective embrace of narcissism, and a Hobbesian war-of-all-against-all have been increasingly nurtured in the last forty years under the rise of a neoliberal form of gangster capitalism, more aptly called neoliberal fascism. Yet, this history of cruelty is not unique to the Trump administration. The attack on the welfare state, a numbing social atomization, the rise of a survivalist ethic, and a growing indifference to human suffering have long been supported by both major political parties. Before Trump's election, America's culture of cruelty resided rhetorically on the margins of power, hidden under the false rhetoric of liberal and conservative politicians who benefited from exploiting the vulnerable in order to further advance the interests of the rich and their own power.

But such attacks have taken on a more aggressive and organizing role under Trump's presidency. This is evident as Trump devotes an inordinate amount of tyrannical energy to the notion that the market and state violence are the primary solution to all social problems and constitute the only legitimate pillars of governance. This decent into the practice of cruel power, cruelty, and barbarism no longer hides in the shadows, and is employed without apology in most of Trump's activities since he was elected. Trump revels in the discourse of bullies. He calls his critics losers, insults world leaders with belittling language, and tacitly supports the violent actions of white supremacists. He endorses state torture, has remilitarized the police, relishes representations of violence, and in one instance tweeted an edited video showing himself body-slamming and punching a man with the CNN logo superimposed on his head during a wrestling match. He has executed polices that bear the weight of domestic terrorism, which partly include breaking up immigrant families and separating young children from their parents while expanding the racially charged reach of the carceral state under his call for "law and order." He has called Latinos "animals," Mexicans rapists and drug dealers, and a number of African nations "shithole countries," all of which echoes the dark and dangerous racially charged rhetoric of the Nazis in the 1930s.

Trump's embrace of the culture of cruelty also drives policies rooted in an ongoing process of dehumanization, rancor, and a racially inspired hatred—one that views with disdain basic human emotions such as compassion, empathy, and care for the other. How else to explain his $1.3 trillion tax cut for the ultra-rich and big corporations along with a massive increase in military spending. This dreadful and harmful legislation accompanies policies that produce unprecedented cuts in low-income housing, impose punitive work requirements for those on welfare, eliminate job training programs, slash food assistance programs for the poor, decrease quality health care for the poorest populations, cut nutrition programs for new mothers and their infants, and remove billions from desperately needed programs such as the Children's Health Insurance Program (CHIP). All of these polices serve to redistribute wealth upward while an alarming 43 percent of American families cannot afford basic needs such as housing, child care, food, or even a cell phone and millions of the most vulnerable Medicaid recipients risk losing their health care. Philip Alston, the United Nations monitor on poverty, in an interview with the *Guardian*, has warned that Trump is not only producing policies that reward the ultra-rich, he is also punishing the poor and most vulnerable as a result of "a systematic attack on America's welfare program that is undermining the social safety net." Alston states that by removing "any sense of government commitment, you quickly move into cruelty."

It gets worse. A new level of hatred, exhibition of ferocity, and state sanctioned cruelty are on full display in Trump's willingness to end the DACA program, risking the expulsion of over 700,000 immigrants brought to the country as children; moreover, Trump has put in play executive orders that end temporary protected status for more than 425,000 immigrants, including 86,000 Hondurans, and 200,000 people from El Salvador, many whom have lived in the US for decade. There is a genocidal mentality at work here amplified by a hatred that suggests a disgust for those who do not fit into Trump's embrace of racial purity, white nationalism, and a "cleansed" public space.

This culture of cruelty has a long history in the United States and has to be connected with the intensifying and accelerating practices of a neoliberal fascism which is more than willing to exercise cruel power in the interest of accumulating capital and profits without any consideration of social costs to humanity or the planet itself. The culture of cruelty is not simply about character, however deformed Trump's might be. On the contrary, it has to be connected to structural and ideological forces in the service of a financial elite. Rather than simply produce moral outrage, the culture of cruelty should point to a convergence of power, politics, and newly emerging structures of domination that are as unjust as they are cruel. Gangster capitalism is the root cause of such cruelty because of its concentration of power, ongoing destruction of democratic values, and its continued production of a machinery of terminal exclusion, disposability, social abandonment, and social death.

Neoliberal fascism as a form of extreme capitalism views democracy as the enemy, the market as the exclusive arbiter of freedom, and the ethical imagination as an object of disdain. It is a form of zombie politics that produces a ruling elite that represents a twenty-first-century version of the walking dead. To quote *New York Times* film critic A. O. Scott, these zombie politicians and power brokers serve as a dystopian "reminder of not only our fears but [also] what we have become." The coarsening of American culture and society has solidified into a state sanctioned language in which the tyranny of authoritarian zombies has become domesticated, if not normalized. What we are now witnessing is the death of compassion, a repudiation of our obligations to the most vulnerable, the death of the social, and a dishonorable discharge from the obligations of a democracy. Under neoliberalism's form of gangster capitalism, the United States has lost its sense of decency and collapsed into a society of lawlessness and moral indifference. Trump is the end point of a country that has become a criminogenic society, one in which, as Pankaj Mishra has written, promotes "a widely sanctioned ruthlessness . . . that does not make for an understanding of the tangled roots of human suffering." The current culture of cruelty is both a symptom of the war on democracy and a mirror that reveals the collapse of the United States into the abyss of fascism.

MK: YOU ARGUE THAT THERE IS A CONNECTION BETWEEN NEOLIBERALISM AND FASCISM. CAN YOU SPEAK TO THAT CONNECTION?

HAG: Actually, I bring the two terms together in the phrase neoliberal fascism, which I define as both a project and a movement. Neoliberalism is an enabling force that weakens, if not destroys, the commanding institutions of a democracy while undermining its most valuable principles. It is part of what Sheldon Wolin called a totalitarian imaginary that constitutes a revolutionary break from democracy. This is a form of fascism in which state rule is replaced by corporate sovereignty and a culture of fear, insecurity, and precarity reinvigorates executive power and the rise of the punishing state. Consequently, neoliberalism as a form of gangster capitalism provides a fertile ground for the unleashing of the ideological architecture, poisonous values, and racist social relations sanctioned and produced under fascism. As I have mentioned earlier in this book, neoliberalism and fascism conjoin and advance in a comfortable and mutually compatible project and movement that connects the worst excesses of capitalism with fascist ideals: the veneration of war and a hatred of reason and truth; a populist celebration of ultra-nationalism and racial purity; the suppression of freedom and dissent; a culture which promotes lies, spectacles of disparagement, and a demonization of the other; a discourse of decline; brutal exploitation; and ultimately state violence in heterogeneous forms. All vestiges of the social are replaced by an idealization of individualism and all forms of responsibility are reduced to individual agents. Neoliberalism creates a failed democracy and in doing so opens up the fascists' use of fear and terror to transform a state of exception into a state of emergency. As a project, it destroys all the commanding institutions of democracy and consolidates power in the hands of a financial elite. As a movement, it produces and legitimates massive economic inequality and suffering, privatizes public goods, dismantles essential government agencies, and individualizes all social problems. Also, it transforms the political state into the corporate state, and uses the tools of surveillance, militarization, and law and order to discredit the critical press and media, and undermine civil liberties while ridiculing and censoring critics. Moreover, what is distinctive about neoliberal fascism is its aggressive war on youth, especially Black youth, its war on women, and its despoiling of the planet.

In addition, corporate control of the cultural apparatuses provide the public with endless spectacles of violence, toxic and banal illusions, the celebration of market-driven values, and an empty obsession and worship of celebrity culture. With the collapse of the social state, the punishing neoliberal fascist state emerges in full force, criminalizing a range of behaviors that are in fact expressions of social problems such as homelessness, mental illness, and poverty. The model of the prison and the state sanctioned embrace of violence and lawlessness are now unleashed with impunity on youth, people of color, undocumented immigrants, and all those others considered disposable. Massive inequality horribly accentuated by neoliberal policies that destroy basic social services, needed infrastructures, and essential public goods, provide a fertile ground for advancing a sinister turn towards a collective anger and resentment open to a newly charged populism willing to embrace white supremacist ideology, state violence, and authoritarian beliefs. Neoliberalism is the face of a new fascism. After decades of the neoliberal nightmare in the United States and abroad, the mobilizing passions of fascism have been unleashed unlike anything we have seen since the 1930s and 1940s. Extreme capitalism has destroyed any vestige of a substantive democracy, produced massive economic suffering, tapped into a combination of fear and a cathartic cruelty, and emboldened a savage lawlessness aimed at those considered disposable. It is time to repudiate the notion that capitalism and democracy are the same thing, renew faith in the promises of a democratic socialism, create new political formations around an alliance of diverse social movements, and take seriously the need to make education central to the sphere of politics. As Walter Benjamin reminds us, fascism is the product often of failed democracies, and under the reign of neoliberalism we are in the midst of not simply a dysfunctional democracy, but in the grip of an extreme form of gangster capitalism wedded to unbridled forms of corporate power that produce massive inequalities in wealth and power and aggressively wage war on everything crucial to a vibrant democratic society.

Notes

INTRODUCTION: THE LANGUAGE OF NEOLIBERAL EDUCATION

1. Parts of this interview first appeared in Mitja Sardoč, ed. *Solslo Polje* 1–2 (2018) as Mitja Sardoč and Henry A. Giroux, "The Language of Neoliberal Education: An Interview with Henry Giroux," 97–106.
2. Darrin S. Murray, "The Precarious New Faculty Majority: Communication and Instruction Research and Contingent Labor In Higher Education," *Communication Education* 2, no. 68 (2019): 235–263.
3. Christopher Newfield, *The Great Mistake* (Baltimore: Johns Hopkins University Press, 2016).
4. Pankaj Mishra, "A Gandhian Stand Against the Culture of Cruelty," *New York Review of Books,* May 22, 2018, http://www.nybooks.com /daily/2018/05/22/the-culture-of-cruelty/.
5. Joshua Sperling cited in Lisa Appignanesi, "Berger's Ways of Being," *New York Review of Books*, May 9, 2019, https://www.nybooks.com/articles /2019/05/09/john-berger-ways-of-being.

CHAPTER ONE: NEOLIBERALISM'S WAR ON DEMOCRACY

1. These themes are taken up extensively in David Harvey, *A Brief History of Neoliberalism* (New York: Oxford University Press, 2005), David Harvey, *The Enigma of Capitalism* (New York: Oxford University Press, 2010), and Colin Crouch, *The Strange Non-Death of Neoliberalism* (Cambridge:

Polity, 2011).

2. This quote is from Andrew Reszitnyk, "Beyond Difference and Becoming: Towards a Non-Differential Practice of Critique," a paper presented as part of his 2013 doctoral comprehensive exam. For other sources on neoliberalism, see Manfred B. Steger and Ravi K. Roy, *Neoliberalism: A Very Short Introduction* (New York: Oxford University Press, 2010); Juliet B. Schor, *Plenitude: The New Economics of True Wealth* (New York: Penguin Press, 2010); Henry A. Giroux, *Against the Terror of Neoliberalism* (Boulder, CO: Paradigm Publishers, 2008); Harvey, *Brief History of Neoliberalism*; and John Comaroff and Jean Comaroff, eds., *Millennial Capitalism and the Culture of Neoliberalism* (Durham, NC: Duke University Press, 2001). On the moral limits and failings of neoliberalism, see Michael J. Sandel, *What Money Can't Buy* (New York: Farrar, Straus and Giroux, 2012). And for positing a case for neoliberalism as a criminal enterprise, see Jeff Madrick, *Age of Greed: The Triumph of Finance and the Decline of America, 1970 to the Present* (New York: Vintage, 2011); Charles Ferguson, *Predator Nation: Corporate Criminals, Political Corruption, and the Hijacking of America* (New York: Crown Business, 2012); Henry A. Giroux, *Zombie Politics in the Age of Casino Capitalism* (New York: Peter Lang, 2010).

3. João Biehl, *Vita: Life in a Zone of Social Abandonment* (Berkeley and Los Angeles: University of California Press, 2005). These zones are also brilliantly analyzed in Chris Hedges and Joe Sacco, *Days of Destruction, Days of Revolt* (New York: Knopf, 2012).

4. For instance, see Henry A. Giroux, *Youth in a Suspect Society* (New York: Routledge, 2010) and Annette Fuentes, *Lockdown High* (New York: Verso, 2013).

5. Zygmunt Bauman, "Does 'Democracy' Still Mean Anything? (And in Case It Does, What Is It?)" *Truthout*, January 21, 2011, http://truth-out .org/index.php?option=com_k2&view=item&id=73:does-democracy -still-mean-anything-and-in-case-it-does-what-is-it.

6. Lauren Berlant cited in Michael Dawson, *Blacks In and Out of the Left* (Cambridge, MA: Harvard University Press, 2013), 181–182.

7. George Lakoff and Glenn W. G. Smith, "Romney, Ryan and the Devil's Budget," *Reader Supported News*, August 22, 2012, http://blogs.berkeley .edu/2012/08/23/romney-ryan-and-the-devils-budget-will-america-keep -its-soul/.

8. Robert Reich, "Mitt Romney and the New Gilded Age," *Reader Supported News*, June 30, 2012, http://robertreich.org/post/26229451132.

9. David Theo Goldberg, "The Taxing Terms of the GOP Plan Invite Class Carnage," *Truthout*, September 20, 2012, http://truth-out.org/news /item/11630-the-taxing-terms-of-the-gop-plan-invite-class-carnage.

10. Paul Krugman, "Galt, Gold, and God," *New York Times*, August 23, 2012.

11. Ibid.

12. Marian Wright Edelman,"Ending Child Poverty: Child Poverty in America: 2011," Children's Defense Fund, http://www.childrensdefense.org/child-research-data-publications/data/2011-child-poverty-in-america.pdf.
13. Marian Wright Edelman, "Ryanomics Assault on Poor and Hungry Children," *Huffington Post,* September 14, 2012, http://www.huffingtonpost.com/marian-wright-edelman/ryanomics-assault-on-poor_b_1885851.html.
14. Richard D. Wolff, "The Truth about Profits and Austerity," *MR Zine,* March 31, 2013, http://mrzine.monthlyreview.org/2013/wolff310313.html. Wolff develops this position in Richard D. Wolff, *Democracy at Work: A Cure for Capitalism* (Chicago: Haymarket Books, 2012).
15. Igor Volsky, "Pick Your Poison," *Progress Report,* March 4, 2013, http://thinkprogress.org/progress-report/pick-your-poison/?mobile=nc.
16. ThinkProgress War Room, "Sequester: "A Fancy Word for a Dumb Idea," *Think Progress,* March 1, 2013, http://thinkprogress.org/progress-report/?mobile=nc.
17. Reich, "Mitt Romney and the New Gilded Age"; Ferguson, *Predator Nation*; Daisy Grewal, "How Wealth Reduces Compassion: As Riches Grow, Empathy for Others Seems to Decline," *Scientific American,* April 10, 2012, http://www.scientificamerican.com/article.cfmid=how-wealth-reduces-compassion.
18. Bauman, "Does 'Democracy' Still Mean Anything?"
19. Lewis H. Lapham, "Feast of Fools: How American Democracy Became the Property of a Commercial Oligarchy," *Truthout,* September 20, 2012, http://truth-out.org/opinion/item/11656-feast-of-fools-how-american-democracy-became-the-property-of-a-commercial-oligarchy.
20. Ibid.
21. Zygmunt Bauman, *This Is Not a Diary* (Cambridge: Polity Press, 2012), 102.
22. Lapham, "Feast of Fools."
23. Eric Lichtblau, "Economic Downturn Took a Detour at Capitol Hill," *New York Times,* December 26, 2011, http://www.nytimes.com/2011/12/27/us/politics/economic-slide-took-a-detour-at-capitol-hill.html?pagewanted=all.
24. Peter Grier, "So Much Money, So Few Lobbyists in D.C.: How Does the Math Work?" *DC Decoder,* February 24, 2012, http://www.csmonitor.com/USA/DC-Decoder/Decoder-Wire/2012/0224/So-much-money-so-few-lobbyists-in-D.C.-How-does-that-math.work.
25. Bill Moyers and Bernard Weisberger, "Money in Politics: Where Is the Outrage?" *Huffington Post,* August 30, 2012, http://www.huffingtonpost.com/bill-moyers/money-in-politics_b_1840173.html.
26. Erika Eichelberger, "See How Citigroup Wrote a Bill So It Could Get a Bailout," *Mother Jones,* May 24, 2013, http://www.motherjones.com/politics/2013/05/citigroup-hr-992-wall-street-swaps-regulatory

-improvement-act.

27. The inhumanity of such modes of punishment is captured brilliantly in Lorna A. Rhodes, *Total Confinement: Madness and Reason in the Maximum Security Prison* (Berkeley and Los Angeles: University of California Press, 2004).

28. It is difficult to access this study because Citigroup does its best to make it disappear from the Internet. See the discussion of it by Noam Chomsky in "Plutonomy and the Precariat: On the History of the U.S. Economy in Decline," *Truthdig*, May 8, 2012, http://www.truthdig.com /report/item/plutonomy_and_the_precariat_the_history_of_the_us _economy_in_decline_201205/.

29. Chrystia Freeland, *Plutocrats: The Rise of the New Global Super-Rich and the Fall of Everyone Else* (New York: Penguin, 2012).

30. See Olivia Ward's interview with Chrystia Freeland. Olivia Ward, "The Rise of the Super-rich: Is the Economy Just Going Through a Bad Patch?" *Truthout*, April 1, 2013, http://truth-out.org/news/item/15452 -the-rise-of-the-super-rich-is-the-economy-just-going-through-a-bad -patch.

31. Salvatore Babones, "To End the Jobs Recession, Invest an Extra $20 Billion in Public Education," *Truthout*, August 21, 2012, http://truth-out.org /opinion/item/11031-to-end-the-jobs-recession-invest-an-extra-$20-billion -in-public-education.

32. John Atcheson, "The Real Welfare Problem: Government Giveaways to the Corporate 1%," *Common Dreams*, September 3, 2012, http://www .commondreams.org/view/2012/09/03-7.

33. John Cavanagh, "Seven Ways to End the Deficit (Without Throwing Grandma Under the Bus)," *Yes! Magazine*, September 7, 2012, http://www .yesmagazine.org/new-economy/seven-ways-to-end-the-deficit-without -throwing-grandma-under-the-bus.

34. Ibid.

35. Joseph Stiglitz, "Politics Is at the Root of the Problem," *European Magazine*, April 23, 2012, http://theeuropean-magazine.com/633-stiglitz -joseph/634-austerity-and-a-new-recession.

36. Lynn Parramore, "Exclusive Interview: Joseph Stiglitz Sees Terrifying Future for America If We Don't Reverse Inequality," *AlterNet*, June 24, 2012, http://www.alternet.org/economy/155918/exclusive_interview %3A_joseph_stiglitz_sees_terrifying_future_for_america_if_we_don %27t_reverse_inequality.

37. Editorial, "America's Detainee Problem," *Los Angeles Times*, September 23, 2012, http://articles.latimes.com/2012/sep/23/opinion/la-ed -detention-20120923.

38. Glenn Greenwald, "Unlike Afghan Leaders, Obama Fights for Power of Indefinite Military Detention," *Guardian*, September 18, 2012, www.guardian.co.uk/commentisfree/2012/sep/18/obama-appeals-ndaa -detention-law. See also Glenn Greenwald, "Federal Court Enjoins

NDAA," *Salon*, May 16, 2012, www.salon.com/2012/05/16/federal
_court_enjoins_ndaa/. See also Henry A. Giroux, *Hearts of Darkness:
Torturing Children in the War on Terror* (Boulder, CO: Paradigm Publi-
hers, 2010).

39. Charlie Savage, "Judge Rules against Law on Indefinite Detention," *New
York Times*, September 12, 2012, www.nytimes.com/2012/09/13/us
/judge-blc:ks-controversial-indefinite-detention-law.html?_r=0.

40. Karen J. Greenberg, "Ever More and Ever Less," *TomDispatch*, March
18, 2012, www.tomdispatch.com/archive/175517/.

41. Catherine Poe, "Federal Judge Emails Racist Joke about President
Obama," *Washington Times*, March 1, 2012, http://communities
.washingtontimes.com/neighborhood/ad-lib/2012/mar/1/federal-judge
-emails-racist-joke-about-president-o/.

42. Amanda Turkel and Sam Stein, "Mitt Romney, on *60 Minutes*, Cities
Emergency Room as Health Care Option for Uninsured," *Huffington
Post*, September 23, 2012, www.huffingtonpost.com/2012/09/23
/mitt-romney-60-minutes-health-care_n_1908129.html?.

43. Editorial, "Why Romney Is Slipping," *New York Times*, September 25,
2012.

44. Brennan Keller, "Medical Expenses: Top Cause of Bankruptcy in the
United States," *GiveForward*, October 13, 2011, www.giveforward.com
/blog/medical-expenses-top-cause-of-bankruptcy-in-the-united-states.

45. Stanley Aronowitz, *Against Schooling: For an Education That Matters*
(Boulder, CO: Paradigm Publishers, 2008), xviii.

46. Reuters, "Goldman Sachs CEO Lloyd Blankfein Says Banks Do 'God's
Work,'" *Daily News*, November 9, 2009, http://articles.nydailynews.com
/2009-11-09/news/17938614_1_year-end-bonuses-goldman-sachs-lloyd
-blankfein.

47. Paul Krugman, "Defining Prosperity Down," *New York Times*, August 1,
2010.

48. Zygmunt Bauman is the most important theorist writing about the politics
of disposability. Among his many books, see *Wasted Lives* (London: Polity
Press, 2004).

49. Bauman, *Wasted Lives*, 5.

50. Robert Reich, "The Rebirth of Social Darwinism," *Robert Reich's Blog*,
November 30, 2011, http://robertreich.org/post/13567144944.

51. Tony Judt, *Ill Fares the Land* (New York: Penguin, 2010).

52. This argument has been made against academics for quite some time,
though it has either been forgotten or conveniently ignored by many fac-
ulty. See, for example, various essays in C. Wright Mills, "The Powerless
People: The Role of the Intellectual in Society" in C. Wright Mills, *The
Politics of Truth: Selected Writings of C. Wright Mills* (Oxford: Oxford
University Press, 2008), 13–24; Edward Said, *Humanism and Democratic
Criticism* (New York: Columbia University Press, 2004); and Henry
A. Giroux and Susan Searls Giroux, *Take Back Higher Education* (New

York: Palgrave, 2004).

53. On the university's relationship with the national security state, see David Price, "How the CIA Is Welcoming Itself Back Onto American University Campuses: Silent Coup," *CounterPunch*, April 9–11, 2010, www.counterpunch.org/price04092010.html. See also Nick Turse, *How the Military Invades Our Everyday Lives* (New York: Metropolitan Books, 2008); and Henry A. Giroux, *The University in Chains: Confronting the Military-Industrial-Academic Complex* (Boulder, CO: Paradigm Publishers, 2007).

54. Robert McChesney, *The Problem of the Media* (New York: Monthly Review Press, 2004). See the interesting table by Ashley Lutz, "These Six Corporations Control 90% of the Media in America," *Business Insider*, June 14, 2012, www.businessinsider.com/these-6-corporations-control-90-of-the-media-in-america-2012-6.

55. See, for instance, Chris Mooney, *The Republican War on Science* (New York: Basic Books, 2005).

56. Frank Rich, "Could She Reach the Top in 2012? You Betcha," *New York Times*, November 20, 2010.

57. Cornelius Castoriadis, "Democracy as Procedure and Democracy as Regime," *Constellations* 4, no. 1 (1997): 5.

58. Toni Morrison, "How Can Values Be Taught in This University," *Michigan Quarterly Review* (Spring 2001): 278.

59. Stephen Holden, "Perils of the Corporate Ladder: It Hurts When You Fall," *New York Times*, December 10, 2010.

60. Hart Research Associates, *American Academics: Survey of Part Time and Adjunct Higher Education Faculty* (Washington, DC: AFT, 2011);Steve Street, Maria Maisto, Esther Merves, and Gary Rhoades, *Who Is Professor "Staff" and How Can This Person Teach So Many Classes?* (Los Angeles: Center for the Future of Higher Education, 2012).

61. Andrew Martin and Andrew W. Lehren, "A Generation Hobbled by the Soaring Cost of College," *New York Times*, May 12, 2012.

62. Paul Buchheit, "Five Ugly Extremes of Inequality in America—the Contrasts Will Drop Your Chin to the Floor," *AlterNet*, March 24, 2013, www.alternet.org/economy/five-ugly-extremes-inequality-america-contrasts-will-drop-your-chin-floor.

63. For an excellent defense of critical thinking not merely as a skill, but as a crucial foundation for any democratic society, see Robert Jensen, *Arguing for Our Lives* (San Francisco: City Lights Books, 2013).

64. Cited in Richard J. Bernstein, *The Abuse of Evil: The Corruption of Politics and Religion since 9/11* (London: Polity Press, 2005), 7–8.

65. Paul Buchheit, "Now We Know Our ABCs and Charter Schools Get an F," *CommonDreams*, September 24, 2012, https://www.commondreams.org/view/2012/09/24-0.

66. See Giroux, *The University in Chains*.

67. See, for instance, Robert B. Reich, "Slashed Funding for Public Universi-

ties Is Pushing the Middle Class Toward Extinction," *AlterNet*, March 5, 2012, www.alternet.org/education/154410/slashed_funding_for _public_universities_is_pushing_the_middle_class_toward_extinction. For a brilliant argument regarding the political and economic reasons behind the defunding and attack on higher education, see Christopher Newfield, *Unmaking the Public University: The Forty-Year Assault on the Middle Class* (Cambridge, MA: Harvard University Press, 2008).

68. Les Leopold, "Crazy Country: 6 Reasons America Spends More on Prisons Than on Higher Education," *AlterNet*, August 27, 2012, www .alternet.org/education/crazy-country-6-reasons-america-spends -more-prisons-higher-education?paging=off. On this issue, see also the classic work by Angela Y. Davis, *Are Prisons Obsolete?* (New York: Open Media, 2003) and Michelle Alexander, *The New Jim Crow: Mass Incarceration in the Age of Colorblindness* (New York: New Press, 2012).

69. Leopold, "Crazy Country."

70. Zygmunt Bauman, *The Individualized Society* (London: Polity, 2001), 4.

71. See, for instance, Rebecca Solnit, "Rain on Our Parade: A Letter to the Dismal Left," *TomDispatch*, September 27, 2012, www.tomdispatch.com /blog/175598/tomgram%3A_rebecca_solnit,_we_could_be_heroes/. *TomDispatch* refers to this article as a call for hope over despair. It should be labeled as a call for accommodation over the need for a radical democratic politics. For an alternative to this politics of accommodation, see the work of Stanley Aronowitz, Chris Hedges, Henry Giroux, Noam Chomsky, and others.

72. This term comes from Daniel Bensaïd. See Sebastian Budgen, "The Red Hussar: Daniel Bensaïd, 1946–2010," *International Socialism* 127 (June 25, 2010), http://www.isj.org.uk/?id=661.

73. Castoriadis, "Democracy as Procedure," 5.

74. Archon Fung, "The Constructive Responsibility of Intellectuals," *Boston Review*, September 9, 2011, www.bostonreview.net/BR36.5/archon _fung_noam_chomsky_responsibility_of_intellectuals.php.

75. Heather Gautney, "Why Do Political Elites All Hate Democracy?" *LA Progressive*, September 19, 2012, www.laprogressive.com/hate-democracy.

76. Stuart Hall and Les Back, "In Conversation: At Home and Not at Home," *Cultural Studies* 23, no. 4 (July 2009), 681.

77. Guy Standing, *The Precariat: The New Dangerous Class* (New York: Bloomsbury, 2011), 20.

CHAPTER TWO: DYSTOPIAN EDUCATION
IN A NEOLIBERAL SOCIETY

1.   Some important sources include: Henry A. Giroux, *Education and the Crisis of Public Values* (Boulder, CO: Paradigm Publishers, 2012); Kenneth J. Saltman, *The Failure of Corporate School Reform* (Boulder, CO: Paradigm Publishers, 2012); Diane Ravitch, *The Death and Life of the Great American School System: How Testing and Choice Are Undermining Education* (New York: Basic Books, 2011); Gaston Alonso, Noel S. Anderson, Celina Su, and Jeanne Theoharis, *Our Schools Suck: Students Talk Back to a Segregated Nation on the Failures of Urban Education* (New York: NYU Press, 2009).

2.   Graeme Turner, *What's Become of Cultural Studies* (New York: Sage, 2011), 183.

3.   See, for example, Madrick, *Age of Greed: The Triumph of Finance and the Decline of America*; Ferguson, *Predator Nation*; Giroux, *Zombie Politics in the Age of Casino Capitalism.*

4.   David Theo Goldberg, "The Taxing Terms of the GOP Plan Invite Class Carnage," *Truthout*, September 20, 2012, http://truth-out.org/news/item/11630 -the-taxing-terms-of-the-gop-plan-invite-class-carnage.

5.   Jolle Fanghanel, *Being an Academic* (New York: Routledge, 2012), 15.

6.   See, for example, Gaye Tuchman, *Wannabe U: Inside the Corporate University* (Chicago: University of Chicago Press, 2009); Martha C. Nussbaum, *Not for Profit: Why Democracy Needs the Humanities*, (Princeton, NJ: Princeton University Press, 2010); Michael Bailey and Des Freedman, eds., *The Assault on Universities: A Manifesto for Resistance* (London: Pluto Press, 2011); Henry A. Giroux, *Twilight of the Social: Resurgent Politics in the Age of Disposability* (Boulder, CO: Paradigm Publishers, 2012).

7.   On the religious Right, see Chris Hedges, *American Fascists: The Christian Right and the War on America* (New York: Free Press, 2008) and Clyde Wilcox and Carin Robinson, *Onward Christian Soldiers? The Religious Right in American Politics* (Boulder, CO: Westview Press, 2010).

8.   I have taken up the attack on higher education in a number of books. See, for example, Giroux and Searls Giroux, *Take Back Higher Education* and *The University in Chains.*

9.   David Theo Goldberg, "The University We Are For," *Huffington Post*, November 28, 2011, http://www.huffingtonpost.com/david-theo-goldberg/university -california-protests_b_1106234.html.

10. Marc Bousquet, *How the University Works: Higher Education and the Low-Wage Nation* (New York: NYU Press, 2008).

11. For a sustained analysis of how inequality undermines democracy and public services, see Richard Wilkinson and Kate Pickett, *The Spirit Level: Why Equality Is Better for Everyone* (New York: Penguin, 2010).

12. John Atcheson, "The Real Welfare Problem: Government Giveaways to the Corporate 1%," *Common Dreams*, September 3, 2012, www.commondreams.org

/view/2012/09/03-7.

13. See Joseph E. Stiglitz, *The Price of Inequality* (New York: W. W. Norton, 2012) and Michael Sandel, *What Money Can't Buy* (New York: FSG Publishing, 2012).

14. Goldberg, "The Taxing Terms of the GOP Plan."

15. Sandel, *What Money Can't Buy*.

16. Les Leopold, "Hey Dad, Why Does This Country Protect Billionaires, and Not Teachers?" *AlterNet*, May 5, 2010, www.alternet.org/module /printversion/146738.

17. David Glenn, "Public Higher Education Is 'Eroding from All Sides,' Warns Political Scientists," *Chronicle of Higher Education*, September 2, 2010, http:// chronicle.com/article/Public-Higher-Education-Is/124292/.

18. Noam Chomsky, "Public Education Under Massive Corporate Assault— What's Next? *AlterNet*, August 5, 2011, www.alternet.org/story/151921/ chomsky%3A_public_education_under_massive_corporate_assault_%E2 %80%94_what's_next.

19. Peter Seybold, "The Struggle Against the Corporate Takeover of the University," *Socialism and Democracy* 22, no. 1 (March 2008): 1–2.

20. Nancy Hass, "Scholarly Investments," *New York Times*, December 6, 2009.

21. Diane Ravitch, "Two Visions for Chicago's Schools," *Common Dreams*, September 14, 2012, www.commondreams.org/view/2012/09/14-3?print.

22. See Christopher Robbins, *Expelling Hope: The Assault on Youth and the Militarization of Schooling* (Albany: SUNY Press, 2008); Giroux, *Youth in a Suspect Society*; Fuentes, *Lockdown High*; Sadhbh Walshe, "US Education Orientation for Minorities: The School-to-Prison Pipeline," *Guardian*, August 31, 2012, www.guardian.co.uk/commentisfree/2012/aug/31/us-education-orientation -minorities. See also the ACLU report *Locating the School-to-Prison Pipeline*, www.aclu.org/racial-justice/school-prison-pipeline.

23. I have taken this issue up in Henry A. Giroux (co-authored with Susan Searls Giroux), "Scandalous Politics: Penn State and the Return of the Repressed in Higher Education," *JAC* 32, no. 1–2.

24. Charles M. Blow, "Plantations, Prisons and Profits," *New York Times*, May 25, 2012, www.nytimes.com/2012/05/26/opinion/blow-plantations-prisons-and -profits.html. For a detailed analysis of the racist prison-industrial complex, see Angela Y. Davis, *Abolition Democracy: Beyond Empire, Prisons, and Torture* (Seven Stories Press, 2005); Michelle Brown, *The Culture of Punishment: Prison, Society and Spectacle* (New York: NYU Press, 2009); Alexander, *The New Jim Crow*.

25. Amanda Terkel, "Arizona Expands Its Discrimination: Teachers with Heavy Accents Can't Teach English, Ethnic Studies Are Banned," *ThinkProgress*, April 30, 2010, http://thinkprogress.org/politics/2010/04/30/94567 /arizona-teachers/.

26. Miriam Jordan, "Arizona Grades Teachers on Fluency," *Wall Street Journal*, April 30, 2010, http://online.wsj.com/article/SB10001424052748703572504575213883276427528.html.

27. Zygmunt Bauman, *Society under Siege* (Malden, MA: Blackwell, 2002), 170.

28. Salvatore Babones, "To End the Jobs Recession, Invest an Extra $20 Billion in Public Education," *Truthout,* August 21, 2012, http://truth-out.org/opinion/item/11031-to-end-the-jobs-recession-invest-an-extra-$20-billion-in-public-education.

29. FT's Lex blog, "U.S. Defense Spending: What's the Real Figure?," *Globe and Mail,* May 28, 2012, www.theglobeandmail.com/report-on-business/international-business/us-defence-spending-whats-the-real-figure/article4217831/.

30. Daniel Trotta, "Cost of War $3.7 Trillion and Counting, 258,000 Dead," Reuters, June 28, 2011, http://uk.reuters.com/article/2011/06/29/uk-usa-war-idUKTRE75S76R20110629.

31. Dominic Tierney, "The F-35: A Weapon That Costs More Than Australia," *Atlantic,* November 11, 2011, www.theatlantic.com/national/archive/2011/03/the-f-35-a-weapon-that-costs-more-than-australia/72454/.

32. Babones, "To End the Jobs Recession."

33. Cited in Zygmunt Bauman, *Liquid Life* (Cambridge: Polity Press, 2005), 138.

34. Bill Readings *The University in Ruins* (Cambridge, MA: Harvard University Press,) 11, 18.

35. Zygmunt Bauman, *In Search of Politics* (Stanford, CA: Stanford University Press, 1999), 170.

36. Bauman, *Society under Siege,* 70.

37. Lynn Worsham and Gary A. Olson, "Rethinking Political Community: Chantal Mouffe's Liberal Socialism," *Journal of Composition Theory* 19, no. 2 (1999): 178.

38. Cavanagh, "Seven Ways to End the Deficit."

39. Ibid.

40. Noam Chomsky, "Paths Taken, Tasks Ahead," *Profession* (2000): 34.

41. Pierre Bourdieu, "For a Scholarship of Commitment," *Profession* (2000): 44.

42. Jacques Derrida, "Intellectual Courage: An Interview," trans. Peter Krapp, *Culture Machine* 2 (2000): 9.

43. A conversation between Lani Guinier and Anna Deavere Smith, "Rethinking Power, Rethinking Theater," *Theater* 31, no. 3 (Winter 2002): 34–35.

CHAPTER THREE: AT THE LIMITS
OF NEOLIBERAL HIGHER EDUCATION

1. This theme is taken up powerfully by a number of theorists. See C. Wright Mills, *The Sociological Imagination* (New York: Oxford University Press, 2000); Richard Sennett, *The Fall of Public Man* (New York: Norton, 1974); Zygmunt Bauman, *In Search of Politics* (Stanford, CA: Stanford University Press, 1999); and Henry A. Giroux, *Public Spaces, Private Lives* (Lanham, MD: Rowman and Littlefield, 2001).

2. Stuart Hall interviewed by James Hay, "Interview with Stuart Hall," *Communication and Critical/Cultural Studies* 10, no. 1 (2013): 11.

3. Vivian Yee, "Grouping Students by Ability Regains Favor in Classroom," *New York*

Times, June 10, 2013, www.nytimes.com/2013/06/10/education/grouping
-students-by-ability-regains-favor-with-educators.html?pagewanted=all&
_r=0.

4. Craig Calhoun, "Information Technology and the International Public
    Sphere," in *Shaping the Network Society: The New Role of Society in Cyber-
    space,* ed. Douglas Schuler and Peter Day (Cambridge, MA: MIT Press,
    2004), 241.

5. Michael D. Yates, "Occupy Wall Street and the Significance of Political Slo-
    gans," *Counterpunch,* February 27, 2013, www.counterpunch.org/2013/02/27
    /occupy-wall-street-and-the-significance-of-political-slogans/.

6. Zaid Jilani, Faiz Shakir, Benjamin Armbruster, George Zornick, Alex Seitz-
    Wald, and Tanya Somanader, "Rewarding Corporations While Punishing
    Workers," *Progress Report,* March 18, 2011, http://pr.thinkprogress.org/2011/03
    /pr20110318/index.html.

7. Jeffrey Sachs, "America's Deepening Moral Crisis," *Guardian,* October 4, 2010,
    www.guardian.co.uk/commentisfree/belief/2010/oct/04/americas-deepening
    -moral-crisis.

8. Classic examples of this can be found in the work of Milton Friedman and the
    fictional accounts of Ayn Rand. It is a position endlessly reproduced in con-
    servative foundations and institutes such as the American Enterprise Institute,
    Heritage Foundation, Hudson Institute, Manhattan Institute for Policy Re-
    search, and the Hoover Institute. One particularly influential book that shaped
    social policy along these lines is Charles Murray, *Losing Ground* (New York:
    Basic Books, 1994).

9. Jacques Rancière, *Hatred of Democracy* (London: Verso 2006).

10. Ellen Schrecker, *The Lost Soul of Higher Education* (New York: The New Press,
    2010), 3.

11. A number of important critiques of the Browne Report and the conservative-lib-
    eral attack on higher education include: Simon Head, "The Grim Threat to Brit-
    ish Universities," *New York Review of Books,* January 13, 2011, www.nybooks
    .com/articles/archives/2011/jan/13/grim-threat-british-universities/; An-
    thony T. Grafton, "Britain: The Disgrace of the Universities," *New York
    Review of Books,* March 10, 2010, 32; Nick Couldry, "Fighting for the
    Life of the English University in 2010," unpublished manuscript; Ste-
    fan Collini, "Browne's Gamble," *London Review of Books* 32, no. 21
    (November 4, 2010) 23–25; Stanley Fish, "The Value of Higher Ed-
    ucation Made Literal," *New York Times,* December 13, 2010, http://
    opinionator.blogs.nytimes.com/2010/12/13/the-value-of-higher-education
    -made-literal/; Aisha Labi, "British Universities and Businesses Are Forming
    Stronger Research Ties," *Chronicle of Higher Education,* October 4, 2010, http://
    chronicle.com/article/British-Universities-and/124814; and Terry Eagleton,
    "The Death of Universities," *Guardian,* December 17, 2010, www.guardian
    .co.uk/commentisfree/2010/dec/17/death-universities-malaise-tuition-fee.

12. Michael Collins, "Universities Need Reform—but the Market Is Not the An-
    swer," *OpenDemocracy.net,* November 23, 2010, www.opendemocracy.net

/ourkingdom/michael-collins/universities-need-reform-but-market-is-not
-answer.

13. Luke Johnson, "Marco Rubio on Climate Change: 'The Government Can't
Change the Weather,'" *Huffington Post*, February 13, 2013, www.huffingtonpost
.com/2013/02/13/marco-rubio-climate-change_n_2679810.html.

14. Ibid.

15. Collini, "Browne's Gamble."

16. Head, "The Grim Threat to British Universities."

17. Stanley Aronowitz, "Introduction," *Against Schooling: For an Education That
Matters* (Boulder, CO: Paradigm Publishers, 2008), xv.

18. Kathryn Masterson, "Off Campus Is Now the Place to Be for Deans," *Chronicle
of Higher Education*, March 6, 2011, http://chronicle.com/article/For-Deans
-Off-Campus-Is-Now/126607/.

19. Jason Del Gandio, "Neoliberalism and the Academic-Industrial Complex,"
Truthout, August 12, 2010, www.truth-out.org/neoliberalism-and-academic
-industrial-complex62189.

20. Scott Jaschik, "New Tactic to Kill Faculty Unions," *Inside Higher Ed*, March 3,
2011, www.insidehighered.com/news/2011/03/03/ohio_bill_would_kill_faculty
_unions_in_unexpected_way.

21. The Coalition on the Academic Workforce, *A Portrait of Part-Time Faculty
Members: A Summary of Findings on Part-Time Faculty Respondents to the
Coalition on the Academic Workforce Survey of Contingent Faculty Members*
(Washington, DC: CAW, June 2012), www.academicworkforce.org/CAW
_portrait_2012.pdf.

22. Schrecker, *The Lost Soul of Higher Education*, 206–215.

23. Evan McMorris-Santoro, "Conservative Think Tank Seeks Michigan Profs'
Emails About Wisconsin Union Battle . . . and Maddow," *Talking Points
Memo*, March 29, 2010; Paul Krugman, "American Thought Police," *New
York Times*, March 27, 2011, A27.

24. I take up these attacks in great detail in *The University in Chains*.

25. Stanley Aronowitz, "The Knowledge Factory," *Indypendent*, March 16, 2011,
www.indypendent.org/2011/03/17/the-knowledge-factory/.

26. John Pilger, "The Revolt in Egypt Is Coming Home," *Truthout*, February 10,
2011, www.truth-out.org/the-revolt-egypt-is-coming-home67624.

27. Courtney E. Martin, *Do It Anyway: A New Generation of Activists* (Boston:
Beacon Press, 2010).

28. Courtney E. Martin, "Why Class Matters in Campus Activism," *American
Prospect*, December 6, 2010, www.prospect.org/cs/articles?article=why_class
_matters_in_campus_activism.

29. Cited in ibid.

30. Mark Edelman Boren, *Student Resistance: A History of the Unruly Subject* (New
York: Routledge, 2001), 227.

31. Simeon Talley, "Why Aren't Students in the U.S. Protesting Tuition, Too?" *Campus Progress*, December 23, 2010, http://www.campusprogress.org/articles/why
_arent_students_in_the_u.s._protesting_tuition_too.

32. Susan Searls Giroux, *Between Race and Reason: Violence, Intellectual Responsibility, and the University to Come* (Stanford: Stanford University Press, 2010), 79.

33. Boren, *Student Resistance*, 228.

34. Robert Reich, "The Attack on American Education," *Reader Supported News*, December 23, 2010, www.readersupportednews.org/opinion2/299-190/4366 -the-attack-on-american-education.

35. Ibid.

36. There are many books and articles that take up this issue. One of the most incisive commentators is Jeffrey Williams, "Student Debt and the Spirit of Indenture," *Dissent* (Fall 2008), www.dissentmagazine.org/article /?article=1303.

37. David Mascriotra, "The Rich Get Richer and the Young Go into Deep Debt," *BuzzFlash*, December 6, 2010, http://blog.buzzflash.com/node/12045.

38. Head, "The Grim Threat to British Universities."

39. Jean-Luc Nancy, *The Truth of Democracy*, trans. Pascale-Anne Brault and Michael Naas (New York: Fordham University Press, 2010), 9.

40. Tom Engelhardt, "An American World War: What to Watch for in 2010," *Truthout*, January 3, 2010, www.truth-out.org/topstories/10410vh4. See also Andrew Bacevich, *The New American Militarism* (New York: Oxford University Press, 2005); and Chalmers Johnson, *Nemesis: The Last Days of the American Empire* (New York: Metropolitan Books, 2006).

41. Eric Gorski, "45% of Students Don't Learn Much in College," *Huffington Post*, January 21, 2011, www.huffingtonpost.com/2011/01/18/45-of-students-don't -learn_n_810224.html. The study is taken from Richard Arum and Josipa Roksa, *Academically Adrift: Limited Learning on College Campuses* (Chicago: University of Chicago Press, 2011).

42. Surely there is a certain irony in the fact that the work of Gene Sharp, a little-known American theorist in nonviolent action, is inspiring young people all over the world to resist authoritarian governments. Yet his work is almost completely ignored by young people in the United States. See, for instance, Sheryl Gay Stolberg, "Shy U.S. Intellectual Created Playbook Used in Revolution," *New York Times*, February 16, 2011, A1. See, in particular, Gene Sharp, *From Dictatorship to Democracy* (London: Serpent's Tail, 2012).

43. Sheldon S. Wolin, *Democracy Incorporated: Managed Democracy and the Specter of Inverted Totalitarianism* (Princeton, NJ: Princeton University Press, 2008), 259–260.

44. Zygmunt Bauman, *Does Ethics Have a Chance in a World of Consumers?* (Cambridge MA: Harvard University Press, 2008), 159.

45. Ibid., 235. I have also taken up this theme in great detail in *Youth in a Suspect Society*.

46. Zygmunt Bauman, *The Individualized Society* (London: Polity, 2001), 55.

47. Alex Honneth, *Pathologies of Reason* (New York: Columbia University Press, 2009), 188.

48. John Comaroff and Jean Comaroff, "Reflections on Youth from the Past to the

Postcolony," in *Frontiers of Capital: Ethnographic Reflections on the New Economy*, ed. Melissa S. Fisher and Greg Downey (Durham, NC: Duke University Press, 2006), 268.

49. Ibid.

50. Cited in Pascale-Anne Brault and Michael Naas, "Translator's Note," in Nancy, *The Truth of Democracy*, xii.

CHAPTER FOUR: INTELLECTUAL VIOLENCE IN THE AGE OF GATED INTELLECTUALS

1. This issue has been taken up in detail in Schrecker, *The Lost Soul of Higher Education*, and Edward J. Carvalho and David Downing, eds., *Academic Freedom in the Post-9/11 Era* (New York: Palgrave, 2011).

2. Theodor Adorno, *Authoritarian Personality* (New York: Harper & Row, 1950).

3. Lutz Koepnick, "Aesthetic Politics Today—Walter Benjamin and Post-Fordist Culture," *Critical Theory—Current State and Future Prospects*, ed. Peter Uwe Hohendahl and Jaimey Fisher (New York: Berghahn Books: 2002), 96.

4. Mumia Abu-Jamal, "The U.S. Is Fast Becoming One of the Biggest Open-Air Prisons on Earth," *Democracy Now!*, February 1, 2013, www.democracynow.org /2013/2/1/mumia_abu_jamal_the_united_states.

5. Michel Foucault, *Society Must Be Defended: Lectures at the College de France 1975–1976*, (New York: Picador, 2003), 47.

6. Ibid., 256.

7. Ibid., 56.

8. On this see, in particular, Bauman, *Society under Siege*.

9. Brad Evans and Mark Duffield, "Biospheric Security: How the Merger Between Development, Security & the Environment [Desenex] Is Retrenching Fortress Europe," in *A Threat Against Europe? Security, Migration and Integration,* eds. Peter Burgess and Serge Gutwirth (VUB Press: Brussels, 2011).

10. This critique of instrumental reason was a central feature of the Frankfurt School and is most notable in the work of Herbert Marcuse. See also Zygmunt Bauman's brilliant critique in *Modernity and the Holocaust* (Ithaca, NY: Cornell University Press, 2010), reprint edition.

11. See, for example, World Bank and Carter Centre, *From Civil War to Civil Society*, (Washington, DC: World Bank and Carter Centre, 1997).

12. Cited in Matt Phillips, "Goldman Sachs' Blankfein on Banking: 'Doing God's Work,'" *Marketbeat* (blog), *Wall Street Journal*, November 9, 2009, http://blogs.wsj.com/marketbeat/2009/11/09/goldman-sachs-blankfein-on -banking-doing-gods-work/.

13. C. Wright Mills, *The Politics of Truth: Selected Writings of C. Wright Mills* (New York: Oxford University Press, 2008), 200.

14. Aronowitz, *Against Schooling*, xii. See also http://archive.truthout.org/the -disappearing-intellectual-age-economic-darwinism61287 - 13.

15. Kate Zernike, "Making College 'Relevant,'" *New York Times*, January 3, 2010.

16. While this critique has been made by many critics, it has also been made recently by the president of Harvard University. See Drew Gilpin Faust, "The University's Crisis of Purpose," *New York Times*, September 6, 2009.

17. Harvey cited in Stephen Pender, "An Interview with David Harvey," *Studies in Social Justice* 1, no. 1 (Winter 2007): 14.

18. See, in particular, Giorgio Agamben, *Homo Sacer: Sovereign Power and Bare Life* (Stanford, CA: Stanford University Press, 1995); and Giorgio Agamben, *State of Exception* (Chicago: University of Chicago Press, 2005).

19. This term is first developed in Henry A. Giroux, *Twilight of the Social* (Boulder, CO: Paradigm Publishers, 2012).

20. David Theo Goldberg, *The Threat of Race: Reflections on Racial Neoliberalism* (Malden, MA: Wiley-Blackwell, 2009), 338-339.

21. Zygmunt Bauman, "Has the Future a Left?" *The Review of Education/Pedagogy/Cultural Studies* (2007): 2. Henry Giroux takes up the issue of gated intellectuals in greater detail in Henry A. Giroux, *The Education Deficit and the War on Youth* (New York: Monthly Review Press, 2013).

22. Judith Butler, *Frames of War: When Is Life Grievable?* (London: Verso, 2009), 3,4.

23. Ibid., 4.

24. Henry Giroux, "Counter-Memory & the Politics of Loss," *Truthout*, September 13, 2011, www.truth-out.org/counter-memory-and-politics-loss-after-911/1315595429.

25. Marjorie Cohn, ed., *The United States and Torture: Interrogation, Incarceration, and Abuse* (New York: NYU Press, 2011); Medea Benjamin, *Drone Warfare* (London: Verso Press, 2013); Nick Turse and Tom Englehardt, *Terminator Planet: The First History of Drone Warfare, 2001–2050* (New York: Dispatch Press, 2012).

26. Roger Simon, "A Shock of Thought," *Memory Studies* (February 21, 2011).

27. See Michael Hardt and Antonio Negri, *Declaration* (New York: Argo Navis Author Services, 2012).

28. Simon Critchley, "September 11 and the Cycle of Revenge," *The Stone* (blog), *New York Times*, September 8, 2011, http://opinionator.blogs.nytimes.com/2011/09/08/the-cycle-of-revenge/.

29. Jacques Derrida, *On Cosmopolitanism and Forgiveness* (New York: Routledge, 2005), 32.

30. Ibid., 37.

31. Brad Evans, *Liberal Terror* (Cambridge: Polity Press, 2013).

32. Leo Lowenthal, "Atomization of Man," *False Prophets: Studies on Authoritarianism* (New Brunswick, NJ: Transaction Books, 1987), 181–182.

33. Walter Benjamin, "Critique of Violence," in *Reflections: Essays, Aphorisms, Autobiographical Writings*, ed. Peter Demetz (Schocken Books: New York, 1986), 277–300.

34. Stanley Aronowitz, "Introduction," in Paulo Freire, *Pedagogy of Freedom* (Boulder, CO: Rowman and Littlefield, 1998), 7.

35. Michel Foucault, "Preface," in Gilles Deleuze and Felix Guattari, *Anti-Oedipus:*

Capitalism and Schizophrenia (London: Continuum, 2003), xv.

36. Gilles Deleuze, *Desert Islands and Other Texts, 1953–1974*, ed. David Lapoujade, trans. Michael Taormina (New York: Semiotext[e], 2004), 139–140.

37. Stuart Hall, "Epilogue: Through the Prism of an Intellectual Life," in *Culture, Politics, Race, and Diaspora: The Thought of Stuart Hall*, ed. Brian Meeks (Miami: Ian Rundle Publishers, 2007), 289–290.

38. See also Giroux and Searls Giroux, *Take Back Higher Education*.

39. Jacques Rancière, *On the Shores of Politics* (London: Verso Press, 1995), 3.

40. Edward Said, *Humanism and Democratic Criticism* (New York: Columbia University Press, 2004), 50.

41. C. Wright Mills, "Culture and Politics: The Fourth Epoch," in *The Politics of Truth: Selected Writings of C. Wright Mills* (New York: Oxford University Press, 2008), 199.

42. Editors, "A Conversation with David Harvey," *Logos: A Journal of Modern Society & Culture* 5, no. 1 (2006).

CHAPTER FIVE: ON THE URGENCY
FOR PUBLIC INTELLECTUALS IN THE ACADEMY

1. Audre Lorde, "Poetry is not a Luxury," *Sister Outsider: Essays and Speeches* (Freedom, CA: The Crossing Press, 1984), 38.

2. I have taken this idea of linking Lorde's notion of poetry to education from Martha Nell Smith, "The Humanities Are a Manifesto for the Twenty-First Century," *Liberal Education* (Winter 2011): 48–55.

3. Debra Leigh Scott, "How the American University Was Killed, in Five Easy Steps," The Homeless Adjunct Blog, August 12, 2012, http://junctrebellion.wordpress.com/2012/08/12/how-the-american-university-was-killed-in-five-easy-steps/.

4. Ferguson, *Predator Nation*, 21.

5. Nicholas Lemann, "Evening the Odds: Is There a Politics of Inequality?" *New Yorker*, April 23, 2012, www.newyorker.com/arts/critics/atlarge/2012/04/23/120423crat_atlarge_lemann.

6. Reihaneh Hajibeigi, "Resisting Corporate Education: Is 'Business Productivity' Coming to the University of Texas?" *Nation of Change*, June 13, 2013, www.nationofchange.org/resisting-corporate-education-business-productivity-coming-university-texas-1371133921.

7. Joseph E. Stiglitz, "The Price of Inequality," *Project Syndicate*, June 5, 2012, www.project-syndicate.org/commentary/the-price-of-inequality.

8. Ibid.

9. Ferguson, *Predator Nation*, 8

10. Ibid.

11. Andrew Gavin Marshall, "The Shocking Amount of Wealth and Power Held by 0.001% of the World Population," *AlterNet*, June 12, 2013, www.alternet.org

/economy/global-power-elite-exposed?akid=10567.40823.Q_uvw_&rd=1 &src=newsletter854356&t=3.

12. Alex Honneth, *Pathologies of Reason* (New York: Columbia University Press, 2009), 188.

13. Buchheit, "Five Ugly Extremes."

14. Zygmunt Bauman, *Collatoral Damage: Social Inequalities in a Global Age* (Cambridge, UK: Polity Press, 2011), 39.

15. I have taken these figures from Paul Buchheit, "Five Facts That Put America to Shame," *Common Dreams*, May 14, 2012, www.commondreams.org/view /2012/05/14-0.

16. Cornelius Castoriadis, *A Society Adrift: Interviews & Debates 1974–1997*, trans. Helen Arnold (New York: Fordham University Press, 2010), 7.

17. The genealogy from anti-intellectualism in American life to the embrace of illiteracy as a virtue is analyzed in the following books: Richard Hofstadter, *Anti-Intellectualism in American Life* (New York: Vintage, 1966); Susan Jacoby, *The Age of American Unreason* (New York: Pantheon, 2008); Charles P. Piece, *Idiot America: How Stupidity Became a Virtue in the Land of the Free* (New York: Anchor Books, 2009).

18. Castoriadis, *A Society Adrift*, 8.

19. Mills, *The Politics of Truth*, 200.

20. Frank B. Wilderson III, "Introduction: Unspeakable Ethics," in *Red, White, & Black* (London, UK: Duke University Press, 2012), 2.

21. Stanley Aronowitz, "Against Schooling: Education and Social Class," in *Against Schooling* (Boulder, CO: Paradigm Publishers, 2008), xii.

22. See most recently Kelly V. Vlahos, "Boots on Campus," *AntiWar.com*, February 26, 2013, http://original.antiwar.com/vlahos/2013/02/25/boots-on -campus/; and David H. Price, *Weaponizing Anthropology* (Oakland, CA: AK Press, 2011).

23. Kelley B. Vlahos, "Boots on Campus: Yale Flap Highlights Militarization of Academia," *Truthout*, February 27, 2013, http://truth-out.org/news/item /14837-boots-on-campus-yale-flap-highlights-militarization-of-academia.

24. Ibid.

25. Greg Bishop, "A Company that Runs Prisons Will Have Its Name on a Stadium," *New York Times*, February 19, 2013, www.nytimes.com/2013/02/20 /sports/ncaafootball/a-company-that-runs-prisons-will-have-its-name-on-a -stadium.html?_r=0.

26. Dave Zirin, "Victory! The Stopping of Owlcatraz," *Common Dreams*, April 3, 2013, www.commondreams.org/view/2013/04/03.

27. Ibid.

28. Scott Travis, "GEO Withdraws Gift, Naming Rights for FAU Stadium," *South Florida Sun-Sesntinel*, April 1, 2013, www.sun-sentinel.com/news/palm-beach /fl-fau-geo-stadium-20130401,0,6857150.story.

29. Zirin, "Victory! The Stopping of Owlcatraz."

30. Zernike, "Making College 'Relevant.'"

31. Scott Jaschik, "Making Adjuncts Temps—Literally," *Inside Higher Education*, August 9, 2010, www.insidehighered.com/news/2010/08/09/adjuncts.

32. Martha C. Nussbaum, *Not for Profit: Why Democracy Needs the Humanities* (Princeton, NJ: Princeton University Press, 2010), 142.

33. Greig de Peuter, "Universities, Intellectuals, and Multitudes: An Interview with Stuart Hall," in *Utopian Pedagogy: Radical Experiments against Neoliberal Globalization*, eds. Mark Cote, Richard J. F. Day, and Greig de Peuter (Toronto: University of Toronto Press, 2007), 111.

34. Nussbaum, *Not for Profit*.

35. On the militarization of higher education, see Giroux, *The University in Chains*. See also Philip Zwerling, ed., *The CIA on Campus: Essays on Academic Freedom and the National Security State* (Jefferson, NC: McFarland and Company, 2011); David H. Price, *Weaponizing Anthropology* (Petrolia, CA: CounterPunch, 2011).

36. Castoriadis, "Democracy as Procedure and Democracy as Regime," 5.

37. George Scialabba, *What Are Intellectuals Good For?* (Boston: Pressed Wafer, 2009) 4.

38. Toni Morrison, "How Can Values Be Taught in This University,"*Michigan Quarterly Review* (Spring 2001): 278.

39. Scialabba, *What Are Intellectuals Good For?*

40. James Baldwin interview by Mel Watkins, *New York Times Book Review*, September 23, 1979, 3.

41. Zoe Williams, "The Saturday Interview: Stuart Hall," *Guardian*, February 11, 2012, www.guardian.co.uk/theguardian/2012/feb/11/saturday-interview -stuart-hall.

42. Sheldon S. Wolin, *Democracy, Inc.: Managed Democracy and the Specter of Inverted Totalitarianism* (Princeton, NJ: Princeton University Press, 2008), 43.

43. Morrison, "How Can Values Be Taught in This University," 276.

44. On this issue, see the brilliant essay by Susan Searls Giroux, "On the Civic Function of Intellectuals Today," in *Education as Civic Engagement: Toward a More Democratic Society*, eds. Gary Olson and Lynn Worsham (Boulder, CO: Paradigm Publishers, 2012), ix–xvii.

45. Martin Luther King, Jr., "The Trumpet of Conscience," in *The Essential Writings and Speeches of Martin Luther King, Jr.*, ed. James M. Washington (New York: Harper Collins, 1991), 644.

46. Arundhati Roy, *Power Politics* (Cambridge, MA: South End Press, 2001), 6.

47. de Peuter, "Universities, Intellectuals, and Multitudes," 113–114.

48. Ibid., 117.

49. Cited in Madeline Bunting, "Passion and Pessimism," *Guardian*, April 5, 2003, http:/books.guardian.co.uk/print/0,3858,4640858,00.html.

50. Irving Howe, "This Age of Conformity," *Selected Writings 1950–1990* (New York: Harcourt Brace Jovanovich, 1990), 27.

51. Giovanna Borriadori, ed., "Autoimmunity: Real and Symbolic Suicides—a Dialogue with Jacques Derrida," in *Philosophy in a Time of Terror: Dialogues with Jurgen Habermas and Jacques Derrida* (Chicago: University of Chicago

Press, 2004), 121.

52. Cornelius Castoriadis, "Democracy as Procedure and Democracy as Regime," *Constellations* 4, no. 1 (1997): 10.

53. Edward Said, *Out of Place: A Memoir* (New York: Vintage, 2000), 294–299.

54. Said, *Out of Place*, 7.

55. Stephen Howe, "Edward Said: The Traveller and the Exile," *Open Democracy*, October 2, 2003, www.opendemocracy.net/articles/ViewPopUpArticle.jsp?id =10&articleId=1561.

56. Hannah Arendt, *Between Past and Future: Eight Exercises in Political Thought* (New York: Penguin, 1977), 149.

57. Edward Said, "On Defiance and Taking Positions," *Reflections on Exile and Other Essays* (Cambridge, MA: Harvard University Press, 2001), 504.

58. Edward Said, *Humanism and Democratic Criticism* (New York: Columbia University Press, 2004), 70.

59. Howe, "This Age of Conformity," 36.

60. See, especially, Christopher Newfield, *Unmaking the Public University: The Forty-Year Assault on the Middle Class* (Cambridge, MA: Harvard University Press, 2008).

61. See Henry A. Giroux, "Academic Unfreedom in America: Rethinking the University as a Democratic Public Sphere," in Edward J. Carvalho, ed., "Academic Freedom and Intellectual Activism in the Post-9/11 University," special issue of *Works and Days* 51–54 (2008–2009): 45–72. This may be the best collection yet published on intellectual activism and academic freedom.

62. Gayatri Chakravorty Spivak, "Changing Reflexes: Interview with Gayatri Chakravorty Spivak," *Works and Days* 28, no. 55/56 (2010): 8.

63. Bill Moyers, "Interview with William K. Black," *Bill Moyers Journal*, April 23, 2010, www.pbs.org/moyers/journal/04232010/transcript4.html.

64. Ibid.

65. See, especially, Hannah Arendt, *The Origins of Totalitarianism*, third edition, revised (New York: Harcourt Brace Jovanovich, 1968); and John Dewey, *Liberalism and Social Action* (New York: Prometheus Press, 1999/1935).

66. See Frederick Douglass, "West India Emancipation," speech delivered at Canandaigua, New York, August 4, 1857, in *The Life and Writings of Frederick Douglass*, vol. 2, ed. Philip S. Foner (New York: International, 1950), 437.

67. Aronowitz, "The Winter of Our Discontent," 68.

68. Jacques Derrida, "No One Is Innocent: A Discussion with Jacques About Philosophy in the Face of Terror," The Information Technology, War and Peace Project, www.watsoninstitute.org/infopeace/911/derrida_innocence.html.

69. Howe, "This Age of Conformity," 49.

CHAPTER SIX: THE PROMISE OF EDUCATION IN DIFFICULT TIMES

1. See, especially, Stuart Hall, "The Neoliberal Revolution," in *The Neoliberal Crisis*, ed. Jonathan Rutherford and Sally Davison (London: Lawrence Wishart, 2012), http://wh.agh.edu.pl/other/materialy/678_2015_04_21 _22_04_51_The_Neoliberal_Crisis_Book.pdf; David Harvey, *A Brief History of Neoliberalism* (New York: Oxford University Press, 2005); Sheldon S. Wolin, *Democracy Incorporated: Managed Democracy and the Specter of Inverted Totalitarianism* (Princeton: Princeton University Press, 2008). Wendy Brown, *Undoing the Demos: Neoliberalism's Stealth Revolution* (New York: Zone Books, 2015). Virginia Eubanks, *Automating Inequality* (New York: St. Martin's Press, 2017); George Monbiot, *Out of the Wreckage* (New York: Verso Press, 2017); Henry A. Giroux, *American Nightmare: Facing the Challenge of Fascism* (San Francisco: City Lights, 2018).

2. Charles Derber, *Welcome to the Revolution: Universalizing Resistance for Social Justice and Democracy in Perilous Times* (New York: Routledge, 2017); Heinrich Geiselberger, ed., *The Great Regression* (London: Polity, 2017).

3. George Steiner, "Some Thoughts on Narrative," in *Art and Interpretation: An Anthology of Readings in Aesthetics and the Philosophy of Art*, ed. Eric Dayton (New York: Broadview Press, 1999), 325.

4. Jon Nixon, "Hannah Arendt: Thinking Versus Evil," *Times Higher Education*, February 26, 2015, https://www.timeshighereducation.co.uk/features /hannah-arendt-thinking-versus-evil/2018664.article?page=0%2C0.

5. Stephen Hopgood, "One Question Fascism: Is Fascism making a comeback?" (Part Two)," *State of Nature Blog*, December 4, 2017, http:// stateofnatureblog.com/one-question-fascism-part-two/.

6. Associated Press, "A One-Year-Old Boy Had a Court Appearance Before an Immigration Judge in Phoenix," *Time*, July 8, 2018, http://time .com/5332740/immigration-judge-boy/.

7. Leon Wieseltier, "Among the Disrupted," *New York Times*, January 7, 2015, https://www.nytimes.com/2015/01/18/books/review/among-the-disrupted .html.

8. Richards J. Evans, "A Warning from History," *The Nation*, February 28, 2017, https://www.thenation.com/article/the-ways-to-destroy-democracy/. See also Robert O. Paxton, *The Anatomy of Fascism* (New York: Alfred A. Knopf, 2004).

9. Henry A. Giroux, *American Nightmare: Facing the Challenge of Fascism* (San Francisco: City Lights, 2018).

10. See, for example, the classic essay: Jerome Kohn, "Totalitarianism: The Inversion of Politics," *The Hannah Arendt Papers at the Library of Congress Essays and Lectures—"On the Nature of Totalitarianism: An Essay in Understanding"* (Series: Speeches and Writings File, 1923–1975, n.d.), http:// memory.loc.gov/ammem/arendthtml/essayb1.html.

11. Angela Y. Davis, *Freedom Is a Constant Struggle: Ferguson, Palestine and the Foundations of a Movement*, ed. Frank Barat. (Chicago: Haymarket Books,

2016), 83.

12. Henry A. Giroux, "Cultural Studies, Public Pedagogy, and the Responsibility of Intellectuals," *Communication and Critical/Cultural Studies* 1, no. 1, (March 2004) 68.

13. Roger Simon, "Empowerment as a Pedagogy of Possibility," *Language Arts* 64, no. 4 (April 1987): 372.

14. Hannah Arendt, *The Origins of Totalitarianism* (New York: Harcourt, Brace, Jovanovich, 1973), 474.

15. Danielle Allen, "What is Education For?," *Boston Review*, May 9, 2016, http://bostonreview.net/forum/danielle-allen-what-education.

16. Stefan Collini, "Browne's Gamble," *London Review of Books* 32, no. 21, November 4, 2010, http://www.lrb.co.uk/v32/n21/stefan-collini/brownes-gamble.

17. Byung-Chul Han, *The Burnout Society*, trans. Erik Butler (Stanford: Stanford University Press, 2015), 12.

18. Byung-Chul Han, *In the Swarm: Digital Prospects*, trans. Erik Butler (Cambridge: MIT Press, 2017). For an excellent commentary on neoliberalism and global policy, see Ourania Filippakou, "Towards a New Epistemic Order: Higher Education After Neoliberalism," in *Higher Education in Austerity Europe*, ed. Jon Nixon (London: Bloomsbury, 2017).

19. Gayatri Chakravorty Spivak, "Changing Reflexes: Interview with Gayatri Chakravorty Spivak," interview by Edward J. Carvalho, *Works and Days* 28, nos. 55/56 (2010): 8.

20. Stefan Collini, "Browne's Gamble."

21. Melvin Rogers, "Democracy Is a Habit: Practice It," *Boston Review*, July 25, 2019, http://bostonreview.net/politics/melvin-rogers-democracy-habit-practice-it.

22. William Rivers Pitt, "Lies, Lies, Lies, Lies, Lies, Lies, Lies, Lies, Lies, Lies, Lies," *Truthout,* February 6, 2019, https://truthout.org/articles/lies-lies-lies-lies-lies-lies-lies-lies-lies-lies/.

23. Mike DeBonis and Seung Min Kim, "Trump Lashes Out as Democrats Step Up Inquiries of President and Administration," *Washington Post,* February 6, 2019, https://www.washingtonpost.com/powerpost/trump-lashes-out-as-democrats-step-up-inquiries-of-president-and-administration/2019/02/06/a80b76c4-2a38-11e9-984d-9b8fba003e81_story.html?utm_term=.a5facc8954bf&wpisrc=nl_most&wpmm=1.

24. Frank Rich, "This Constitutional Crisis Probably Won't Be Trump's Last," *New York Magazine,* May 5, 2019, http://nymag.com/intelligencer/2019/05/frank-rich-this-constitutional-crisis-wont-be-trumps-last.html.

25. Brad Evans and Henry A. Giroux, *Disposable Futures: The Seduction of Violence in the Age of the Spectacle* (San Francisco: City Lights, 2016).

26. Ulrich Beck, *Twenty Observations on a World in Turmoil* (London: Polity Press, 2010), especially 53–59.

27. Christopher Newfield, "Faculty Need to Do Better Than This,"

Remaking the University, August 20, 2018, http://utotherescue.blogspot.com/2018/08/faculty-need-do-better-than-this.html.

28. Terry Eagleton, "The Ambition of Advanced Capitalism Is Not Simply to Combat Radical Ideas—It Is to Abolish the Very Notion That There Could Be a Serious Alternative to the Present," *Red Pepper,* October 13, 2013, https://www.redpepper.org.uk/death-of-the-intellectual/.

29. Brad Evans, "A World Without Books," in *Atrocity Exhibition: Life in the Age of Total Violence* (Los Angeles: Los Angeles Review of Books, 2019), 177.

30. Robin D. G. Kelley, "Sorry, Not Sorry," *Boston Review,* September 13, 2018, http://bostonreview.net/race-literature-culture/robin-d-g-kelley-sorry-not-sorry.

31. Anthony DiMaggio and Paul Street have addressed this issue in a number of brilliant books and articles.

32. Teju Cole, "Resist, Refuse," *New York Times,* September 8, 2018, https://www.nytimes.com/2018/09/08/magazine/teju-cole-resistance-op-ed-resist-refuse.html.

33. Michael Hayden, "The End of Intelligence," *New York Times,* April 28, 2018, https://www.nytimes.com/2018/04/28/opinion/sunday/the-end-of-intelligence.html.

34. Anonymous, "I Am Part of the Resistance Inside the Trump Administration," *New York Times,* September 5, 2018, https://www.nytimes.com/2018/09/05/opinion/trump-white-house-anonymous-resistance.html?module=inline.

35. Ibid.

36. Henry A. Giroux, "The Politics of Neoliberal Fascism," *Tikkun,* August 21, 2018, https://www.tikkun.org/newsite/the-politics-of-neoliberal-fascism.

37. Christopher R. Browning, "The Suffocation of Democracy," *New York Review of Books* 65, no 16, October 25, 2018, https://www.nybooks.com/articles/2018/10/25/suffocation-of-democracy/; Cass R. Sunstein, "It Can Happen Here," *New York Review of Books,* June 28, 2018, http://www.nybooks.com/articles/2018/06/28/hitlers-rise-it-can-happen-here/.

38. Marc Margolis, "Brazil's Mercurial Courts Undermine Democracy," *Bloomberg Opinion,* July 15, 2018, https://www.bloomberg.com/opinion/articles/2018-07-15/brazil-s-mercurial-courts-undermine-growth-and-democracy; Rubens Glezer, "Presidential Corruption Verdict Shows Just How Flawed Brazil's Justice System Is," *Conversation,* January 29, 2018, http://theconversation.com/presidential-corruption-verdict-shows-just-how-flawed-brazils-justice-system-is-90794.

39. See, for instance, Jason Hirthler, "The Pieties of the Liberal Class," *Counter-Punch,* October 19, 2018, https://www.counterpunch.org/2018/10/19/the-pieties-of-the-liberal-class/.

40. Michelle Alexander, "We Are Not the Resistance," *New York Times,* September 21, 2018, https://www.nytimes.com/2018/09/21/opinion/sunday/resistance-kavanaugh-trump-protest.html.

41. Alex Seitz-Wald, "Sanders' Wing of the Party Terrifies Moderate Dems. Here's How They Plan To Stop It," *NBC News,* July 20, 2018, https://www .nbcnews.com/politics/elections/sanders-wing-party-terrifies-moderate -dems-here-s-how-they-n893381.

42. Grace Lee Boggs with Scott Kurashige, *The Next American Revolution: Sustainable Activism for the Twenty-First Century* (Oakland: University of California Press, 2012), 36.

43. Rob Nixon, *Slow Violence and the Environmentalism of the Poor* (Cambridge: Harvard University Press, 2011), x.

44. George P. Lakoff and Gil Duran, "Trump Has Turned Words into Weapons. And He's Winning the Linguistic War," *Guardian,* June 13, 2018, https://www.theguardian.com/commentisfree/2018/jun/13/how-to-report -trump-media-manipulation-language.

45. Christal Hayes, "Nearly Half of Republicans Think Trump Should Be Able to Close News Outlets: Poll," *USA Today,* August 7, 2018, https://www.usatoday .com/story/news/politics/2018/08/07/trump-should-able-close-news-outlets -republicans-say-poll/925536002/.

46. Editorial, "As Lincoln Advised, This, Too, Shall Pass," *Herald Tribune,* August 16, 2018, http://www.heraldtribune.com/opinion/20180816/editorial -as-lincoln-advised-this-too-shall-pass.

47. Kevin Liptak, "Trump Says He Doesn't Regret Signing Immigration Order," *CNN Politics,* June 25, 2018, https://www.cnn.com/2018/06/25 /politics/trump-immigration-order/index.html.

48. See, for example, Jason Stanley, *How Fascism Works: The Politics of Us and Them* (New York: Random House, 2018); Henry A. Giroux, *American Nightmare: Facing the Challenge of Fascism* (San Francisco: City Lights Books, 2018); Timothy Snyder, *The Road to Unfreedom* (New York: Tim Duggan Books, 2018); Brian Klaas, *The Despot's Apprentice: Donald Trump's Attack on Democracy* (New York: Hot Books, 2017).

49. Pierre Bourdieu and Günter Grass, "The 'Progressive' Restoration: A Franco-German Dialogue," *New Left Review* 14 (March–April, 2002): 2.

50. Pierre Bourdieu, *Acts of Resistance* (New York: Free Press, 1998), 11.

51. Terry Eagleton, "The Slow Death of the University," *The Chronicle of Higher Education,* April 6, 2015, http://chronicle.com/article/The-Slow-Death-of -the/228991/.

52. Brad Evans, *The Atrocity Exhibition* (Los Angeles: Los Angeles Review of Books, 2019).

53. Kenneth J. Saltman, *Scripted Bodies: Corporate Power, Smart Technologies, and the Undoing of Public Education* (New York: Routledge, 2016); Diane Ravitch, *Reign of Error* (New York: Knopf, 2014); Henry A. Giroux, *Education and the Crisis of Public Values* (New York: Peter Lange, 2015).

CHAPTER SEVEN: HIGHER EDUCATION, NEOLIBERALISM, AND THE POLITICS OF DISPOSABILITY

1. Steven Levitsky and Daniel Ziblatt, *How Democracies Die* (New York: Crown, 2018); Henry A. Giroux, *America at War with Itself* (San Francisco: City Lights Books, 2016).

2. See the introduction.

3. "Oprah Winfrey Interviews Donald Trump on the Role Genetics Play in Success," March 22, 1998, YouTube, https://www.youtube.com /watch?v=YclB7UDbnKQ.

4. Sarah Jones, "Trump Has Turned the GOP into the Party of Eugenics," *New Republic*, February 15, 2017, https://newrepublic.com/article/140641 /trump-turned-gop-party-eugenics.

5. Manny Fernandez and Katie Benner, "The Billion-Dollar Business of Operating Shelters for Migrant Children," *New York Times,* June 21, 2018, https://www.nytimes.com/2018/06/21/us/migrant-shelters-border-crossing .html.

6. Colleen Long, "At Least 4,500 Abuse Complaints at Migrant Children Shelters," *Truthdig*, February 27, 2019, https://www.truthdig.com/articles /at-least-4500-abuse-complaints-at-migrant-children-shelters/.

7. Farnel Maxime, "Zero-Tolerance Policies and the School to Prison Pipeline," *Shared Justice*, January 18, 2018, http://www.sharedjustice.org /domestic-justice/2017/12/21/zero-tolerance-policies-and-the-school-to -prison-pipeline.

8. All of the latter examples are taken from David Leonhardt and Ian Prasad Philbrick, "Donald Trump's Racism: The Definitive List," *New York Times,* January 15, 2018, https://www.nytimes.com/interactive/2018/01/15 /opinion/leonhardt-trump-racist.html.

9. Paul Krugman, "The GOP Goes Full Authoritarian," *New York Times*, December 10, 2018, https://www.nytimes.com/2018/12/10/opinion/trump -gop-authoritarian-states-power-grab.html.

10. Frank Rich, "With State of the Union Disinvitation, Pelosi Outmaneuvers Trump Once Again," *New York* magazine, January 17, 2019, http://nymag .com/intelligencer/2019/01/frank-rich-pelosi-outmaneuvers-trump-on-sotu -disinvitation.html.

11. Frank Rich, "Mueller's Steady Stream of Russia Revelations Is Driving Trump Crazy," *New York* magazine, November 29, 2018, http://nymag .com/intelligencer/2018/11/mueller-revelations-drive-trump-crazy.html.

12. George Packer, "The Corruption of the Republican Party," *Atlantic,* December 14, 2018, https://www.theatlantic.com/ideas/archive/2018/12 /how-did-republican-party-get-so-corrupt/578095/

13. Chantal Da Silva, "Donald Trump Says Migrants Bring 'Large Scale Crime and Disease' to America," *Newsweek*, December 11, 2018, https://www. newsweek.com/donald-trump-says-migrants-bring-large-scale-crime -and-disease-america-1253268.

14. Cited in Richard A. Etlin, "Introduction," in *Art, Culture, and Media Under the Third Reich* (Chicago: University of Chicago Press, 2002), 14.
15. Lawrence M. Eppard, Dan Schubert, and Henry A. Giroux, "The Double Violence of Inequality: Precarity, Individualism, and White Working-Class Americans," *Sociological Viewpoints* 32, no. 1 (2018): 58–87.
16. Etlin, "Introduction," in *Art, Culture, and Media*, 3.
17. Ibid., 3.
18. A. K. Thompson, "Premonitions: Fragments of a Culture of Revolt," *Socialist Project: The Bullet,* December 10, 2018, https://socialistproject.ca /2018/12/premonitions-fragments-of-culture-of-revolt/.
19. Giroux, *American Nightmare.*
20. Levitsky and Ziblatt, *How Democracies Die.*
21. See, for instance, Nadja Popovich, Livia Albeck-Ripka, and Kendra Pierre-Louis, "78 Environmental Rules on the Way Out Under Trump," *New York Times,* December 19, 2018, https://www.nytimes.com/interactive/2017/10 /05/climate/trump-environment-rules-reversed.html?emc=edit_nn_p_ 20181227&nl=morning-briefing&nlid=51563793&section=topNews&te=1.
22. Editorial, "Trump Imperils the Planet," *New York Times,* December 26, 2018, https://www.nytimes.com/2018/12/26/opinion/editorials /climate-change-environment-trump.html.
23. Lisa Friedman, "E.P.A. Proposes Rule Change that Would Let Power Plants Release More Toxic Pollution," *New York Times*, December 28, 2018, https:// www.nytimes.com/2018/12/28/climate/mercury-coal-pollution-regulations .html?action=click&module=Top%20Stories&pgtype=Homepage.
24. Eliot Weinberger, "Ten Typical Days in Trump's America," *London Review of Books* 40, no. 20 (October 25, 2018), https://www.lrb.co.uk/v40/n20 /eliot-weinberger/ten-typical-days-in-trumps-america.
25. Caitlin Oprysko, "'I Don't Believe It': Trump Dismisses Grim Government Report on Climate Change," *Politico,* November 26, 2018, https://www .politico.com/story/2018/11/26/trump-climate-change-report-1016494.
26. Miles Kampf-Lassin, "Why is the Political Establishment So Afraid of Ocasio-Cortez's Green New Deal," *In These Times,* February 7, 2019, http:// inthesetimes.com/article/21726/alexandria-ocasio-cortez -green-new-deal-democrats-legislation-nancy-pelosi.
27. Ted Steinberg, "Capitalism, the State and the Drowning America," *Counter-Punch,* September 8, 2017, https://www.counterpunch.org/2017/09/08 /capitalism-the-state-and-the-drowning-of-america/
28. David Cutler and Francesca Dominici, "A Breath of Bad Air: Cost of the Trump Environmental Agenda May Lead to 80,000 Extra Deaths per Decade," *JAMA Forum,* June 12, 2018, https://jamanetwork.com/journals /jama/fullarticle/2684596?appid=scweb&appid=scweb&alert=article.
29. Ibid.
30. Ibid.
31. Teju Cole, "Unmournable Bodies," *New Yorker,* January 9, 2019, https:// www.newyorker.com/culture/cultural-comment/unmournable-bodies.

32. Luke Darby, "GOP Congressman Calls Two Children Dying in Border Detention an 'Excellent Record,'" *GQ Magazine*, December 29, 2018, https://www.gq.com/story/peter-king-dead-kids-excellent.

33. On this issue, see C. Wright Mills, *The Sociological Imagination* (New York: Oxford University Press, 1959).

34. Ian Hughes, "Entrepreneurs of Hate," *OpenDemocracy*, October 2, 2018, https://www.opendemocracy.net/transformation/ian-hughes/entrepreneurs-of-hate.

35. Bill Blum, "The Judiciary Won't Save American Democracy," *Truthdig*, February 25, 2019, https://www.truthdig.com/articles/the-judiciary-wont-save-american-democracy/.

36. Hannah Arendt, *The Origins of Totalitarianism* (New York: Houghton Mifflin Harcourt, 2001), 468.

37. Erik Wemple, "Tucker Carlson in October: 'I Have Complete Editorial Freedom and the Support of the Company,'" *Washington Post*, December 19, 2018, https://www.washingtonpost.com/opinions/2018/12/19/tucker-carlson-october-i-have-complete-editorial-freedom-support-company/?utm_term=.4b357e88ce23.

38. Robinson Woodward-Burns, "Trump Wants to Change the Rules of Citizenship. Here Are Three Reasons His Proposal Might Be Unconstitutional," *Washington Post*, October 31, 2018, https://www.washingtonpost.com/news/monkey-cage/wp/2018/10/31/trump-wants-to-change-the-rules-of-citizenship-here-are-three-reasons-his-proposal-might-be-unconstitutional/?utm_term=.6cccb22ef8be.

39. Hannah Arendt, "Ideology and Terror: A Novel Form of Government," in *Origins of Totalitarianism*, 460–479.

40. Paul Mason, "Reading Arendt Is Not Enough," *New York Review of Books*, May 9, 2019, https://www.nybooks.com/daily/2019/05/02/reading-arendt-is-not-enough/.

41. Arendt, *The Origins of Totalitarianism*, 458.

42. Leo Löwenthal, "Atomization of Man," in *False Prophets: Studies in Authoritarianism* (New Brunswick: Transaction Books, 1987), 182–183.

43. Chantal Mouffe, *For a Left Populism* (Verso, London: 2018), 24.

44. Chantal Mouffe, "The Populist Moment," *Open Democracy*, November 21, 2016, https://www.opendemocracy.net/democraciaabierta/chantal-mouffe/populist-moment.

45. Leo Löwenthal, "Atomization of Man," 184–185.

46. Cited in Chris Hedges, "Suffering? Well You Deserve It," *Truthdig*, March 2, 2014, http://www.truthdig.com/report/item/suffering_well_you_deserve_it_20140302

47. An excellent analysis of the underlying causes of the teacher strikes can be found in Stan Karp and Adam Sanchez, "The 2018 Wave of Teacher Strikes: A Turning Point for Our Schools?" *Rethinking Schools* 32, no. 4 (Summer 2018), https://www.rethinkingschools.org/articles/the-2018-wave-of-teacher-strikes.

48. See, for instance, Anthony J. Nocella II, Priya Parmar, and David Stovall, eds., *From Education to Incarceration: Dismantling the School-to-Prison Pipeline* (New York: Peter Lang, 2018).

49. Mark Fisher, *Capitalist Realism: Is There No Alternative?* (Winchester, UK: Zero Books, 2009), 2.

50. Ibid., 16.

51. John Cassidy, "Trump's Speech Was a Big Non-Event," *New Yorker*, January 9, 2019, https://www.newyorker.com/news/our-columnists/trumps-presidential-address-was-a-big-non-event.

52. Sam Fulwood III, "The Media Is Overlooking the Purpose of Trump's Border Wall," *ThinkProgress*, January 11, 2019, https://thinkprogress.org/media-have-trumps-wall-all-wrong-d90d2665070a/.

53. Trip Gabriel, "Before Trump, Steve King Set the Agenda for the Wall and Anti-Immigrant Politics," *New York Times*, January 10, 2019, https://www.nytimes.com/2019/01/10/us/politics/steve-king-trump-immigration-wall.html.

54. Ibid.

55. "Full Transcript: Michael Cohen's Opening Statement to Congress," *New York Times*, February 27, 2019, https://www.nytimes.com/2019/02/27/us/politics/cohen-documents-testimony.html.

56. Maegan Vazquez, "Trump Keeps Mum on King's Comments while Separately Stoking Racism," *CNN Politics*, January 14, 2019, https://www.cnn.com/2019/01/14/politics/donald-trump-steve-king-white-nationalism-supremacy/index.html.

57. Wendy Brown, "Apocalyptic Populism," *Eurozine*, September 5, 2017, http://www.eurozine.com/apocalyptic-populism/.

58. Chantal Mouffe, "The Populist Moment."

59. I want to thank Michael Lerner for helping me clarify this point.

60. See for instance, Zygmunt Bauman, *Liquid Times: Living in an Age of Uncertainty* (London: Polity Press, 2007).

61. Francis Wilde interviews Pankaj Mishra, "'The Liberal Order Is the Incubator for Authoritarianism': A Conversation with Pankaj Mishra," *Los Angeles Review of Books*, November 15, 2018, https://lareviewofbooks.org/article/the-liberal-order-is-the-incubator-for-authoritarianism-a-conversation-with-pankaj-mishra/#!.

62. Nicholas Gane and Les Back, "C. Wright Mills 50 Years On: The Promise and Craft of Sociology Revisited," *Theory, Culture, & Society* 29, nos. 7–8 (January 3, 2013), https://journals.sagepub.com/doi/10.1177/0263276412459089

63. Tracy K. Smith, "Politics and Poetry," *New York Times*, December 10, 2018, https://www.nytimes.com/2018/12/10/books/review/political-poetry.html.

64. Ibid.

65. Rob Nixon, *Slow Violence and the Environmentalism of the Poor*, (Cambridge: Harvard University Press, 2013), x.

66. C. Wright Mills, *The Sociological Imagination* (New York: Oxford Univer-

sity Press, 1959), 27.

67. Dylan Moore, "The Poet and the Public Intellectual," *Wales Arts Review*, October 25 2012, https://www.walesartsreview.org/longform-the -poet-and-the-public-intellectual/.

68. Ronald Aronson, *We: Reviving Social Hope*, (Chicago: University Chicago Press, 2017).

69. Mark Fisher, *Capitalist Realism*, 79.

70. A. K. Thompson, "Premonitions: Fragments of a Culture of Revolt," *Bullet*, December 10, 2018, https://socialistproject.ca/2018/12 /premonitions-fragments-of-culture-of-revolt/.

71. Fredric Jameson, "Future City," *New Left Review* 21 (May–June 2003), https://newleftreview.org/II/21/fredric-jameson-future-city.

72. Frederick Douglass, "The Meaning of July Forth for the Negro," in *The Life and Writings of Frederick Douglass: Volume II Pre-Civil War Decade 1850–1860* in ed. Philip S. Foner (New York: International Publishers Co., Inc 1950), https://www.pbs.org/wgbh/aia/part4/4h2927t.html.

73. Antonio Gramsci, *Selections from the Prison Notebooks*, ed. and trans. Quintin Hoare and Geoffrey Nowell Smith (New York: International Publishers, 1971), 275–276.

74. Melvin Rogers, "Democracy Is a Habit: Practice It," *Boston Review*, July 25, 2019; http://bostonreview.net/politics/melvin-rogers-democracy-habit -practice-it.

CONCLUSION: HIGHER EDUCATION AND THE THREAT OF FASCISM

1. Parts of this interview first appeared in *Truthout*.

Index

About Haymarket Books

Haymarket Books is a radical, independent, nonprofit book publisher based in Chicago.

Our mission is to publish books that contribute to struggles for social and economic justice. We strive to make our books a vibrant and organic part of social movements and the education and development of a critical, engaged, international left.

We take inspiration and courage from our namesakes, the Haymarket martyrs, who gave their lives fighting for a better world. Their 1886 struggle for the eight-hour day—which gave us May Day, the international workers' holiday—reminds workers around the world that ordinary people can organize and struggle for their own liberation. These struggles continue today across the globe—struggles against oppression, exploitation, poverty, and war.

Since our founding in 2001, Haymarket Books has published more than five hundred titles. Radically independent, we seek to drive a wedge into the risk-averse world of corporate book publishing. Our authors include Noam Chomsky, Arundhati Roy, Rebecca Solnit, Angela Y. Davis, Howard Zinn, Amy Goodman, Wallace Shawn, Mike Davis, Winona LaDuke, Ilan Pappé, Richard Wolff, Dave Zirin, Keeanga-Yamahtta Taylor, Nick Turse, Dahr Jamail, David Barsamian, Elizabeth Laird, Amira Hass, Mark Steel, Avi Lewis, Naomi Klein, and Neil Davidson. We are also the trade publishers of the acclaimed Historical Materialism Book Series and of Dispatch Books.

Also Available from Haymarket Books

Against Apartheid: The Case for Boycotting Israeli Universities
Edited by Ashley Dawson and Bill V. Mullen, Foreword by Ali Abunimah

Badass Teachers Unite! Writing on Education, History, and Youth Activism
Mark Naison

Education and Capitalism: Struggles for Learning and Liberation
Edited by Jeff Bale and Sarah Knopp

The Future of Our Schools: Teachers Unions and Social Justice
Lois Weiner

A Marxist Education: Learning to Change the World
Wayne Au

More Than a Score: The New Uprising Against High-Stakes Testing
Edited by Jesse Hagopian, Foreword by Alfie Kohn,
Preface by Diane Ravitch

Schooling In Capitalist America: Educational Reform and the Contradictions of Economic Life
Samuel Bowles and Herbert Gintis

This Is Not A Test: A New Narrative on Race, Class, and Education
José Vilson, Foreword by Karen Lewis, Afterword by Pedro Noguera

Uncivil Rites: Palestine and the Limits of Academic Freedom
Steven Salaita

ABOUT THE AUTHOR

Henry A. Giroux currently holds the Global TV Network Chair Professorship at McMaster University in the English and Cultural Studies Department and a Distinguished Visiting Professorship at Ryerson University. His most recent books include *Youth in Revolt: Reclaiming a Democratic Future* (Paradigm Publishers, 2013) and *America's Educational Deficit and the War on Youth* (Monthly Review Press, 2013).